the COMPOST COACH

Make compost, build soil and grow a
regenerative garden – wherever you live!

the
COMPOST
COACH

KATE FLOOD
Compostable Kate

Photography by Honey Atkinson

murdoch books
Sydney | London

CONTENTS

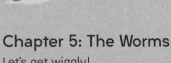

A NOTE ABOUT QR CODES

You'll find QR codes sprinkled throughout this book. When you scan each one with your smartphone camera, a short-form video from my Instagram page will pop up, featuring a clip that will bring to life the topic you're reading about. These videos are just a small sample of the educational (and fun!) compost content on my Instagram platform. Head to @compostable.kate to see more.

HELLO!

I'm Kate, the Compost Coach, and you're holding my guide to creating black gold – also known as luscious compost. I've helped thousands of people master the dark art of making perfect compost, and in that time I've noticed some common pain points:

- It stinks!
- There are flies!
- It's not breaking down!

I've written this book to solve your composting problems and to simplify the technicalities of soil science, so you can become a confident compost creator.

If you're a newbie composter, you can get overwhelmed with scientific mumbo jumbo and then throw in the towel because it all feels too hard. There's a lot of conflicting information about composting because it's not an exact science. Googling 'how to compost' is a minefield because there are so many variables at work. Lots of articles are full of technical jargon that is intimidating and boring. Rejoice! That is not the tone of this book. I'm going to hold your hand along the way and make sure you feel empowered to go out into your yard (or apartment's lobby), yelling out a rallying cry: 'I'm a Compost Creator – hear me ROAR!'

I'm happiest when I'm teaching people about compost, reading about it, or elbow deep in the stuff. I'm a compost nerd and sustainability educator, and for the past three years I've been on a mission to help others re-use their household waste. From my home in a small town on the east coast of Australia, I spread the word on black gold via workshops for councils, community gardens and corporations. I'm not a soil scientist by any stretch of the imagination, but I've experimented with and tested just about everything in this book so you don't have to do the work.

COMPOST AND CLIMATE CHANGE

Over the years, I've found that a common barrier to giving composting a red–hot go is the perceived inconvenience. People assume that it's a hard skill to master, it's time–consuming, it's smelly, and you need a lot of outdoor space for it to work. I'm a mum of three busy little dirt–babies, and I know that time is the most precious commodity. I'll show you that making compost is fun, not smelly when managed correctly, and requires hardly any space, time or effort. This book will help you find the right compost solution to match your lifestyle and home.

I want you to feel excited about making compost because it's the coolest form of climate activism that we can all do in our own homes. Climate change is a heavy concept. I bet you sometimes feel like vomiting, screaming or crying (or all three) when you think about where the world might be heading. But if we become nihilistic about the big 'CC', then we're not going to take any personal action (or demand change) on a systemic level. So, I hope this book won't only help you to master compost making, but also motivate you to make other small but significant changes in your life to stem the climate crisis. I believe that individual actions – when done collectively – can make a massive positive impact.

There is no doubt that the past few years have been ... a lot. But one real positive that has come from the wild ride is the confluence of Covid gardening, climate–change awareness, indoor–plant jungles and a surge in urban edible gardening, which has prompted people from all walks of life to start thinking about the importance of soil.

SAVING THE SOIL

For too long we've used and abused our soil, filling it with petrochemical–based fertilisers, yanking plants out of the earth (roots and all),

ANYONE (AND EVERYONE!) WHO HAS ACCESS TO SOIL IN THEIR YARD CAN TURN THEIR GARDENS INTO FOOD BOWLS.

overworking it and then expecting plants to grow abundantly. Vast areas of once–healthy soil have been exploited by industrial agriculture and turned into dust bowls that are considered biologically dead. The impending threat of soil extinction (where soil loses its organic content and irreversibly transforms into barren, lifeless sand) is only further motivation to make soil from scraps.

Anyone (and everyone!) who has access to soil in their yard can rewrite this narrative and turn their gardens into food bowls, growing produce and recycling waste in a way that sequesters carbon and builds healthy soil. In the second half of this book, I'll share some simple yet extremely effective (and exciting) regenerative gardening practices that go beyond compost, which can be used in your own backyard to restore and rejuvenate your soil.

We need to stop having a dysfunctional relationship with our soil and start treating it like the earthy goddess that it is. The best partnerships are based on giving just as much as – if not more than – you take. Composting is a way of using overlooked and underappreciated things such as kitchen scraps, grass clippings, cardboard, weeds and fallen leaves to repay our seriously overdue debt to the earth.

We don't have any time to waste (or 'waste' to waste, either), so let's jump right into it. Come on – let's get dirty!

1.

THE WHAT

WHAT IS COMPOST?

Composting is a microbial–driven process of decomposition. It turns organic matter into a valuable amendment that feeds the life in your soil. This sounds a bit technical, doesn't it? To put it more simply, compost is the transformational process that turns 'waste' into a resource. It's real–life alchemy – changing scraps into black gold.

Do you want to hear something that may seem obvious but is actually quite reassuring to anyone who has attempted to make compost and has ended up with a stinking, slimy mess? Ready for it? Compost happens every single day in nature without human intervention. Pull back the leaves on a forest floor, and you'll find the most fabulous decomposing organic matter, heaving with worms and life. Compost in nature never follows an exact recipe. One season, it may be full of fallen leaves with welcome additions of berries, pine cones and manure dropped from passing native animals. The next season, it could have the carcass of a dead animal and the branch of a fallen tree.

Anything that was once alive decomposes eventually. Backyard composting simply speeds up the process by providing the perfect environment for bacteria, fungi and other organisms (such as worms, beetles, slaters and beneficial nematodes) to do their work. Regardless of whether it's you or Mother Nature making it, compost requires four universal elements: nitrogen (the juicy stuff), carbon (the dead, dry stuff), oxygen and water. I'll talk about these in detail later, when I show you how to make stellar compost.

WHAT IS ORGANIC MATTER?

I'm going to use the term 'organic matter' a lot in this book, so let me explain what it means now. Organic matter is an umbrella term for any living or dead animal or plant material. Here are some examples of organic matter: fresh green leaves or fallen brown leaves; an animal carcass – bones and all – from your cooking (hello, roast chicken!) or, more gruesomely, from roadkill; woodchips or a whole branch of a tree; commercial pelletised chicken manure or cow (or human!) manure; freshly pulled weeds; and dried straw. Organic matter comprises the raw materials that can be transformed into compost.

WHAT DOES COMPOST DO?

Compost builds healthy soil. If you become a compost creator rather than just a plant cultivator, you'll eventually be able to wean yourself off using artificial fertilisers as well as toxic pesticides and herbicides. This is because compost feeds the life in your soil, which grows strong plants, and this helps to build a healthy ecosystem in your own backyard.

Shop-bought fertilisers never fix poor soil; they provide a temporary bandaid solution but ultimately kill off soil biology. If your garden doesn't have a thriving soil food web (this term is used to describe what eats what in your soil), then your plants will become more susceptible to pests and diseases. This leads to an increased use of pesticides and herbicides that indiscriminately kill everything they land on: the harmful pests and the beneficial pollinators, predators and biology in your soil. This quick-fix style of gardening may seem like an easy solution, but it creates more problems that you'll have to deal with in the long term.

When you become a compost creator, you may find yourself becoming more tolerant of a background population of pests in your patch. You'll start to realise that pests are part of the food chain and help to sustain the beneficial predators and pollinators we all know and love – hello, gorgeous ladybirds, lacewings and praying mantises, not to mention all of the microscopic life forms in your soil that protect your plants, too. If you learn to live with all sorts of bugs in the soil and on your plants – the cute, the annoying and even the icky – then you'll notice the natural balance of your patch developing.

BIODIVERSE BISTRO

Did you know that one of the top ways to increase biodiversity in your garden is to create a backyard compost bin or pile? Compost heaps work hard for you – not only are you paid in black gold at the end of the process, but your pile is also a food source and hangout for bucketloads of life.

THE POWER OF COMPOST

Homemade compost contains billions of life forms, some we can see (such as worms, beetles and springtails) but most we can't (such as bacteria, nematodes and fungi). These soil superstars work together to cycle nutrients that allow the soil to function and your plants to grow.

COMPOST PROVIDES PLANTS WITH A LIVING SOURCE OF NUTRITION.

Here are just some of the things that compost does:

- Compost dramatically increases the amount of life in soil. It introduces beneficial microbes, in the same way that a baker introduces yeast to bread dough. If you have soil that lacks nutrients, compost will introduce microbiology that helps to extract minerals from the sand, silt or clay in your soil, and this will allow you to grow healthy crops. Hardworking and productive edible gardens are hungry, and compost provides plants with a living source of nutrition that is delivered slowly and steadily.
- Compost helps to suppress plant pests and diseases. It introduces billions of soil superheroes (beneficial bacteria, invertebrates and fungi, to name just a few) that can outcompete the villains (pathogens and pests) for food sources. The microorganisms in compost also become a food source for soil biology higher up the food chain. Various compost microorganisms protect plants from pathogens by surrounding the fine root hairs and forming a barrier layer that pathogens can't break through. All of these factors help to make the soil ecosystem robust and more resilient to pests as well as fungal and bacterial diseases.
- Compost improves the structure of all soil types over time. It enhances sandy soil by improving its water- and nutrient-holding capacity. Compost opens up clayey soil by providing air pockets that improve drainage.
- Humus-rich compost helps to buffer the pH of soil. Compost doesn't dramatically change the pH of soil, but it helps plants that are sensitive to the extremes of acidity or alkalinity to access nutrients and grow.

- Composting stores more carbon in the soil than it emits to the air, which means it helps with carbon sequestration (the process of capturing carbon dioxide [CO_2] in the soil so that it's not released into the atmosphere and can't contribute to climate change). This is a big string in our bow when it comes to our battle to save this glorious planet.

SO, HOW ON EARTH CAN COMPOST DO ALL THAT?

Healthy soil is a heaving, thumping, pumping party of life. A wee teaspoon of healthy soil can hold up to 10 billion living things! In one of my favourite books, *Soil*, Matthew Evans notes that a handful of soil can contain:

- 5000 insects, arachnids, worms and molluscs (from up to 500 species)
- 100,000 protozoa (from up to 500 species)
- 10,000 nematodes (from up to 100 species)
- 500 metres of plant roots (from up to 50 species)
- 100 billion bacteria (from up to 10,000 species)
- algae, archaea and more.

Don't just let these big numbers roll over you. I know it's hard to conceptualise this amount of life getting down and dirty in the soil of your backyard. But if you've been regularly feeding your patch with homemade compost, then this is the reality of the guest list for this somewhat inconceivable soil soiree.

Fascinatingly, the life in your soil is more important than the nutrients it contains when it comes to your plants' ability to access and gobble up these nutrients. As Evans says, 'The ecosystem under the ground drives what happens above ground ... Soil is the medium, life is the result.' The microscopic world of a healthy soil ecosystem cycles nutrients from compost into a form that plants can take up in the root zone. So, as gardeners we need

to provide tender, loving care to our soil first and foremost, and then our plants will look after themselves.

Whatever type of soil you have – sandy, clayey, silty or loamy – and regardless of whether it's in a container garden, a potted patch or a garden bed directly on the earth, compost will improve it. Now, hold on to your hats … this next bit is a little scientific but worth getting your head around, as it will reveal one of compost's biggest benefits.

Compost is a living soil conditioner that works by adding humus to the soil. Humus (not hommus, the chickpea dip, which is delicious but different) is stable organic matter that forms when plants and animals decay. It acts like glue, holding on to nutrients and water in soil. Compost's high humus content greatly increases the water- and nutrient-holding capacity of all soils, which means you need to feed and water your plants less. We know that our future gardens are going to be hotter and drier than ever before, so the fact that compost holds moisture is a huge benefit to all gardeners.

When added to your soil, compost continues to decompose and slowly release nutrients. Plants take up these nutrients, which is why it's a good idea to add new compost to your garden every year, but compost continues to improve your garden's soil even after all of the organic matter and nutrients have been consumed. This is because humus remains in your soil and coats the soil particles. Over time, this creates the gorgeous crumb structure of healthy soil.

Applying homemade compost over several years can completely transform sandy and clayey soil into a friable (crumbly) substrate in which plants will thrive. Compost binds with soil particles and forms aggregates (the scientific word for crumbs) that open up more space for oxygen to sit within the soil, which is essential for healthy root growth. The spaces created by these crumbs also improve drainage during extreme rain events (hello, La Niña!). In addition, humus contains chemical elements that help to 'lock up' any heavy metals in your soil so the metals don't get sucked up by plants, making your edible plants safer to eat.

TOP:
A teaspoon of compost can contain up to 10 billion living things!

OPPOSITE:
This illustration shows a zoomed-in view of compost microorganisms.

MICROBIAL MAGIC

Hipsters and homesteaders seem to be onto something with their desire to make slow food: to shape and bake sourdough; to ferment kombucha, sauerkraut and booze; and to transform milk into sumptuous cheeses that ooze. These slow and utterly delicious processes all happen by harnessing the majesty of microbes, which transform simple ingredients such as flour, water and salt into something far superior to its component parts (bread!). The same is true in gardening for the kitchen scraps, brown leaves, weeds and shredded paper in our compost when microbes enter the mix: the sum is greater than the parts.

Worms often receive all the attention as the major decomposers within compost. They're fabulous, don't get me wrong, but it's bacteria and fungi that do most of the heavy lifting, multiplying and eating of your waste. As on a forest floor, you can't make good compost at home without harnessing the power of composting microorganisms and all forms of life within the soil food web.

Your innocent compost bin hidden behind your garden shed actually hosts a wild 24-hour orgy – some of which you can see (hello, worms!), but much of which is invisible to the naked eye (thank goodness, otherwise it might make you blush).

All of the life forms buzzing around your compost bin are hardworking, hungry and – dare I say – horny! There's a titillating amount of copulation happening in your heap; if there wasn't, then the process wouldn't work. You need to provide the life forms in your compost with a balanced diet of greens (nitrogen) and browns (carbon), as well as plenty of oxygen and an adequate amount of hydration to sustain their vigour. Otherwise, they'll go on strike – and you'll end up with a pile of stinky scraps that don't do much at all, aside from annoying your neighbours. I'll outline the ingredients and inputs that make balanced compost in Chapter 3, but first let's take a deep dive into why making compost is so important.

2.

THE
WHY

IT'S NOT WASTE UNTIL IT'S WASTED

From the moment we wake up, our lives involve the consumption of resources: turning on a light, going to the bathroom, making a cuppa and some toast, getting dressed, driving to work. The result of most of this consumption is waste – and this is something that doesn't simply 'go away'. Food waste becomes a major climate liability if it's not handled mindfully.

Why not just chuck food scraps in the rubbish? Surely they'll break down? Food waste that is thrown away in plastic bags breaks down far more slowly than you think. Bagged scraps piled on top of one another in landfill have limited exposure to oxygen, aerobic microbes and bugs (the three things that quickly turn food waste into soil-enriching compost – more on this later). In the smelly, oxygen-free environment of landfill, decomposition happens very slowly; an innocent apple core or broccoli stem will slowly mummify, ooze toxic leachate and release enormous amounts of methane gas.

I can't sugar-coat the food-waste facts. They're eye-watering, especially because this information isn't new. We've known for an awfully long time that food waste turns into climate poison when it's placed in landfill. Yet most developed countries still handle these scraps like they're trash, not treasure.

FOOD WASTE FEEDS CLIMATE CHANGE

We all urgently need to stop overlooking and ignoring the massively detrimental impact of food waste in the climate–change debate. We know that the burning of fossil fuels (coal, natural gas and oil) produces carbon dioxide, which is atmospheric poison. But did you know that methane released from landfill areas overflowing with food waste is 28–34 times more potent than carbon dioxide at trapping heat in the atmosphere? This greenhouse gas contributes disproportionately to global warming. It's shocking that the source of methane is not something toxic, but rather something we all handle and consume every day.

Food that is produced but not eaten – because it never leaves the farm, gets damaged or lost during distribution, or is thrown away by supermarkets, cafés, restaurants, hotels, schools or home kitchens – represents 8–10 per cent of global greenhouse–gas emissions. I think that it's important to put this figure into perspective:

- The global emissions from wasted food are four times larger than the global emissions from the airline industry (1.9 per cent), and more than all of the emissions from the plastic we produce (3.8 per cent) and from extracting oil (3.8 per cent).
- The food wasted just in the United States is equivalent to 32.6 million cars' worth of greenhouse–gas emissions.

If global food waste were a country, it would be the third–largest emitter of greenhouse gases in the world, behind the United States and China. So, what individuals, communities and countries do with their food waste matters – quite a lot!

FOOD WASTE BECOMES A MAJOR CLIMATE LIABILITY IF IT'S NOT HANDLED MINDFULLY.

EMPTY BELLIES

Food waste is not only an environmental catastrophe, but also a humanitarian one. Today, one in nine people does not have enough food to eat; that's 793 million people who regularly go hungry. If as little as one–quarter of the food wasted could be saved, it would be enough to feed 870 million hungry people.

THROW–AWAY SOCIETY

Worldwide, humans have a big food–waste problem. It's estimated that about 40 per cent of all the food produced in the world is wasted. Households in Australia lose between $2000 and $2500 a year in wasted groceries. This wastage equals about 312 kilograms of food per person – or one in five bags of groceries – being tossed into landfill.

Almost half of all fruits and vegetables grown globally is wasted (that's 3.7 trillion delicious apples!). The fresh, edible food wasted from farms alone could feed the world's undernourished population almost four times over. In Australia, 25 per cent of farmers' crops never leave the farm on which they were grown – not because they're inedible, but because they're a bit ugly. The visual specifications outlined by some of the major Australian supermarkets prevent wonky, flawed and imperfect produce being sold in our fresh fruit and vegie aisles.

According to Horticulture Australia, at least 277,700 tonnes of fruits and vegetables (which represents around 25 per cent of the major production lines) are wasted each year in Australia; in other words, they're grown, picked and then dumped. This has negative consequences for everyone: it's bad for the farmer's bottom line, it makes food more expensive for the consumer, and it's obviously a disaster for the environment. When food is produced but not eaten, all of the energy, water and resources it takes to grow, harvest, package, transport and prepare it are wasted, too.

Thankfully, some major supermarkets have started to act upon consumer outrage. At selected stores, you can now find a small aisle of perfectly imperfect produce (such as stick–straight bananas or blemished apples) – but they're often sold in plastic, which is a point of contention for another day!

If you're anything like me, you'll find these food–waste figures deeply depressing. The

good news is that reducing food waste is the third most effective way we can all address climate change. Throwing food in the bin at home can be convenient, but I'll show you easy strategies for taking ownership of this waste. Leftovers, kitchen scraps and rotting food lurking in the back of your fridge are full of nutrients, but when we put them in plastic bags and send them to landfill, the nutrients are lost.

Composting 'waste' at home returns nutrients to the soil, where they belong. We don't need to rely on others to collect our waste, drive it to a facility, process it and then transport the finished products back to the community. Home composting involves no miles, no energy–inefficient processes and no packaging.

TOP:
Household food scraps (such as mandarin peels, carrot tops and watermelon rinds) can be transformed into compost to feed your soil.

OPPOSITE:
Ugly produce is perfectly delicious when you eat it.

3.

THE
HOW

THE FOUR UNIVERSAL INGREDIENTS

I hope you're starting to think about your compost as a living system, rather than a static pile of decomposing scraps, because this will help you to get your head around the creation and care of your compost.

First of all, you need to know the four universal elements that compost requires:

1. nitrogen (the juicy green stuff)
2. carbon (the dead, dry, brown stuff)
3. oxygen
4. water.

Like all life on Earth, your compost microbes need air to 'breathe', water to 'drink' and a balanced diet of 'greens' and 'browns'. So, let's examine the composting requirements to keep your compost happy (breaking down efficiently) and healthy (smelling fab).

1

2

3

4

NITROGEN (THE GREENS)

We all know that most garden prunings, seaweed, grass clippings, weeds, Granny Smith apples, spinach and lettuce are green. But did you know that compost is colourblind? It also treats the following items as nitrogen-rich greens:

- coffee grounds, manure and leftover lentil curry
- orange and carrot peels and rockmelon rinds
- strawberry tops, tomato skins and Pink Lady apple cores
- squeezed lemons, banana skins and pineapple tops.

You get the idea …

Regardless of the colour, greens are the inputs into your compost that are generally lush and juicy, due to their high water content. They're full of nitrogen, which provides nutrition for compost microbes so they can grow and reproduce, and which – when applied to your garden in your finished compost – will help your plants to grow. Greens are readily available to anyone who gardens, cooks, eats and shops for food and is left with garden waste, kitchen scraps and leftovers.

It can be tempting to simply load up your compost bin with your food scraps alone. You may feel like you're doing the right thing by diverting this waste away from landfill, but if you have a nitrogen-heavy compost it will turn into a mini landfill in your own backyard and release methane. Totally shocking, but true! It's essential to balance your food and green garden waste with carbon, also known as browns.

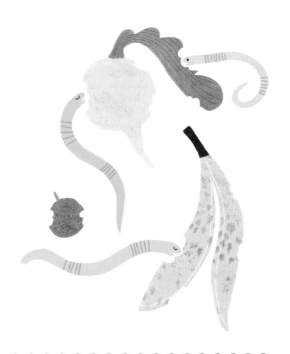

TOP:
Food scraps are full of nitrogen, which is an essential nutrient that helps plants grow abundantly.

CARBON (THE BROWNS)

When I talk about compost with people, I often hear horror stories of slimy, smelly, cockroach-ridden, anaerobic messes (anaerobic is a fancy word for oxygen-free). These tales of woe are easily fixed by adding carbon materials (fibrous, dry and woody ingredients such as dried leaves, newspaper and aged woodchips) – along with your regular inputs of nitrogen – to the composting system.

Adding carbon is the secret to making good compost and is often the solution to composting problems. Putting in a generous amount of brown matter with every bucket of food waste is a must. Adding carbon is important because it provides compost microorganisms with the energy they need to multiply and consume your waste. Carbon helps to create structure and bulk in your pile, which means more compost. It makes the finished product far more moisture retentive. Carbon also creates air pockets in your pile, which ensures that your bin won't stink. Your neighbourhood will be grateful!

Sorry people, but there is no excuse for not having enough carbon matter on hand. Honestly, just look around – there are literally piles of free brown stuff almost everywhere (especially in autumn). Brown leaves, dunny rolls, torn newspapers, ripped cardboard boxes, your kids' artworks (shh ... I won't tell if you don't), cut-up egg cartons, woodchips being

given away for free by many councils and going begging – I could go on and on.

A lot of what you put in your paper recycling bin could instead be placed in your compost bin. Shockingly, paper products account for more than 40 per cent of landfill volume, as a lot of them are contaminated with grease and can't be recycled. Like food waste, paper products stubbornly resist breaking down in the anaerobic environment of landfill. So, taking ownership of our household carbon means that these nutrients are actually kept in circulation and returned to the soil. (To learn how to safely compost manufactured carbon, turn to page 168.)

I'll talk about composting ratios in more detail on pages 32–3, but in simple terms, all you need to do is follow my mantra: 'Brown is best, then chuck in the rest.' This means that you need to add at least equal amounts of browns (carbon) to greens (nitrogen) every time you add scraps to your compost. You'll experience the sweet smell of successful compost when you follow this simple rule. Carbon is often the missing link in helping to create well-balanced compost that is full of life, has a rich deep brown colour and has a deliciously distinctive earthy scent.

Brown is best, then chuck in the rest.

OXYGEN

You and I are not that different from the microbes in your compost pile – seriously! Just like us, your compost critters need to breathe. You can make compost using lots of different methods and equipment: in a compost bin, in a tumbler, in a worm farm or in an open pile directly on the ground. Regardless of the method and equipment used, these composting systems all rely on aerobic (oxygen–rich) decomposition. The air–breathing aerobic bacteria and soil organisms that break down all of your greens and browns need oxygen to survive, thrive and multiply.

Oxygen may not feel like a tangible ingredient to add to your compost because you can't touch or hold it. But you can physically add it via the process of aeration (a fancy word for turning your compost). You can also capture air within your compost in the way that you layer and build your compost, and in your mix of ingredients. Adequate aeration is important if you want finished compost fast, as oxygen fuels the fire of your compost.

As a compost creator, you wield a lot of power: the amount of air that gets into your pile is entirely within your control. Adding carbon of varying sizes to your compost – such as chunky woodchips, sticks, brown leaves or cardboard – is a simple method to help oxygenate your heap. This is because these chunky and robust inputs create greater pore spaces that allow oxygen to enter and be trapped within your compost pile during the initial active stages of decomposition.

When your compost is actively decomposing, the microbial populations are working hard. The aerobic bacteria will eventually use up most of the oxygen in the middle of the pile. Also, as your scraps and other organic matter in your compost decompose, their particle size shrinks; less air is able to be captured in the pore spaces within your pile. This is why it's so important to turn your compost, as this opens up the core of the pile to let in air. If you don't do this, anaerobic bacteria (those that don't need oxygen) may take over, and your compost will start to stink.

BREAKING THE RULES

Bokashi composting is the one exception to the compost–needs–oxygen rule. It's an anaerobic process that ferments your scraps in an airtight container. (To learn all about Bokashi, turn to pages 91–105.)

TOP:
A compost aerator is a fabulous tool that introduces oxygen into your compost.

An anaerobic compost will still decompose, but at a much slower rate. The problem with this is that the oxygen–free environment favours an undesirable group of bacteria called anaerobes. When anaerobes start breaking down your compost in an oxygen–free environment, they release methane and hydrogen sulphide (the technical term for rotten–egg gas). This stench is disgustingly distinctive; your nose knows when anaerobes have gate–crashed the party. Pass a peg, please! Aerating your compost is essential when this happens because these bacteria can produce phototoxic compounds that are harmful to your plant babies. They can also create compost that is too acidic.

I enjoy the physical nature of turning my compost. If you aren't able to do this (as compost can get quite heavy), here are four alternative aerating hacks:

1. Wiggle a star picket (metal garden stake) through the mass of compost, all the way down to the bottom of the bin, to allow air to flow.
2. Get your hands on a PVC pipe that has been cut to the internal height of your compost bin. Drill numerous holes all over it, and position the pipe in the centre of your compost heap or bin. It will act like a lung and draw oxygen into your pile.
3. Fashion a small–diameter tube from stainless–steel mesh that is tall enough to run from the bottom of your bin to the top, but is short enough for the lid to go back on if you're using an enclosed bin.
4. Tie a bunch of sticks or cornstalks together, and position the bundle in the centre of your bin. The sticks and stalks will eventually break down, but they can be replaced with fresh materials when they no longer hold their form.

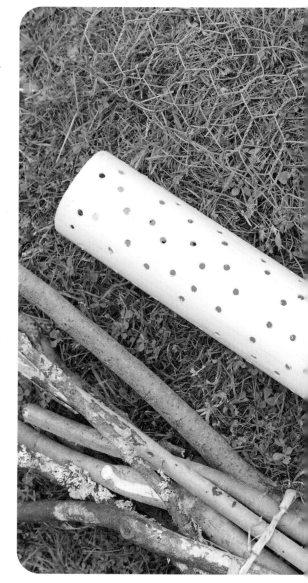

TOP:
Air will flow freely in your compost if you build layers of organic matter around one of these DIY lungs.

OPPOSITE:
The organic matter in your compost needs to be kept lightly moist at all times to encourage active microbial decomposition.

WATER

All life needs water, and the microbes and bug buddies in your compost are no different. Compost works best with 40–60 per cent hydration. These figures seem like a clearly definable amount, but what does this actually mean in practice? The organic matter in your compost needs to stay moist at all times, but what I don't want you to do is to get trigger-happy with your hose and saturate your compost.

The best way to test the moisture content of your compost is to grab a handful and give it a squeeze. You only want a drop or two of liquid to come out; if you have more than this, then you have a problem. A happy heap will feel just like a wrung-out sponge – all the organic matter is coated with water, but there are air spaces in between.

There should be a thin, barely visible film of water covering all of the compost particles when they're actively breaking down. This is because microbial decomposition happens most rapidly in that layer of water surrounding the particles of organic matter. Depending on the weather, you may need to add extra water (as dry compost will just sit there, doing next to nothing). But be careful not to over-wet the contents of your bin, as the compost will become anaerobic and start to stink, and the decomposition will slow down. If things become a little slimy, then add dry carbon to balance out your food and garden waste.

A HAPPY HEAP WILL FEEL JUST LIKE A WRUNG-OUT SPONGE.

THE C:N RATIO EXPLAINED

To make great compost, you need to provide a balanced diet of greens and browns to feed your compost microbes. In compost language, we call this balance the C:N ratio (carbon to nitrogen ratio).

The C:N ratio allows us to work out how much carbon relative to nitrogen is in each of our composting ingredients, and therefore our pile. Our green scraps, for example, always have a low C:N ratio. Kitchen waste typically has a ratio of 15:1, which means that these scraps have 15 units of carbon for each unit of nitrogen. On the other hand, our browns have lots more available carbon and have a high C:N ratio. Cardboard, for instance, typically has a C:N ratio of 500:1, so this means there are 500 units of carbon for each unit of nitrogen.

Why does the numerical ratio of carbon to nitrogen matter? Well, the microbes in your compost have a C:N ratio, too, which is close to 8:1. To survive and thrive in your heap, they need access to enough carbon and nitrogen to maintain this balance in their bodies. These busy little microbes burn lots of carbon as a source of energy, and a lot is also lost as carbon dioxide when they exhale, so not all of the carbon they consume actually remains in their systems. To obtain enough carbon and nitrogen to maintain their bodies, power their energy needs and stay alive, these microbes need a diet with a C:N ratio near 24:1. This gives microbes 16 parts of carbon to use for energy (which allows them to feast on your scraps and have enough stamina for sexy times – when each microbe divides into two new ones) and eight parts for bodily maintenance (bulking up).

So, what happens when we add a compost ingredient with a higher C:N ratio to the soil or our compost, such as sawdust with a C:N ratio of around 440:1? Since sawdust contains a much greater proportion of carbon to nitrogen than the 24:1 ratio that is ideal for microbes, they can only consume the sawdust if they source additional nitrogen from their environment to balance the excess carbon. That is why we always need to add greens with our browns – if we don't, a pile of carbon such as woodchips will take years to decompose.

On the other hand, if you load up your compost with ingredients that have a low C:N balance, such as grass clippings (12:1), the microbes will quickly consume these inputs. The excess nitrogen will be lost as ammonia gas, causing stinky smells. There's no point losing this nitrogen; we want to capture it for our plants, and we do that by mixing it with carbon.

THE MAGIC RATIO

So, if we consider the energy needs of the microbes in our compost, wouldn't a C:N ratio of 24:1 be ideal? Interestingly, this amount of carbon is too low. It actually needs to be around 30:1, which can be achieved by combining different organic materials with a low and high C:N – such as coffee grounds (20:1) with sawdust (440:1). A ratio of 30:1 allows the microbes to readily decompose your compost pile and also leaves a little food and structure to feed and shelter the microbes after the compost is applied to the soil. Throughout the composting process, the C:N ratio will slowly decrease from 30:1 to a final ratio of around 10–15:1 for the finished, cured compost.

There's a very complicated mathematical equation you can use if you want to be super precise about the C:N ratio, but who has the time to get bogged down in calculations for all of the various compost ingredients? I'm not expecting you to get out your scales and calculator. You can create optimal composting conditions simply by using a combination of materials, some high in carbon and others high in nitrogen. So, mix and match the ingredients

MATERIALS HIGH IN CARBON	MATERIALS HIGH IN NITROGEN
Small branches/twigs (500:1)	Garden waste (30:1)
Hardwood chips or shavings (450–800:1)	Horse manure (20–50:1)
Corrugated cardboard (350–600:1)	Coffee grounds (20:1)
Sawdust (200–750:1)	Seaweed (19:1)
Softwood chips or shavings (200–300:1)	Grass clippings (12:1)
Newspaper (175–250:1)	Vegetable scraps (10–20:1)
Mixed paper (150–200:1)	Fish guts (10:1)
Pine needles (80:1)	Hair/fur (10:1)
Straw (50–150:1)	Aged chicken manure (7–10:1)
Autumn leaves (30–80:1)	Dried blood meal (3:1)

listed in the boxes above to create the perfect combination – for example, for one bucket of fruit and vegie scraps, add one bucket of hardwood woodchips or two buckets of autumn leaves. (Please note that I've listed approximate ratio ranges because each item can vary widely.) Experiment and see what blends work best for you.

It's handy to know that carbon is more accessible when it has smaller-sized particles. Woodchips and sawdust made from the same timber will contain the same amount of carbon, but according to composting experts Nancy M. Trautmann and Marianne E. Krasny, 'the larger surface area in the sawdust makes its carbon more readily available for microbial use'. Consequently, you need to add a lot less sawdust than woodchips to have the same amount of available carbon in your compost heap.

THE SQUEEZE TEST

All organic matter has some amount of carbon and nitrogen, and a quick way to guesstimate the ratio is by conducting a squeeze test. As a general rule, juicy nitrogen-rich greens contain more water than drier and more fibrous carbon-rich browns. If you give the item in question a squeeze and it's a green, then it's likely you'll be able to see a small bead of water forming. A brown with a lot of carbon present won't contain any moisture when squeezed.

The creeping vines of peas or the stalks of chilli plants have a relatively balanced C:N ratio, so you may not be able to squeeze out a droplet of water, but you'll feel the presence

of moisture if you snap the plant material and rub it between your fingers. This squeeze test is a useful practice when you're first starting out, even though there are exceptions to this rule (such as coffee grounds, which are dry but very high in nitrogen).

Freshly cut or pulled herbaceous plants, weeds or grass clippings are high in nitrogen and moisture. If you leave these plant materials to dry out before redoing the squeeze test, then you'll find that very little moisture can be extracted. This is because nitrogen is not stable, and it can be leached away or released as gas into the atmosphere. So, if you have an abundance of greens that would make your compost unbalanced if you added them all at once, then dry some out to reduce their level of nitrogen before composting them.

SLOW VS HOT COMPOSTING

There are two major methods of aerobic composting: hot and cold. In this book, I'm going to refer to cold composting as slow composting, because this method has moments of being cool, lukewarm and occasionally hot. It gets confusing if you place an emphasis on the cold temperature; instead, I'll focus on the speed at which you make compost with this method.

SLOW COMPOSTING

Slow composting is what most of us do in our backyards when we first dip our toe into the world of decomposition. This is because it is by far the simplest method, as we're replicating what happens in nature. Natural decomposition occurs over several months – if not years – on forest floors, and it yields luscious results.

In a slow composting system, your food scraps, garden waste and carbon are added bit by bit over many months. Just like on a forest floor, the temperature of the organic matter in your compost will stay at a similar level to the outdoor ambient temperature.

WHY CHOOSE SLOW COMPOSTING?

Making slow compost is a satisfyingly simple process and a busy person's best choice. You can add your scraps to your bin, bay or pile on an ad hoc basis and, for the most part, ignore the compost. Honestly, this is no harder than throwing your waste into the trash. Later, I'll explain how you can layer your ingredients in a way that captures oxygen, so you don't need to turn your compost regularly (or at all!).

The main drawback of this method is that you'll have to wait patiently before you harvest that black gold. It typically takes anywhere from six months to one year to produce finished compost.

Even though it takes time, don't view slow composting as a second-rate option to hot composting. I know that it's easy to get het-up about heat and view it as the most important mechanism for quick decomposition, but this isn't the case. Finished, cooler compost is actually more beneficial to the soil than the quicker compost that is produced in hot composting systems. Slow compost is luscious stuff because the lower temperature results in less nitrogen off-gassing. If you haven't turned your compost, then it's often fungi-rich – which is heavenly for your soil.

HOW SLOW COMPOSTING WORKS

The two biggest differences between slow composting and hot composting are the required volume and the way that you make it. There are no size specifications for a slow compost bin or pile; it will work big or small, and you can gradually add material to your compost over several months. If you add a lot of organic matter at once, then you may find that your 'cold' compost bin has some moments when it's lukewarm or maybe even a little hot and steamy. This is an indication of bacteria at work (or play) in your compost.

Slow composting relies on the activity of two main groups of bacteria: mesophiles and (to a lesser extent) psychrophiles. Part of the first wave of microbes that take over your compost, psychrophiles are slow and steady workers that do their best work at around 10–20 degrees Celsius. In the deepest, darkest months of winter, psychrophiles are still very slowly decomposing your compost, as they can live in sub-zero temperatures. These microbial mates are resilient but not particularly productive decomposers, and they don't get long in the spotlight before the mesophiles take centre stage.

Most of the decomposition that occurs in your compost bin is due to mesophilic bacteria. These bacteria thrive in a moderate temperature range of 20–40 degrees Celsius. When mesophilic microbes start digesting carbon in your compost, a lot of the carbon is literally burned off and released as heat. That is why you may occasionally see steam rising from a cold compost bin.

The major downside to slow composting is that the temperature doesn't reach high enough – 55–60 degrees Celsius – to kill pathogens, plant diseases and weed seeds. So, to be on the safe side, it's best not to add weeds once they have gone to seed, or meat that hasn't been fermented first in a Bokashi bucket, to your cold compost bin. (To learn about Bokashi, turn to pages 91–105.)

MAKING SLOW COMPOST IS A SATISFYINGLY SIMPLE PROCESS AND A BUSY PERSON'S BEST CHOICE.

HOW TO MAKE SLOW COMPOST

Follow these instructions to achieve beautiful results in a plastic compost bin, box or open pile. I'm giving you all of the dirty details about each step so you can confidently do this at your own place.

1. Set up your compost pile directly on the soil or lawn. If it's an invasive species, such as kikuyu, then cover the grass with cardboard to smother it, and pile your compost on top of this. If you're working with a compost bin or box with an open base, then apply a piece of rodent–proof, stainless–steel mesh to the bottom (see pages 156–9).

2. Start with a 15–centimetre layer of carbon. I like to use chunky woodchips for this foundation layer because air is captured between them; they also help with drainage and act like a sponge to suck up any excess moisture. Fungi love woodchips, too, so it's a win–win situation. Alternatively, you can use robust carbon materials (such as twigs, bark or even stalks from brassicas or corn) mixed with softer carbon sources (such as ripped cardboard or fallen autumn leaves). It's important to use a combination of structural and soft carbon so the foundation layer doesn't decompose too quickly.

3. You'll harvest your finished compost off the top of this carbon layer, so it will get used numerous times before it breaks down. This actually helps to re–seed your new compost with the beneficial bacteria from the previous batch. If this is your first batch of compost, then it's a great idea to add a few handfuls of healthy garden soil, finished compost or a sprinkle or two of worm castings to act as a microbial inoculant. This helps to seed your compost and get the party started.

4. Now it's time to gradually layer your greens (such as grass clippings – in layers no thicker than 3 centimetres – food scraps, seedless weeds, plant prunings, manure, coffee grounds, and so on) and browns (such as shredded paper, cardboard, aged woodchips/shavings/sawdust, autumn leaves, and so on). Keep the green layers thin and the brown layers more generous (for example, 5–centimetre green layers and 7–10–centimetre brown layers). It's a good idea to use a compost turner (see page 120) to mix together your layers. Or you can insert a DIY 'lung' like this drilled PVC pipe (see page 30) into the centre of your bin, and fill around it. Alternatively, you can premix the greens and browns in a container or wheelbarrow before adding them in, so there is direct contact between the nitrogen and carbon sources, as this helps the aerobic microbes work efficiently. This also prevents the centre of the green layer from becoming anaerobic and stinky.

5. As you add each new layer, you may need to add some water, too, as compost must be kept moist. The moisture from your juicy greens will likely provide almost enough water to keep the compost microbes happy during the cooler winter months. During the height of summer, however, it's a good idea to wet your carbon materials before adding them to stop excessive evaporation and maintain the correct hydration. If you want to check whether your compost is thirsty or too wet, grab a handful of organic matter from the centre of your pile and give it a squeeze (see page 31).

6. Always remember to add a layer of carbon materials to top off your scraps, even if you've premixed them with carbon, so your compost doesn't start to attract flies. It's useful to keep a container of carbon next to your compost, so you always have some on hand. Shredded autumn leaves are my favourite material for this job.

7. Each time you add more scraps to your compost, you may notice that the level has sunk rather than risen. This is normal – it can take several months for a slow compost bin to become full to the brim, thanks to the hungry microbes and compost critters. Once the compost bin is full, you can take a hands–off approach to the management

and, for the most part, ignore the compost. Every now and then, check back in to see how it looks. Add a splash of water if it's drying out, or give it a turn if you haven't layered it with sticks or added a DIY 'lung' to the centre (see page 30).

8. After six to twelve months, the bottom layer should be mature enough to use. The finished compost should be crumbly and dark brown – with no visible food scraps – and have an earthy smell. To harvest the bottom layer (if you've used a compost bin), lift off the bin and set it aside. Now move any organic matter that has not finished decomposing, by placing it in a wheelbarrow or tub. Start harvesting the beautifully crumbly black gold from the bottom of the compost. You'll need to remove any larger sticks and put them back into your next batch of compost.

9. Keep harvesting until you hit the bottom foundation layer. Once all that's left at the bottom of your bin or pile is a small amount of compost clinging to the woodchips and sticks, it's time to pop your compost bin back on top. Then place the half–composted materials back into the bin, and now you're ready to start the process all over again.

SPEED DEMONS

If you want to get a little fancy, there are things you can add to your slow compost that will provide trace elements and speed up the process. These include compost activators (see pages 65–6) as well as homemade biochar, bonemeal or shell meal, and rock minerals or dusts (see Chapter 8). Don't overdo these, otherwise your compost will become alkaline.

Another method for speeding up decomposition is to turn your compost. Buy a corkscrew aerator or garden fork, and give your compost a turn each time you add new scraps. If you don't have the time, energy, ability or inclination to manually aerate your compost, that's fine, too. You can create an open structure that will stop the contents of your pile or bin collapsing too much and becoming anaerobic by adding sticks, woodchips and chopped–up hedge prunings between your usual green and brown inputs. For a no–turn compost, it's important to regularly add carbon of different sizes and textures (such as woodchips, sticks, straw/hay, cardboard and autumn leaves), as this creates pore spaces in your compost that capture oxygen. (For more aerating hacks, turn to page 30.)

ANOTHER METHOD FOR SPEEDING UP DECOMPOSITION IS TO TURN YOUR COMPOST WITH A CORKSCREW AERATOR OR GARDEN FORK.

HOT COMPOSTING

It's important that I start this section with a disclaimer: hot composting is a highly addictive process. You'll feel like some dark magic has occurred when you lift the lid off your compost and get hit by a blast of heat and observe steam billowing up. It's seriously thrilling to see the magical results of the heat–loving compost microbes.

WHY CHOOSE HOT COMPOSTING?

This is a winning method if you want to produce finished compost fast. The active decomposition of materials in a hot compost heap can occur in as little as a month because bacteria digest waste materials 32 times faster at 60 degrees Celsius than at 10 degrees Celsius. But you then need to cure your fresh compost for at least this length of time again, so don't get

too ahead of yourself! Hot composting requires a lot more attention and maintenance than slow composting, so don't pick this option if you want a hands–off experience.

HOW HOT COMPOSTING WORKS

The dominant microorganisms in a hot compost pile are thermophilic bacteria. The heat these amazing bacteria generate is actually a by–product of them consuming organic matter. The temperature range and length of time the thermophiles will produce heat depends on the volume of the pile (or size of your bin) and its moisture content, aeration and C:N ratio.

Thermophiles produce temperatures of 40–60 degrees Celsius – and higher, too – but you want to rein them in because if they generate too much heat, a lot of the nutrients in your compost will be burned away. Compost critters survive this scorching thermophilic stage by moving away from the hot core to the edge of your bin or pile, where temperatures are cooler. But most of these critters can't survive at temperatures above 65 degrees Celsius, so it's important to aerate really hot compost to bring the temperature down. Or you can try adding more carbon or spreading out the contents into a thinner and wider layer to cool things down.

Unlike a slow compost bin, which you add to gradually over a long period, a hot compost pile needs to be built all at once, in one fell swoop. You're going to feel like a real compost cook when you make your first hot compost pile, as it's a bit like baking a lasagne. The *mise en place* for the hot compost cook–off is a collection of 50:50 carbon to nitrogen (or 40 per cent greens to 60 per cent browns, depending on their C:N ratio) that you have ready to add all in one go.

You need to chop, mow, shred or mulch the organic matter into similar–sized pieces, as this ensures rapid decomposition of the material and also makes turning your compost pile far easier. Delivering oxygen via regular aerations is critical to the hot composting process. You can't skip this bit in the same way that you can with a slow compost bin. Just like a bonfire, hot compost is fuelled by oxygen.

Interestingly, water is just as important as oxygen in this style of composting. The addition of a generous amount of water when you're building your pile is essential for it to start cooking. You need to wet each layer thoroughly when adding your greens and browns. It's a good idea to have a sprinkler on hand, set on low, which you place on top of your pile after adding each new layer. Microbially induced decomposition in hot compost happens rapidly in the film of water on the surfaces of the organic matter in your compost, and without a moist environment these microbes will die off. So long story short: water and oxygen are indispensable to the life and active decomposition of your hot compost.

Another difference between hot and slow composting is the required volume. When you want to get hot, you have to go big – and I mean really big. The best pile size to ensure consistently hot compost is 1 metre × 1 metre × 1 metre, which is 1 cubic metre or 1000 litres of organic matter. Making a pile of this size works well for people with large gardens, but if you have a smaller yard and want to give hot composting a go, then home compost creators can have blisteringly hot compost with piles of 500 litres or slightly less, if you nail the C:N ratio and add a compost activator. There is no doubt that it's more challenging to create consistently hot compost in smaller volumes, but it's definitely possible.

One thing to note is that volumes of less than 1000 litres don't hold high temperatures for long because they don't have the critical mass to become self–insulating. So, don't add weeds that have gone to seed, diseased plant material or pernicious weeds to small hot compost piles. Your pile needs to reach 55–60 degrees Celsius for a minimum of three consecutive days, otherwise the weeds and diseases are not destroyed; they can then spread back into your soil via the finished compost. Not all batches cook enough when you first start experimenting with the hot compost method, and this can lead to compost heartbreak. So, when building your first hot compost pile, focus on adding disease–free plant matter and seedless weeds. This will allow you to enjoy the process and not stress about the results because, as you learned on pages 34–5, lukewarm and slow (cold) composting are still kick–arse – the compost just takes more time to be ready!

HOW TO MAKE HOT COMPOST

Follow the instructions below to get hot and steamy using plastic compost bins of 400–600 litres (you can't go any smaller than this, but you can absolutely go bigger if you have a bin or the space to accommodate this). You can also follow the steps below for bigger open piles, boxes and bays.

1. You'll need to pop on your compost-coloured glasses and go hunting for greens and browns because you need to stockpile enough ingredients to fill your compost bin all at once. This can be a bit tricky to manage when you have perishable scraps such as food waste. That's why I love Bokashi bins – they give me a place to store my household food waste while I'm gathering enough greens and browns for my latest batch of hot compost. (To learn about the wonders of Bokashi, turn to pages 91–105.)
2. Position your open-to-the-ground compost bin or pile directly on the soil to allow bugs, bacteria and fungi to travel into the organic matter to help break it down. If you're placing the pile directly on your lawn, it's a good idea to gently dig up sections of the grass (or at least wiggle a garden fork into the grass) to help with drainage. This step isn't essential, as the grass will be covered in organic matter and will eventually decompose (unless it's an invasive species such as kikuyu, which should be smothered with cardboard).
3. Add a generous foundation layer of 'fluffy' carbon-rich materials. Woodchips are best, but sticks and twigs work well, too. It should measure about 15 centimetres in height.
4. Water well.
5. Seed this carbon layer with a few handfuls of healthy garden soil, worm castings or well-cured compost.
6. Now add your first nitrogen-rich layer. It could be seaweed, animal manure, Bokashi compost, coffee grounds, spent plants, and so on. Make this layer about 7 centimetres thick.

7. Add a slightly thicker layer of carbon, aiming for about 10 centimetres. (I'm not expecting you to get out a measuring tape – eyeballing it is fine). This layer can be made from shredded brown leaves, aged woodchips or sawdust, weathered hay, shredded paper/cardboard, and so on.
8. Water well.
9. Now continue adding layers of greens and browns (watering in between) until your bin is full or your open pile is 1.5 metres high (it will shrink down to 1 metre). If you're concerned about nailing the C:N ratio, then measure out your ingredients in buckets. Depending on their C:N ratio (see pages 32–3), add one bucket of greens for every one bucket of browns if you're using a carbon-rich input (such as woodchips), or one bucket of greens for every one and a half to two buckets of browns with an input that has less available carbon (such as shredded brown leaves).
10. Once your bin is full or you've built your pile, it's important to leave it for four days to become active. This is especially vital if you've added material from a Bokashi bin, as it allows the effective microorganisms (EM) in the Bokashi material to inoculate the organic matter in your compost, which speeds up the decomposition.
11. Your compost should get hot within 24–36 hours after building it. If it doesn't get hot, then something is off and needs to be tweaked (it's usually down to the C:N ratio or lack of moisture at this point – if there is room in your bin, squeeze in some more moist greens and browns). If it's getting hot and sitting around 40–50 degrees Celsius, then you know that the thermophiles are at work. When composting in volumes that are less than 1000 litres, you can encourage hotter temperatures by adding more greens and browns as the level of your compost drops. These fresh ingredients should give rise to a further fiery peak in temperatures.

HERE'S A HOT TIP

The secret ratio for hot composting in small volumes is 50 per cent carbon (make sure at least 20 per cent is aged woodchips to improve airflow), 40 per cent nitrogen (from food scraps, manure or green garden waste) and 10 per cent nitrogen–rich activators (such as blood and bone, chicken manure or Bokashi material).

12. Decomposition is now occurring rapidly during the thermophilic stage (40–60 degrees Celsius). This period can last for several weeks in big compost piles, depending on your ingredient mix. In 400–600–litre compost bins, it generally lasts somewhere between three and ten days. This stage is really important for destroying pathogens, fly larvae and weed seeds (if you've added plants that have gone to seed). In my experience, your compost needs to be 55–60 degrees Celsius for at least three consecutive days to guarantee this. It's useful to get yourself a hot composting thermometer that has a temperature range up to at least 80 degrees Celsius, so you can monitor the temperature of your compost.

13. After four days, you need to give your compost a thorough aeration. The easiest method when working with a compost bin is to use a corkscrew aerator. Screw it through the layers and then pull it up. The first time you turn your compost will be the hardest, especially if you haven't chopped everything down to size. Use some muscle and persistence to get the job done. If you have two compost bins or bays next to each other, then you can use a garden fork to move the contents from the full section to the empty one. Find a method that works for you because ideally you'll aerate your compost every second day for two weeks. Monitor the moisture each time you turn your compost and add water when needed. If the organic matter dries out, the heat will quickly dissipate, so keep a watering-can handy.

14. Turning the compost and noticing any changes with your eyes and nose is important across the next few weeks. If you dig into the core of your compost and smell an unpleasant odour or see the development of a white ashy substance, it can be an early indication that anaerobic conditions are starting to take over. Give your compost a thorough turn to introduce more oxygen.

15. This process of aeration will result in temperature peaks, especially the first few times you do it, because you're introducing more oxygen and moving organic matter from the cooler outside of the pile to the inside where the real action occurs. After the thermophilic phase, the compost temperature will drop, and it won't be restored by turning or mixing. This is totally normal, so don't get too disappointed when this happens. As the heat–loving thermophilic bacteria die off, mesophilic bacteria that thrive at temperatures between 20–40 degrees Celsius will repopulate your pile and continue the composting process.

16. Once your compost has completely cooled down, it's essential to leave it for at least six weeks to cure. (To learn about curing, turn to pages 50–6.) So be patient, and you'll soon end up with beautiful black gold for your garden.

ESSENTIAL INGREDIENTS

I can't provide you with a single 'recipe' for hot compost because every batch is different, depending on the season, but some inputs that I always try to add are nitrogen–rich activators such as Bokashi material, fresh seaweed, small amounts of blood and bone, and manure from our chooks (no more than 5 per cent of the total volume). Adding compost activators is important when filling a bin with a volume that is less than 1000 litres. (To learn more about activators, turn to pages 65–6.) I usually add a handful or two of grey and black material, too, in the form of rock minerals or dusts and biochar. These are magical ingredients that really energise the hot composting microbes. (For more about grey and black material, turn to pages 229–32.)

OPPOSITE:
It was a privilege to make hot compost with Robyn Rosenfeldt, the founder and publisher of Australia's PIP Magazine, at her permaculture property in Pambula on the far south coast of New South Wales.

ALESSANDRO VITALE

THE URBAN COMPOSTER

ALESSANDRO VITALE – also known as Spicy Moustache – is an urban gardener in London who has captured the imagination of city dwellers yearning to green up their homes. The gardening advice and inspiration that Alessandro shares in his book, *Rebel Gardening*, and on his social-media platforms focus on transforming small yards, balconies and even windowsills into highly productive and beautifully immersive spaces. Alessandro shows us how living soil, creatures and plants can coexist in concrete jungles, and how this green space can become a sanctuary from the daily grind.

How did you develop your green thumb?

I started gardening with my grandparents when I was a kid, and I learned a lot from them about the living soil and how to cook without wasting any part of the fruits and vegetables we grew. Unfortunately, my grandad passed when I was ten, and I lost that link with nature as I pursued my career. Ironically, moving to London later in life gave me the push I needed to rediscover nature and create my green corner, where I could detach from the busy routine of the city. Over the past seven years, I have moved a lot – but I have never left behind any part of my garden, including soil, raised beds, pots and even my glass greenhouse! I think that everyone has the time to tend to a garden; it is really a question of priorities and how you decide to invest genuine time and effort.

How do you overcome the difficulties of greening up small urban backyards?

The biggest lesson, which I learned from moving house many times, is the importance of planning. Investing time in planning your space can really improve your garden's productivity. In most urban gardens, you don't get sun all day in the whole space. I usually spend at least two weeks observing the sun rotation over the garden before I start deciding what to grow where. I then plant sun-loving plants where I have sunlight for most of the day, and plants that can thrive in shade or semi-shade in all of the other parts of my growing space. This is crucial if you want to make sure that your garden will reach its peak potential!

What space-saving techniques do you employ to maximise your harvest?

Most people tend to see a growing space horizontally, trying to fit as many things as possible on one level, but using vertical gardening could double – if not triple – your output. This is why I recycle a lot of materials to use in my garden. I use plastic type-2 HDPE (high-density polyethylene)

bottles, which are frost- and heat-resistant and don't leak chemicals into the soil, to make hanging containers or vertical gardens. If you do this, you'll reduce your waste and save money in the garden, which is a win-win situation!

To plant my seeds, I use Charles Dowding's multisowing method. It's perfect for maximising the harvest for beetroot, onions for bulbs, spring onions, leeks, radishes, parsnips, peas for shoots and pods, dill, parsley, basil, lettuce for leaves, spinach, mustard and chard. You need to sow four to six seeds for larger plants, or six to eight seeds for smaller plants, in a single cell. You can thin out weak plants later, so you are left with the number that you want in your cluster. The results are impressive, and you can harvest each plant once it is ready, leaving the others in the ground to develop further.

I have tried many techniques when planting out in the garden, but one seems to work better than others for me: square foot gardening by Mel Bartholomew. The basic idea is to make a tiny garden (4 feet by 4 feet or 4 feet by 8 feet is typical), and divide it into a grid of 1–foot squares that you care for individually. Each type of vegetable is represented by one or more squares, and seeds or seedlings are planted there at a density determined by the expected mature size of the plants.

I use other techniques, too, but what I always say is what may work for me may not work for you, so don't be scared to experiment. Even if you fail, it will still be a valuable lesson that can teach you something and improve your skills and knowledge.

What is the most successful repurposed item in your garden?

It would be my raised garden beds, most of which I built using dismantled pallets. I fill them up using the Hügelkultur technique, which doesn't break the bank. You start by laying cardboard at the bottom if you have weeds growing (not a problem in my concrete garden!). You follow up with big logs, making sure to source wood that doesn't inhibit the growth of the plant, then a layer of twigs (apple–tree branches are ideal). You can now add spoiled hay, unfinished compost and kitchen scraps (no dairy, meat or oil), following up with mature compost, soil and a draining material (such as vermiculite). This bed can be planted straight away.

How do you successfully hot compost in your small garden?

In my garden, I repurposed an old barrel, drilled holes all around the sides and at the bottom, and transformed it into a hot compost bin. It worked great for a few years but harvesting the final product was hard, as I had to remove the top layer and slowly start digging until the barrel was light enough to be lifted and tilted.

LEFT:
You can hot compost in a small urban garden using a system like Alessandro's 'bio reactor'.

I found a much better solution thanks to my dear friend, Michael Kennard. Using an old pallet and some mesh looped and joined by cable ties, we created a system that he likes to call a 'bio reactor'. You can replicate this in pretty much any location and size. I insert two to four poles or branches inside the compost bin, and then layer the materials around them in the same way as a normal composting system. Once the bin is full, I slide out the poles/branches – this increases oxygen and helps to speed up the decomposition by microorganisms, resulting in a final product that will establish and then feed a healthy soil food web. I manage to produce quite a good amount of compost and worm castings in my garden, which helps me to not only save money but also understand my soil biology and know exactly what I'm adding to my growing space.

Which small-space sustainable solutions soften your impact on the planet?

To me, gardening is about not only growing food but also trying to be sustainable in every aspect of my life. There are many things that you could do more sustainably, even if you live in the middle of the city like me. I usually buy from zero-waste shops, or refill shops where you bring old jars, paper bags, and so on. This is a great way to reduce the amount of plastic coming into your home.

What we don't grow in the garden, we buy from local farmers' markets to support small businesses; this also means that the food doesn't have to travel long distances and is not packaged but delivered fresh. We also preserve most of our food by dehydrating, fermenting, canning, pickling or freezing it, so we can enjoy fresh produce throughout the year. I highly recommend that you start by saving your own seeds and growing your own produce, which are two of the most empowering actions that any individual can take – and so you don't have to rely on big corporations to supply the food chain.

CURING YOUR COMPOST

Curing is the process of allowing compost that has finished the active phase of decomposition time to mature. It's an essential step for a number of reasons:

- Compost that is too fresh and has not been cured can damage sensitive plant roots.
- It allows time for the compost to become stable, and for beneficial fungi, worms, beetles and other critters in your garden to make their way into the compost.
- Microorganisms can recover nitrogen from the remaining woody particles that degrade during the curing process, which results in mature compost being higher in nitrogen than freshly decomposed compost.

Curing compost is especially important if you build a hot compost pile. People are often surprised to learn that hot compost will often have no worms present until the curing phase. Many creatures of the compost cannot stand the heat, so they make a quick escape until the thermophilic microbes have done their thing and conditions have cooled.

In hot composting, worms act like a litmus test to help you to determine when the compost is ready to use. When worms start returning to your pile, there will be other microorganisms helping to cure it, too, such as fungi, protozoa and nematodes. Many of these composting buddies are sneaky little suckers, as they're completely invisible to the naked eye, so the worm becomes the compost maker's indicator species.

ABOVE:
If space is an issue, then you can cure your compost in an empty garden bed (ideally for at least six weeks) before you plant it out.

OPPOSITE:
A garden sieve works well to remove chunky bits of organic matter (such as corncobs), which can be added back into your next batch of compost.

WHEN DOES THE CURING PROCESS START?

With hot compost, you need to wait until the temperature of the compost reaches the ambient outdoor temperature – even if it looks like soil sooner than this – before the curing process starts.

It can be a bit harder to know when to start the 'curing clock' with slow compost, because it doesn't transition from hot to warm to cold. But curing really starts when the compost looks 'ready' (more about this below). Basically, if you can pick out food scraps and grass clippings or big pieces of cardboard, it's not ready to start curing.

HOW DO YOU CURE COMPOST?

To cure the compost, you should ideally make sure that it's in direct contact with the earth. This may mean removing your compost from a tumbler or enclosed bin and shovelling it onto a damp patch of soil in your garden, and placing a tarpaulin over it. If the compost is in a heap or open–based bin on the ground, you can just leave it where it is; but if you have the space, then taking it out of the heap/bin and spreading it out a little on the ground will speed up the process.

If you don't have exposed soil at your place, putting your compost in a bucket or bin out of the rain with a few handfuls of healthy garden soil works almost as well. This helps to introduce soil biology – such as insects, worms and beneficial fungi – to the pile.

Fungi–rich compost is magical for your soil. So, rejoice if you see mushrooms or mycelia bloom during the curing phase. Don't aerate the compost at this stage; if you do, you'll disturb the fungal development.

One thing is certain: throughout the curing process, it's essential that you keep the compost moist at all times. The compost won't continue to process if it dries out.

WHAT ABOUT THE CHUNKS?

Even in finished, cured compost, you'll still find the odd 'chunky bit' – especially in compost that was processed 'cold'. Things such as bones, woodchips, eggshells and corncobs will hang around. You have two choices:

1. Pick out the biggest bits as you spread the compost, or shake the compost through a garden sieve. Don't bother removing small bits such as eggshells, otherwise you'll go mad; they'll break down in the soil over time. You can put the bits you pick out back into a fresh compost pile. They'll help to kickstart the next batch because there'll be beneficial organisms clinging to them.

2. Ignore them because they'll continue to decay once they're in the soil. But remember, it's not a good idea to add compost with a lot of uncomposted woody material to your edible garden (unless it's added as a surface mulch) because it will steal nitrogen from the soil to continue the decomposition.

HOW LONG DOES CURING TAKE?

This stage can be as short as six weeks or as long as six months. It really depends on how patient you are and the sort of ingredients you added. However, as a general rule, the longer the better.

If your compost was primarily built with plant–based scraps, then a minimum curing period of six weeks is usually sufficient. If you added a lot of manure or animal products, then it's best to cure your compost for double this length of time. Twelve weeks allows for the composted manure to become stable and safe to use. Studies have shown that some manure–borne pathogens can persist in hot compost, but they disappear over time as the compost cures.

There are some types of fungi and bacteria found in your pile that are not active at higher temperatures, but will get active when the compost is curing. These organisms will continue to break down tougher plant tissues (including bark and wood) that survive the hot phase. The longer you leave your compost to cure, the finer its texture and the higher its nitrogen content due to the activity of these microorganisms.

WHEN WILL YOUR COMPOST BE READY TO USE?

Compost is ready when it looks, feels and smells like rich, dark earth: it should be a fairly even, dark brown colour; it should be crumbly, without any visible food scraps, leaves or bark; and it shouldn't have any strong or foul odours.

The photo at the top of this page shows what my compost looks like before and after two months of curing.

There are scientific methods of testing the compost for maturity, but they can take some time and involve complicated equipment. So, here are three easy tests that will tell you if your compost is mature and ready to use.

1. Bag test – Put a handful of moist compost into a plastic zip–lock bag and press out the air before sealing it. Leave the bag in a cool, dark cupboard for three days, then open the bag. If you can smell an ammonia or sour odour, then the microorganisms are still at work and your compost needs more time to finish curing (and may also need a thorough aeration). Repeat this test with a new sample taken from your compost a week or two later. Well–cured compost that is

ready to be applied to your garden should not be pungent, but have an earthy smell.

2. Cress test – A germination test is another good way to check if your compost is mature and stable. Put some compost into a pot, and sprinkle it with cress seeds. Cover the seeds with another handful of compost, and give them a gentle water. If 75 per cent of the seeds germinate, and the first two leaves grow without discolouration or deformation, then your compost is ready to use.

3. Compost pH test – Using a pH testing kit, check to see if your cured compost has a pH of 6–8.

Don't freak out if you haven't done any of these tests in the past. I don't test every batch, but it's useful to do a couple of times when you're a beginner compost creator as it gives you a clear answer about when your compost is ready.

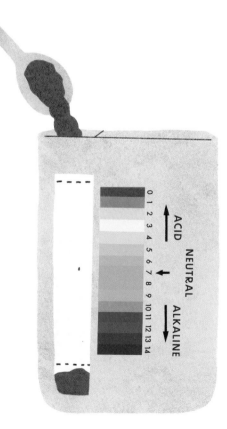

MONITORING COMPOST PH

Testing the pH of your compost a couple of times during the decomposition process is really useful, as it takes away the guesswork. You don't need to do this for every batch of compost you make (unless you love getting firm data), but when you're first getting the hang of the composting process, this info will let you know how your compost is going.

- An aerobic (oxygen-rich) compost that's in the initial stages of decomposition will have a slightly acidic pH (around 5–7) because compost microbes are producing acids and enzymes to break down the cell walls of cellulose (in plant materials) and lignin (in wood). This pH range is ideal, as compost microbes and fungi multiply rapidly in neutral to slightly acidic conditions.

- As aerobic composting continues, the acids will become neutralised. You should see an increase in pH in mature compost that is ready to use. Cured compost generally has a pH between 6 and 8.

- If your compost becomes anaerobic (oxygen-free), you'll not only smell it, but also see from a pH test that it has become acidic (with a pH of 5.5 or lower). Organic acids increase rather than neutralise in anaerobic compost. If this happens in your compost, simply aerate it manually to reintroduce oxygen over several consecutive days. Old-school composting guides often recommend adding a handful of dolomite or garden lime (calcium carbonate), but this causes nitrogen to be lost to the atmosphere as ammonia gas. The release of this gas will actually make your compost smellier, and it also decreases the amount of nitrogen in the finished compost.

- Be aware that your compost may have an alkaline (high) pH if you've added a lot of manure or wood ash, and this can interrupt the natural composting process. So, be mindful of how much you add (especially if your soil is alkaline, too) because this alkalinity won't lower significantly throughout the composting process.

HOW DO YOU USE CURED COMPOST?

All soil, whether it's around your edible or ornamental plants, under your lawn or in pots or raised beds, will benefit from a generous application of homemade compost a couple of times a year. In the past, gardeners would work compost into the soil by digging, tilling or forking it in. We now know that this causes more harm than good to the soil ecosystem, so the methods I've outlined in the following table are all based on gentle applications that work with nature, not against it.

USAGE	HOW TO DO IT
Planting out a vegie patch	It's fine to add a handful of compost into the holes around tender-rooted seedlings in your vegie patch. This won't negatively impact their root development but will provide nutrients right where they need them: at the root zone. Later in the season, when plants go through a growth spurt, you can add a few handfuls or a 1.5–2.5-centimetre layer of compost around the base of the plants. This is especially useful for hungry plants such as tomatoes, cucumbers, capsicums, zucchini, corn and pumpkins. If you have enough compost, add it to the soil's surface around heavy feeders every month during spring and summer, and this will result in bountiful produce.
Maintaining a vegie patch	Top-dress your vegie patch with finished compost. Pull back any mulch material, and apply the compost directly onto the surface of the soil. This is best done after rain or a good soaking with a hose. Ideally, add 2.5–5 centimetres at a time. Cover the compost with dried mulch if you live in a hot, dry climate. The combination of compost and mulch helps to prevent weed growth and makes your plants more drought-tolerant. If slugs are a problem in your patch, then leave off mulch to stop them hiding in it.
Planting out trees and shrubs	When planting out trees and bigger shrubs, it's best to avoid putting compost directly into the planting hole as this can discourage roots from growing beyond the hole. Instead, apply compost to the surface of the soil once you've backfilled the hole. Earthworms and other soil-dwelling critters will gradually incorporate the compost into the soil to feed your plant.
Maintaining established trees	Apply compost as a surface mulch around established trees to their drip line. First, pull back any mulch or grass that is growing between the trunk and the outermost branches (this area is known as the drip line). Add 2.5–5 centimetres of compost to this area. Make sure that the compost doesn't touch the trunk, as this can lead to rotting. Leave a 5-centimetre compost-free moat around the trunk, and cover the compost with mulch (such as hay, woodchips and grass clippings) to keep it moist.

USAGE	HOW TO DO IT
Planting out and maintaining a no dig garden bed	Place cardboard on the surface of your lawn or soil, and top with 10–12 centimetres of compost. Firm this layer down by gently walking on it. This will help the plant roots to have more anchorage and to hold moisture in this new bed. You can plant directly into the compost, and within six months the cardboard will decompose and the plant roots will reach into the native soil below. Add another 5 centimetres of compost to the bed every year. (To learn more about compost and its use in no dig gardening, turn to pages 112–15.)
Maintaining container gardens and potted plants	Potting mixes become depleted of nutrients as plants grow. Adding compost to your potted plants once or twice a year replenishes nutrients. Thoroughly soak the container, pot, tub or box before adding up to 3 centimetres of well–cured compost to the surface of the potting mix. Be aware that a few viable worm eggs may hitch a ride in the compost and hatch in your pots. Worms can live happily in containers if the potting mix and compost is kept moist, so this is not really a concern.
Rejuvenating lawn or turf	Spread well–sieved compost over your lawn as a top dressing twice a year. Use a rake to disperse the compost, and within a week you'll no longer notice it. Lawns are hungry and thirsty, but feeding your turf compost will reduce the need to apply fertilisers and bucketloads of water in summer.
Making a quick soil drench	Steep a handful or two of cured compost in a bucket filled with water for a couple of minutes, give it a thorough mix and then apply as a drench to new seedlings. This helps to spread the compost over a larger surface area and allows the nutrients and microorganisms to penetrate deeper into the soil around the root zone of plants. Pour the drench onto your seedlings from the bucket, as compost chunks will block a watering–can's rose.
Making aerated compost tea	Make aerated compost tea, as the brewing process frees up nutrients and allows the compost microbes to proliferate. This is a gentle plant food, not a fertiliser; however, by adding biology and life to the soil, you'll end up with healthier plants. (For the full recipe and method, turn to pages 234–6.)

WHEN DO YOU APPLY CURED COMPOST?

You can spread cured compost onto your garden whenever it's ready, but you'll see the best results in plant growth and resilience if you apply it to your garden at least one month before each growing season. In most parts of Australia, our climate allows for year-round gardening, which means compost can be applied to gardens almost continuously. However, you'll get more bang for your buck if compost is applied before the two major growing seasons: cool and warm.

If you live in a temperate climate, then aim to spread the bulk of your compost at the start of autumn (to protect plant roots and to conserve moisture over winter) and the beginning of spring. This allows time for microbes and critters to incorporate the compost into your soil and means that the nutrients are more readily available to plants.

If you live in a cold climate with one major growing season, then it's best to apply the bulk of your compost once a year, in autumn before the ground freezes. The compost will slowly decompose during the winter months and help to protect your soil from harsh weather events. As the weather warms, your garden will be ready for planting in spring.

Another benefit of applying compost at least one month before you sow seeds or plant out seedlings is it allows time for any volunteer seedlings to germinate and emerge. I think all compost creators have spread a luscious load of finished compost or worm castings onto their soil, only to come back a few days later to see a veritable sea of tomato, cucumber or pumpkin seedlings springing up. If you use a slow composting process, this is inevitable (without heat to kill them, some seeds will always germinate). But this is not a big deal if you've built in time for this to happen. You can either hand-pull these cheeky surprise seedlings or turn them back through your soil as a bonus green-manure crop.

HOW MUCH SHOULD YOU APPLY?

You can be pretty liberal and generous with the amount of compost you add to your garden. As a general rule, add up to 2.5 centimetres of well-cured compost to soil that is organically rich. You can do a simple 'eyeball test' to determine the quality of your soil. Generally speaking, soil with a high concentration of organic matter will be dark brown to black in colour. Soil that is pale brown, yellow-brown, greyish black, golden brown or light red doesn't contain as much organic matter and will benefit from a generous feed of compost each growing season, as much as 5 centimetres per season if you have enough compost on hand.

Remember, compost is a living soil conditioner rather than a fertiliser. So, to give your edible patch a complete feed, also add nitrogen inputs such as blood and bone, aged chicken manure (pelletised is fine), worm castings, liquid foliar feeds and soil drenches. (To learn about how to make your own organic soil teas, turn to pages 234–40.)

COMPOST PROBLEMS AND SOLUTIONS

Making compost is not an exact science. Each batch will be different due to the seasonal availability of scraps, the changes in the weather and variations in your compost management. It's inevitable that at some point you'll make a batch that goes bad. Thankfully, composting is a forgiving process, and you can always fix a mistake. Here are the most common composting problems and their solutions.

OPPOSITE:
Pull back mulch around plants, and apply cured compost directly onto the surface of the soil. Add mulch back on top, and water in to make the life in your soil happy.

MY COMPOST STINKS

There are three main reasons why your compost pile is on the nose:

1. You've added too many greens and forgotten about the browns. If your C:N ratio is out of whack, then your compost pile will quickly start to smell. Empty out the contents of your compost and rebuild it with layers of carbon-rich materials (such as brown leaves, aged woodchips, torn-up newspaper or hay) between the nitrogen-heavy compost. Then give your compost a big aeration to combine the layers. Adjust moisture levels by adding dry carbon or more water if needed. Doing this will quickly bring your compost back into balance and stop the stench.

2. Your compost is lacking adequate oxygen. The pile will start to reek like rotten eggs as the anaerobic bacteria produce hydrogen sulphide and methane. Introduce oxygen into your compost via active daily aeration (in other words, turning it) until it stops stinking. Adding carbon with different sizes and textures will help, too, as inputs such as small woodchips and sticks create open pore spaces that capture oxygen in your pile and stop your compost from compacting.

3. You've added the right ratio of greens and browns, but they were added in thick layers. If nitrogen-rich scraps (such as a thick layer of grass clippings) are isolated from carbon materials, the organic matter can start to putrefy and

stink. Thankfully, this is easily fixed by turning your compost to mix the layers more thoroughly.

Fix all of these things, and I reckon I'll be able to hear the members of your household (and your neighbours) cheering.

MY COMPOST IS TOO WET

If your compost gets soaked in a downpour or you've been a bit heavy-handed with the hose, then it's important to rectify this before the organic matter becomes anaerobic. To fix a wet, slimy, smelly compost pile, turn the compost daily and add plenty of dry brown materials to absorb some of the moisture.

If your open pile got saturated and you've got the space, then the quickest way to fix it is to spread the contents into a thin layer on the ground on a sunny day. The excessive moisture will quickly evaporate.

MY COMPOST IS NOT BREAKING DOWN

There are several reasons why the organic matter in your compost bin is taking ages to decompose:

- Compost that is dry will break down slowly, as the microbes will go on strike. Grab a handful of scraps from the centre of your compost and give it a squeeze. If you can't squeeze out a droplet of moisture, then you need to add more water to your compost to speed up decomposition.
- Compost that is made from lots of big scraps and plant prunings can take an age to decompose. You'll need to dismantle your compost and go to town with a pair of secateurs or a shredder to cut everything down to size. The smaller the inputs, the more readily they'll decompose.
- If your compost is a bit carbon-heavy, then the rate of decomposition will slow. Add some nitrogen-rich compost activators to get the party reignited. (To learn more, turn to pages 65–6.)

- All of your nitrogen-rich greens (such as food scraps) have broken down, but a lot of the carbon hasn't. This can happen for two reasons: too little nitrogen was added, or your compost was too dry. You can separate the finished compost by sieving out the carbon, and then add the carbon back into your next batch with more greens and some compost activators.
- If your compost is breaking down slowly and you see fungi fruiting and producing mushrooms, please don't despair. This is a great sign, as the fungi are working hard to break down the lignin in woody materials and to make nutrients more available for the compost bacteria.

MY COMPOST IS FULL OF BUGS

Believe it or not, this may not be a problem. An active composting system and worm farm will be alive with all sorts of critters that are busy recycling your waste. I really encourage you to try to get over the ick factor when it comes to creepy crawlies. Bugs are essential workers in the community of microorganisms that consume your scraps and transform them into black gold. However, if flies, ants, cockroaches or rodents are an issue, turn to pages 154–6 to discover how to evict these unwanted visitors.

OPPOSITE:
Heavy-feeding crops (such as tomatoes) love a generous serve of compost once a month during the growing season. Apply it to the drip zone around the plant.

TIPS FOR SUCCESSFUL WINTER COMPOSTING

When the temperature drops and short days arrive, managing an outdoor compost pile can feel like a seriously undesirable chore. There's no doubt that winter puts a chill on composting: the organic material from your garden or neighbourhood become much less plentiful, and cold conditions slow down the activity of the microbes in your pile. However, your compost can keep on chugging along during the cooler months with a bit of planning in autumn and some simple steps in winter.

I should point out that while this section is mostly for people who live in places where the temperature gets down near or below 0 degrees Celsius for extended periods, there are useful things for everyone to know. I also want to make it clear that it's harder – but not impossible – to hot compost throughout winter. The key to success is the size of your pile. Don't attempt to make hot compost with a volume less than 1000 litres in the depths of winter, otherwise you'll be disappointed. The tips below will work for both small slow composting bins and large hot composting piles.

AUTUMN PREP FOR EXISTING PILES

Get your raw materials organised in autumn! You'll produce greens from your kitchen all winter, but browns can be a problem – so, collect as many brown leaves as you can, and stockpile them in autumn. You can store them in large garden bags or bins, or make a tower

from chicken wire and fill it with leaves. (But try to keep some of them dry, for the reasons discussed below.)

Harvest as much cured compost as you can during autumn (as this is one of the best times to apply it to your soil). Now fill your composting system to near capacity with new green and brown material, including plenty of small sticks and dry leaves to create open spaces that capture air. This will give the microbes lots of raw material to work on through the really cold months. Add structural carbon such as small branches and woodchips to trap oxygen within the pile, so you won't have to turn it during winter.

You can insulate your pile by covering it with a generous layer of leaves or straw. This will help to keep in the heat generated by the pile. If you want to add greens, then tuck them under the carbon blanket you've made. If you're composting in a bin, surround it with bales of straw or garden bags filled with leaves; you can move these things easily when you need to access the bin. You can also insulate your compost bin with old woollen blankets or even re–use pieces of bubble wrap. All of these options provide a snuggly compost cover that helps to trap the heat.

LOCATION OF WINTER COMPOSTING SYSTEMS

During winter, compost situated in an open bay in the shade is not going to stay as warm as compost placed in an enclosed black–plastic bin in the sun. So, if you live in an area that gets really cold, think about the type of system and the location of your compost. If you're lucky enough to have a greenhouse, you could put your composting system in there.

If winter brings rain, then you may find that an open compost pile gets too wet. Moisture will come from both the sky and the soil, as the organic matter will suck up excessive water from rain–drenched earth. Remember that while the pile needs to be moist, if it becomes saturated then you're creating an anaerobic environment and the contents will start to rot and become very smelly. So, a fully enclosed bin may be a better option for composting if you live somewhere that gets a lot of winter rain.

If you have an open bay system, then covering the pile with a tarpaulin is a good idea. Don't forget to build your pile on a carbon–rich base layer made from plenty of sticks to elevate your compost from the wet ground. Or you could try building your open pile on top of untreated timber pallets, as this allows for good airflow and drainage. Make sure you add dry browns if the weather is wet and cold (cover your stockpile of leaves, too, or you'll end up adding soggy leaves).

If you're up for some hard yakka, then you can dig a pit at least 30 centimetres deep for the compost pile, regardless of whether it's going to be open or in a bin. This will help to keep the pile insulated and active during winter. (This goes for worm farms, too: an in-ground farm is going to do much better in a cold winter than an above–ground one because the surrounding soil will help to keep the worms warm and snug.) This works well for cold, dry climates; if winter is wet where you live, I don't recommend doing this as water can pool in the base of the compost pit.

If you get a lot of snow, choose the location of your pile based on how much work will be required to get to it in winter. A spot that's part of an area you keep clear of snow is perfect. If you use a tumbler, HOTBIN® or Aerobin®, then you may be able to move it into a garage or greenhouse for winter. Similarly, if you have a worm farm that is above ground, you may want to put it in a shed, garage or other warm location for the winter.

CARE OF COMPOST IN WINTER

You need to keep adding both greens and browns during winter. If you forget to add browns, then you'll end up with a stinky, wet mess come the spring thaw. This is why I told you to stockpile browns in autumn! If you have a bag, bin or tower of leaves next to your pile, then you can toss some in the compost every time you add your kitchen waste.

Add to your compost as infrequently as possible in winter because your pile will lose heat each time you open the lid or pull aside the leaf 'blanket' or tarpaulin. So, keep a compost caddy or bucket (or, better yet, a Bokashi bin) inside to collect green and brown material from your kitchen, and then add as much as you can in one go.

The smaller the 'bits' you add in winter the better because there is more surface area for the microbes to get to work on. So, if you can, dice your kitchen scraps and tear up the bits of paper and cardboard.

If you live somewhere really cold, then it's a good idea to skip aerating your compost in winter (yay!). This is because turning the organic matter will let out a lot of the heat, and this will slow the decomposition process. Instead, add sticks and chunky bits of carbon (such as aged woodchips) to create air pockets in your heap, and then wait until the weather warms up in spring before you turn the pile.

If your compost freezes solid, then many of the microbes will become dormant and not much will happen until the weather warms up. While psychrophilic bacteria are still active in very cold temperatures, they work far more slowly than their hot composting relations. (Adding pelletised chicken manure, blood and bone or other high–nitrogen amendments – such as urine! – will help keep temperatures and microbial activity up.) You can keep adding fresh greens and browns on top of a frozen pile, because at a molecular level the frozen scraps have been transformed and will break down fast once they defrost. Also, frozen scraps don't stink!

If the water in your compost pile has frozen over winter, then it will get released when the pile thaws, which can produce a slimy and smelly pile. If this has happened to your compost, then it's time to aerate the pile and to add more carbon materials: brown leaves (if you have any left from autumn), torn–up cardboard or thin layers of aged hay are all good options.

OTHER WINTER COMPOSTING OPTIONS

Like a lot of activities, composting can come indoors during the frozen months with help from Bokashi bins, soil factories or small worm farms. Ferment kitchen scraps in a Bokashi bin (see pages 91–105) and then process them indoors in a soil factory, or you can add the bin's contents to your outdoor compost.

Processing your food waste indoors in a worm farm is an excellent winter activity. Eventually, you'll have plenty of worm castings ready for your spring garden. Worm farms don't smell when they're managed correctly – adding plenty of carbon is the secret. (For more on worm farms, turn to Chapter 5.)

TIME TO MOISTURISE

If your compost is exposed to low humidity and winter winds, then it can dry out. Wet the pile (sparingly) on days when the water won't immediately freeze, and keep the pile covered if possible to retain the moisture.

CLASH OF THE ASH

If you get a lot of ash from your winter fires, then it can be tempting to add it to the compost. But this can cause more harm than good: wood ash can quickly raise the pH of the compost pile, decreasing microbial activity. Most of the beneficial organisms in compost piles do best when the pH is neutral to slightly acidic. So, add ash sparingly in small handfuls every now and again.

OPPOSITE:
Bokashi material is being mixed with carbon before it's added as an activator to a hot compost pile.

COMPOST ACTIVATORS

If you want to make bread, then you can mix flour and water together and wait; eventually, some native yeast will become active and multiply, but it might take days. But if you want to have bread tomorrow morning, then you add a 'starter' or commercial yeast to your flour and water. Compost is the same. If you mix up green and grown matter and wait, then it will decompose because there are composting microbes present on all organic matter. But if you add an activator, then you can be certain that the decomposition process will kick off almost straight away.

A compost activator's job is to feed the microbial colony in the pile, and to inject extra nitrogen to support the microbes' reproduction. This will fire up your bin fast.

Activators come in many different forms:

- Finished and matured compost, which is loaded with good bugs and bacteria, should be mixed with new organic matter in your composting system to speed things up. Adding a handful of healthy, humus-rich garden soil is an alternative to finished compost if you don't have any on hand, or you could ask a friend for a few handfuls of their compost. Think of it like a sourdough starter: it's the 'mother' of your compost, taking the active microbes from the last batch and dropping them into the new batch to start the process again.
- Bokashi bins (see pages 91–105) are the bee's knees of homemade compost activators. The heat from your compost is a by-product of the microbes breaking down organic material. The faster they do it, the more heat is produced. This is where Bokashi bins come in. Your nitrogen-rich food scraps are fermented in the Bokashi bin, a process whereby microorganisms digest sugars, starches and proteins. Fermenting food increases the digestibility

of the nitrogen by compost bacteria, and this is enough to give the compost process a real kickstart.
- Plants with high levels of minerals are useful additions. Comfrey leaves are king, but dandelion, lucerne (alfalfa), yarrow leaves, stinging nettle and borage leaves are great, too.
- Manure from chickens, cows, sheep and rabbits is rich in nitrogen, potassium and phosphorus. But fresh manure contains a lot of water, and will inhibit the airflow in your pile, so well-aged manure is the good shit (so to speak), and has the added benefit of not being stinky. Some manure, especially from horses, carries weed seeds, so it's important that your compost reaches 60 degrees Celsius for at least three days straight to stop the seeds from germinating. For urban gardeners, pelletised chicken manure, Dynamic Lifter® or blood and bone are useful additions when used sparingly.
- Used coffee grounds are high in nitrogen, so they're a great addition to your compost and they'll help to get the contents of your bin hot and steamy. (To learn more about composting coffee grounds, turn to pages 164–5.)

- Urine is liquid gold, as it contains a lot of nitrogen that will give your compost a quick boost. So, go ahead and wee on your compost pile if you feel like it. (To learn more about safely using urine in your compost, turn to pages 178–9.)

- Protein meal from lucerne (alfalfa) or cottonseed is a good vegetarian substitute for animal manure or blood and bone. It's full of nitrogen, phosphorus and potassium (which you'll see described by NPK values on commercial fertiliser products). Look for organic products if you want to make sure you aren't introducing pesticides and herbicides to your pile. Use protein meal when building a pile in one go by sprinkling it every 15 centimetres or so, and wetting it. If you're gradually adding to your pile, have a bucket full of the stuff nearby and toss in a handful when you add a bucket of scraps and carbon.

- A more adventurous but readily available activator for those living in rural areas is roadkill. Burying a dead animal in the centre of a compost pile you're building in one go will add lots of valuable nutrients. If you want to do this, then you'll need to make sure that you've rodent–proofed your compost and there is good airflow around the carcass because you won't want to turn the pile for a while. Use aged woodchips and small sticks below and around the animal.

- Fish waste is another great compost activator. Deal with it just like roadkill.

There are also other commercially produced compost activators, which will do the job. But if you can make your own at home, then it's better than buying something in plastic packaging.

HOW COMPOSTING KILLS PATHOGENS

If you're wondering whether or not it's safe to compost your meat scraps, diseased plants or roadkill, then the simple answer is: yes. But why is this so?

The first reason is heat. The heat generated in the pile is the number–one killer of pathogens, bacteria and viruses. Thermophilic bacteria should heat your compost to about 60 degrees Celsius, which will knock off almost all of the pathogens in the pile.

The second reason is acidity. In both hot and cold compost and Bokashi bins, the microbes produce organic acids and ammonia, causing the pH to drop and the pile to become acidic. This acidic environment is inhospitable to pathogens.

The third reason is that compost microbes also produce some other cool stuff that pathogens don't like:

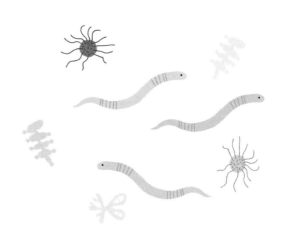

- Some produce killer enzymes that have the ability to destroy pathogenic cells by chemically invading and breaking their outer membrane, in a process known as lysis.
- Others produce chemicals that force certain pathogens to 'germinate' prematurely, rendering them harmless by the time the compost is finished.
- Some compost microorganisms produce antibiotic substances that directly attack pathogens, while others stage attacks via parasitism.

Finally, compost microbes are hungry for nutrients, and they can actually outcompete pathogens for food (this happens in the case of EM bacteria in your Bokashi bin). With not enough food, the pathogens can't reproduce and will be harmless by the time you're ready to use the finished compost.

COMPOST MICROBES ARE HUNGRY FOR NUTRIENTS, AND THEY CAN OUTCOMPETE PATHOGENS FOR FOOD.

COMMUNITY COMPOSTING

Making compost can quickly become an addictive pastime. If you're hooked, then you'll always be looking for scraps. To fuel this habit, you may want to upscale your backyard set-up by opening up the food-waste floodgates: collecting scraps from your neighbours, local cafés and schools or your workplace. If you have the space, time and energy, you may wish to sign up to the free global composting app ShareWaste and become a Compost Host. Or alternatively, you could set up a community composting system so your neighbours can join in on the dirty deed, too.

Community composting can foster a much closer relationship to your neighbours and your wider community. When I used to live in a tiny terrace in Sydney's inner west, I collected waste from my neighbours, local cafés and small businesses (such as newspapers from newsagents, coffee grounds from our local barista and sad, limp fruits and vegies from an obliging greengrocer). I met heaps of people, whom I now consider mates, by accepting and composting their scraps.

Here are some tips that will help you to set up a seamless composting system for your neighbourhood:

- Start small with one or two compost bins and expand if needed.
- Use enclosed bins to keep pests out, smells in and your neighbours onboard. Bokashi bins work a treat, but so do plastic on-ground bins with rodent-proof, stainless-steel mesh on the bottom.
- Ask all participants to remove any fruit stickers, rubber bands and plastic packaging from their scraps. Be aware that this won't be perfect, but because plastic doesn't decompose it's relatively easy to remove these items from the finished compost.

- If you have a couple of enclosed bins in your yard that your neighbours can access, make sure they're labelled with clear signs, such as 'Feed me, I'm hungry' and 'Don't add, I'm full'.
- Set up a separate container near the compost bin that is filled with carbon-rich materials such as brown leaves or woodchips for participants to access.
- Create a clear sign with simple language that outlines the process, for example:
  - Step 1: Add your food scraps.
  - Step 2: Use the compost turner to mix in your food waste.
  - Step 3: Add an equal amount of dry, brown material on top.
  - Step 4: Don't forget to put the lid back on.

Following these tips will help to iron out some of the potential missteps, but things can still go awry – so you'll need to roll up your sleeves and fix the problems as you go. Remember, more carbon and more air (via an active aeration) are often what smelly or anaerobic compost needs. I found it easiest to manage the moisture of my compost bins myself. At the end of the day, don't forget to give yourself a pat on the back because you're helping your community to compost problems and grow solutions.

~~~~~~~~~~~~~~~~~~~~~~~~~~~~

OPPOSITE:
This communal compost area was created by Costa Georgiadis. Costa is an avid community composter and has numerous compost bins and worm farms set up on his street that his neighbourhood can access (see pages 70–3).

COSTA GEORGIADIS

THE COMMUNITY COMPOSTER

Lovable larrikin COSTA GEORGIADIS and I share a deep fascination with compost's ability to turn death into new life. The cycle of growth, decay and regeneration is something that happens every day in suburban gardens and planted street verges. It's a privilege to share Costa's take on how reclaiming urban spaces to make compost and grow plants can, in turn, allow lovely communities to blossom.

Why did you start a shared street garden, and how does it bring your community together?

I wanted to start my street garden because the easiest way to bring an idea into a community is by demonstrating it in public. The garden is at the top of the street, which means roughly 52 households – probably over 200 people – go past it every day. It's a non-intimidating space to demonstrate anything and everything in a slow burn kind of way. The garden amplifies and broadcasts its story to children and families as they walk past. This is the artery of community, and the real estate of opportunity.

Getting as many families as possible – especially children – involved is where the real traction exists. Putting my chicken tractor on the street was the perfect way to engage the children; it provided an opportunity to tell the story and start the conversation about the garden of our imagination.

The other key was that before I started, I did an extensive doorknock. I think it's the best thing you can do because it creates inclusiveness. I told everybody my plan, I gave people a chance to contribute, and I could answer their concerns personally. I would recommend creating a little document, a letter of support for people to sign, which can be used to illustrate community support if you need to. Don't underestimate just how valuable that time is in the process of community engagement.

How did you engage the community to get behind the two big bathtub worm farms and numerous compost bins?

When you're dealing with food waste, you need to be organised and you need to have the capacity to process whatever you get from the community. Composting in a public place requires cleanliness and a rigorous routine. You cannot have insecure food waste that will attract vermin, or a poor routine that will lead to stinky bins, or you will immediately lose support.

The rewards for processing local food scraps at their source are wonderfully rich compost and humus that can be used to increase soil fertility, as well as grow trees for shade, flowers for beauty, and, of course, crops for eating. But a clear, clean and secure system for accepting food scraps and directing them to the correct place is critical to prevent vermin and to ensure that the system operates at optimum capacity.

It's also vital to give feedback. Having a whiteboard or a chalkboard where you can leave encouragement and thanks, or tips and directions, is a simple but important way to maintain community engagement and connection.

The other wonderful opportunity is the chance to give back some worm castings or compost to those who are part of the process. Equally, having a place where crops can be shared is the ultimate closing of the loop, illustrating that what was once food waste is now food again. That's the bit that gives me goosebumps!

What have you learned from any challenges or mistakes?

Not making the process clear is an opportunity for stuff-ups to rear their head. In the case of this system, what I mean is that I ask for people to bring their food scraps in buckets, which I then put into compost bins and worm farms or feed to the chooks. A new household became involved, and I mustn't have walked

them through the process clearly enough. Unbeknown to me, over a period of a couple of weeks they had made multiple drops of food scraps into a compost bin that was in its eight-week maturing stage, when it was cool and full of worms making humus.

Their food scraps became a decomposing glug on top of the compost bin, turning it anaerobic. The worms suffocated, and the maturation process stopped. The aroma when I lifted the lid caused me to gag. I can literally smell it as I type this. Lesson learned!

Create simple signs to place on bins that tell your contributors – actually, partners – whether the bin is taking scraps, needs turning or needs to be left alone. The simpler the graphics, the better.

How have you used your street garden to strengthen your community?

One of my favourite projects I call my 'happiness garden'. I plant out the bottom third of my verge with sunflowers. When I set it out, I put a meandering mulch path through the centre, and some logs for seating at the end. As the sunflowers grow, the path becomes enveloped, which makes for a perfect adventure crawl between the sunflowers until you reach the seating circle. People come from streets around to get photos with the sunflowers, and I generally plant out in late October so that the blooms open and happiness is distributed across the Christmas, New Year and holiday period. It's a really simple way to create a community focal point.

This year, I'm going to extend the visual connection of the sunflower garden by asking neighbours along the street to plant sunflowers, including my buddies Maxi and Alyssa. They will have sunflowers at the end of the street, I will have them at the top, and we will join the dots at a few spots in between.

A neighbour a few streets away grew sweet peas around a power pole. I have done a similar thing, and I'm going to expand that idea by getting more households involved.

Keeping it simple and growing each idea in manageable increments is the way to go. That way you bring the community with you.

What plants have you chosen for your patch, and why?

First, I wanted a visual and acoustic buffer from the main road at the top of the garden, so I planted native species to create a habitat where grasses and ground covers mix into an understorey of native shrubs that surround a bottlebrush tree. The ground covers include warrigal greens, midyim berry, kangaroo grass and club rush. The shrub layer includes tea-tree, prickly Moses, heath and coastal rosemary. Then there are local species: *Banksia marginata*, *B. spinulosa* and *B. serrata*. Spiky plants and low-growing shrubs provide valuable hiding spaces for small birds.

Below the habitat garden, I planted a herb maze that includes rosemary, curry leaf, lemon verbena and a variety of basils – all of which I can shape – plus a mix of lower-growing herbs (such as thyme, oregano, marjoram and parsley).

The next section of the garden I call the 'wild edible garden', and that includes wild rocket, chicory, dandelion, nasturtium and purslane.

The last area is where I grow my annual vegetables, including salad greens and seasonal varieties. This garden is contained by a vetiver grass hedge on the footpath side, and a lemongrass hedge on the roadside, so that when people open their car doors and hit the plants, they release a nice aroma.

Aside from creating community, what other benefits are there to planting a shared garden?

When I was working in the garden one day, a local on her regular walk stopped and said, 'Your garden is really cool.'

I had a bit of a chuckle and said with a smile, 'It must take after the gardener.'

She explained that she could feel a dramatic temperature drop whenever she walked past my garden, and that it smelled like a forest. This was her experience of what the Japanese call 'forest bathing': the opportunity to be in nature and absorb microbes in different landscapes. My street garden is a little forest, and my intention is to share the knowledge so that more little forests can connect the arteries that are our streets, and can grow into corridors that connect all of our open spaces with our rivers, creeks, streams and waterways right up to our ridge tops.

My street garden brings native insects, which bring birdlife and wildlife. The leaf litter and ground covers support myriad decomposers that provide food for worms, beetles, moths, frogs and lizards. It's nature. It's all around us. It is us, and we are it. Support it, provide a place for it, and it returns.

What is the role of street gardening and community composting in broader environmental issues?

A street garden is a non–intimidating way to introduce a connection to nature, which starts conversations about the smaller details of life as well as the bigger picture. Everything we require is built on a food chain in an ecosystem that needs to be in balance to provide a safe habitat for each component to work efficiently, not only to sustain itself but also to regenerate itself.

A street garden is a place to think about the landscape where we live: is it coastal; near a lake, creek or river; on a ridge facing west; or in a gully? How does that affect the plants we grow? Where does water come from and go? Can we capture and store some of that water to use in our gardens or homes? Where does sunlight fall on our block? Could we capture that sunlight, and turn it into foods and fibres? Can we grow an abundance, and then swap it for what other people have? Can we use trees and vegetation to cool the surfaces around our home, to create shade in summer but allow warmth in winter?

These questions allow us to look at our landscape as a naturehood, not simply a neighbourhood with roads, pavements and rooftops. A street garden is a way to reinterpret the world around us with our nature goggles on.

How has making compost from your own waste and your neighbours' waste helped you?

Spending time in my garden is about operating on a different clock. Going out into my garden connects me with nature's clock, where a simple stroll to see if my neighbour has left any food scraps leads to turning the compost, removing some weeds, harvesting a cucumber or two, having a conversation with a neighbour who pulls up in their car, and watering a plant that looks a little thirsty and neglected.

Making compost is a way of collectively turning death into life. We don't have life without the sustenance that death provides, and compost nurtures and grows the cycle of life and death. Composting is the only activity where we turn death into life. What could be better than doing it together with contributions from the collective?

Any final thoughts that might inspire others to start their own green urban sprawl?

Never underestimate the power of doing something small. I mean really small. It's all relative to a story, to a narrative and to an inclusiveness that, like a tiny seed, only needs a sliver of sunlight and a drop of water to germinate and grow into a massive tree.

Do not allow the currency of urgency to lead to fear and hesitation. Action grows outlook, outlook creates perspective, perspective encourages vision, and vision harbours optimism. Optimism turns hope into activism, which is a habit, a routine, a discipline and a certainty that replicates and inspires capacity, clarity and the connection to heart that is the signature ingredient for change.

4.

THE KIT

THE RIGHT COMPOST EQUIPMENT

Working out the best composting kit for your home is an important piece of the puzzle. This can be bewildering, as there are many different commercially available composting systems plus lots more you can make yourself.

The right system will accommodate your climate, as well as the volume and types of waste you produce in your kitchen and garden. It will also fit into your space and match your desired aesthetic – sometimes looks do matter! Just remember that compost microbes don't care if they're in a fancy compost tumbler or a DIY trash–can compost bin with the bottom cut off, so don't get too hung up on one particular product.

For ease of comparison, I've grouped composting equipment into six categories. (The wiggly waste management of worm farms is so useful that I've dedicated Chapter 5 to it.) I'll provide the pros and cons for common equipment in each category so you can pick a winner – but anyone who composts, regardless of what they use, is already a winner! The six categories are:

1. Enclosed bins – These are best for smaller urban gardens or areas with a lot of wildlife, including pests such as rodents.
2. Boxes and bays – These are best for larger gardens that need to process a lot of plant material and garden waste.
3. Bokashi bins – These are best for people with a busy lifestyle, apartment dwellers or homes without gardens.
4. Digesters – These are best for the dirt–averse who shudder at the thought of handling compost and want a hands–off approach.
5. Pit and sheet composting – These are best for people who don't want to move finished compost, as these methods put organic matter exactly where you need it.
6. Electric composters – <u>Don't</u> get one of these! More on this later ...

COMPOST MICROBES DON'T CARE IF THEY'RE IN A FANCY TUMBLER OR A DIY TRASH-CAN BIN.

THINK GREEN!

Please consider the cradle–to–grave life cycle of any bin you're thinking of buying. If you do end up with a composting system made from plastic, ensure that it's made from 100 per cent recycled plastic.

DOES YOUR HOUSEHOLD PRODUCE MOSTLY FOOD WASTE OR GARDEN WASTE?

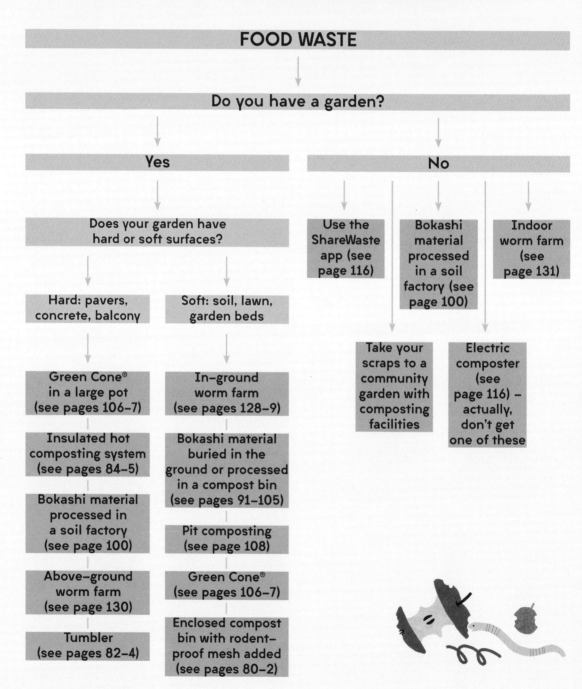

FOOD WASTE

↓

Do you have a garden?

↓ ↓

Yes   **No**

↓

Does your garden have hard or soft surfaces?

↓ ↓

Hard: pavers, concrete, balcony   **Soft: soil, lawn, garden beds**

↓ ↓

Green Cone® in a large pot (see pages 106–7)   **In-ground worm farm (see pages 128–9)**

Insulated hot composting system (see pages 84–5)   **Bokashi material buried in the ground or processed in a compost bin (see pages 91–105)**

Bokashi material processed in a soil factory (see page 100)   **Pit composting (see page 108)**

Above-ground worm farm (see page 130)   **Green Cone® (see pages 106–7)**

Tumbler (see pages 82–4)   **Enclosed compost bin with rodent-proof mesh added (see pages 80–2)**

Under **No** (three branches):

Use the ShareWaste app (see page 116)

Bokashi material processed in a soil factory (see page 100)

Indoor worm farm (see page 131)

↓ ↓

Take your scraps to a community garden with composting facilities

Electric composter (see page 116) – actually, don't get one of these

GARDEN WASTE

↓

Does your yard have animal activity (pets, rodents, wildlife)?

↓   ↓

Yes   **No**

↓   ↓   ↓

**Enclosed compost bin with
rodent–proof mesh added
(see pages 80–2)**

**Box or bay
(see pages 86–90)**

**Sheet composting
(see pages 110–11)**

ENCLOSED BINS

There are so many different enclosed bins available, but I'm going to focus on three main types: plastic compost bins that are open to the ground; tumblers; and insulated hot composting systems. You can get lots of different permutations of these three styles, but I'll focus on the products I've tried, tested and loved.

ABOVE:
I love my Tumbleweed® Gedye Compost Bins and have several scattered around my garden. They're Australian-made from 100 per cent recycled plastic.

PLASTIC COMPOST BINS

Since the day I was brought home from hospital, I've lived in a home with a compost bin. My mum is an avid home composter, but she didn't always get the set-up right. I have a strong memory of her emptying a compost bin in our tiny, inner-city courtyard and a family of mice running from it. I thought they were cute; my mum did not. Despite this memory, I continue to use enclosed compost bins in my own home with great success (and no rodents, either). They're convenient and highly functional when set up correctly.

Here are things to look out for when choosing a plastic, open-based compost bin:

- Millions of these are in use worldwide, so always look for a second-hand bin first. You can often get them cheaply or even for free from Facebook gardening groups, Gumtree, Freecycle websites or the side of the road during a council clean-up. Your council may give you a free compost bin or a generous discount on one, so check that out, too. Alternatively, you can make your own plastic compost bin by cutting off the bottom of a regular rubbish bin and wedging the bin into the soil.
- If you're buying a new bin, then avoid designs with separate pieces that clip together. Over time, the organic matter in the full bin will push against the sides, and the clips will break. Also, these designs are more prone to pest attacks. Rats and mice will diligently nibble their way in through the edges, while blowflies and vinegar flies will access your scraps through any gaps and then set up camp.
- Don't bother with designs that have a harvesting hatch at the bottom, either. Trying to shovel composted material out through the hatch often results in damage to the bin, and you're not getting all the finished black gold, anyway.

- I recommend that you look for a commercial compost bin made from one solid piece of recycled plastic. Emptying these bins involves you lifting the whole bin up and off the compost sitting inside, but it's easy to do this because of the bin's shape.
- I prefer round compost bins rather than square, as organic matter can't get wedged in the corners. Also, there are no joins or corners in which cockroaches can breed.

The good

- They're open to the ground, which allows the soil biology direct access to your tasty scraps. Remember, we want to work with nature, not against it, so having microbial contact with the dirt is a big benefit of this design.
- They come in lots of sizes, so you should be able to find one that fits your space. They're great for small gardens, but if you do have space, try a 400–600-litre commercial compost bin – the bigger the volume, the faster the compost microbes will consume your waste.
- The solid walls and lid help to hold in heat, stop excessive evaporation and keep rain out. This means that you need to manage the moisture levels yourself, though.
- They're easy to move around your garden (if you have the space available), depending on the season.
- They can handle food waste, small garden prunings (when they've been shredded or chopped up) and all your manufactured and natural carbon.
- The enclosed design helps to keep out flies and rodents (when you've added a piece of rodent-proof, stainless-steel mesh to the bottom – see pages 156–9).
- It's easy to harvest and remove finished compost – you simply lift up the bin to access the black gold underneath.

The bad

- As these bins are fully enclosed, compost needs to be turned and aerated by hand regularly – otherwise it can become anaerobic. This can be awkward and heavy work, but also a wonderfully therapeutic activity. I recommend that you use a corkscrew aerator rather than a garden fork to turn compost in these bins.
- Low-quality plastic can become brittle when exposed to sunlight, and lids can split. Buy a quality bin once, or find a second-hand bin instead.
- You really need two of these bins: one that you're filling, and the other that is curing compost.
- Compost leachate will drain from the bottom of these bins and can damage or stain hard surfaces (such as pavers). These bins must be positioned on permeable surfaces (such as grass, mulch or soil) or in a garden bed.
- Rats and mice can easily enter these bins, unless you've added a piece of rodent-proof, stainless-steel mesh to the bottom (see pages 156–9).

The location

Don't hide these bins away; place them where you want the compost and nutrients to go. As they're open to the ground, some nutrients will leach out of the organic matter and end up in your soil – it's worthwhile locating the bins close to your growing space, so you don't lose these nutrients. I have three enclosed bins at the ends of my productive garden beds. Having them front and centre means that I tend to them regularly and can add fresh inputs with ease.

You need to consider your climate, the season and the amount of sun your compost bin will receive. When composting during the temperate shoulder seasons of autumn and spring, position your bin where it will get some morning sun or, better still, all-day sun. This helps to warm the contents of your bin and to buffer temperature fluctuations so the conditions are cosy and hospitable for the mesophilic and thermophilic microbes to do their work.

If you live in a hot climate, you may wish to move your compost bin into a cool, shady spot for the summer months. I personally don't move my bins in summer, and this means that I need to monitor the moisture on very hot days. I bet you can guess where I'm going to tell you to place your compost bin in winter: in the warmest, sunniest spot your yard offers. (To learn more about composting in winter, turn to pages 62–4.)

TUMBLERS

Many people's first compost bin is a tumbler. It seems like such a good idea – it keeps the compost free of pests and rodents, it's clean and tidy, and it's supposedly easy to turn the compost. You imagine a rich harvest of finished compost tumbling out like magic within a couple of months.

But I suspect that tumblers are also many people's last compost bin. Tumblers often end up being hard or impossible to turn; the material inside doesn't decompose uniformly; gooey sludge oozes from the unit; and if you can make some compost, how do you separate it from the bits that haven't decomposed, let alone harvest it through the tiny hatch?

Compost tumblers can definitely work, but your mistakes can't be fixed by worms and other critters easily migrating into your pile, as they can be if your pile is situation on the ground. If you don't get the mix of inputs right, don't keep the moisture at the right level, and don't tumble the contents regularly, then it can all go horribly wrong.

Here are some things to look out for when choosing a tumbler:

- Tumblers are the most common compost bin to get thrown away. This is in part due to misuse, but it also comes down to the design and quality of materials. I recommend that you avoid tumblers made from flimsy plastic that clips together. Tumblers with a solid barrel made from metal or firm plastic are superior in function and longevity.
- Read reviews of the tumbler you're thinking of buying before you commit to it. Some tumblers are very tricky to turn and require a lot of muscle power. To get compost fast, you need to turn the tumbler each time you add new inputs, so take the time to find one that you can actually operate.
- If you're concerned about flies being attracted to your tumbler, then get a solid barrel without perforated holes. Fully enclosed tumblers are also best for decks or paved areas, otherwise you'll end up with compost leachate dripping onto your hard surfaces. You'll need to actively monitor the moisture with these models, as there is no drainage (dry carbon will become your best friend).

If you do want to go with a tumbler, then here are my top ten tips to get the most out of it:

1. The best way to create compost in a tumbler is to make one whole batch at a time rather than add material constantly. This speeds up decomposition, and it means that you can harvest the finished product (before curing it) in one go without trying to separate what you put in six months ago from the kitchen scraps you just added. If you want to add scraps gradually, then you'll need to leave your compost to cure for at least six weeks once the tumbler is full. You can also buy tumblers with two chambers, so you can add to one section while the other side is 'cooking'.

2. Remember to rotate the contents of your tumbler regularly to ensure that your pile is oxygenated. Be aware that the tumbling motion often causes clumps of compost to form. Don't freak out: these will break down when you add them to your soil.

3. As with any composting system, activate a new tumbler by adding a handful of finished compost or healthy garden soil. This will give your compost microbes a head start.

4. Make sure you add equal amounts of browns and greens. Little moisture drains from tumblers, so the contents often become slushy; if this happens, then increase the amount of carbon you're adding. On the other hand, if it feels dry, then add more food waste or a little water. As with any compost pile, the contents should feel like a squeezed-out sponge.

5. The smaller the better when it comes to the size of inputs. This speeds up the decomposition and stops things from clumping. You may think it makes composting less convenient, but it takes five seconds to turn that watermelon rind from one large piece to seven or eight small pieces. Do it as you go. It's time well spent.

6. Position your tumbler in a warm spot, but not in full sun if you live in a hot climate – otherwise it will act like an oven and dry out the organic matter too quickly.

7. Sniff the contents regularly to register any change in smell. If you notice a foul stench, this usually means that the compost ratio is wrong. When a scent resembles ammonia, it's a clear sign that you should add more carbon to the tumbler.

8. To prevent an infestation of vinegar flies, keep your compost moist but not wet and aim for a neutral pH by adding small amounts of wood-fire ash, ground eggshells or bone meal to the mix.

9. There's no need to buy worms for your tumbler. You'll find that some composting worms naturally hatch and live in the organic matter in your tumbler because worm eggs were in the leaf litter you added to your compost. These worms have acclimatised to this environment so should be okay, but mature shop-bought worms will likely perish. For the most part, compost microbes will break down your waste in tumblers.

10. Finally, don't overfill the bin (whether you're making a whole batch or just filling it as you go). If the bin is too full, there won't be enough airflow because the organic matter won't tumble, and you may find that the bin is not robust enough to take the weight. Once the bin is about 75 per cent full, stop adding organic matter; leave it until the compost is ready to remove and cure. During this time, continue tumbling the compost to make sure that no patches become anaerobic.

The good

- If you have a garden without any exposed soil (for example, you only have paving, concrete or a wooden deck), then tumblers are a good option.
- They're also a good solution for renters with picky landlords or yards that have rodent issues.
- When managed correctly, tumblers make aerating your compost easy.

- Tumblers come in a large variety of sizes, so you'll find one that meets your waste requirements.

The bad

- When mismanaged, which is easy to do, tumblers quickly become difficult to turn and extremely heavy.
- Tumblers are expensive and often made from plastic that will end up in landfill when they break.
- Depending on the style, tumblers may have small hatches that make it hard to retrieve compost.
- If you have a tumbler with a single chamber, then your compost will need to be added to a maturation bin to cure before use on your garden (see pages 50–6). Doing this extra step is a bit inconvenient, but it will free up space in your tumbler so no food waste ends up in landfill.

The location

Tumblers can be positioned on hard surfaces (ideally, they should be fully enclosed, so leachate doesn't drip from the barrel). They should be moved into the shade during summer and into the sun in winter.

INSULATED HOT COMPOSTING SYSTEMS ARE FULLY ENCLOSED, AND THIS HELPS TO KEEP RODENTS OUT.

INSULATED HOT COMPOSTING SYSTEMS

The final off–the–shelf enclosed bins I'll cover are insulated hot composting systems. These bins act in a similar way to a thermos flask in that they have a double wall that helps to retain heat generated by the composting microbes. These bins are more expensive than other composting bins, but they're effective when used correctly. They're good options for renters or yards with hard surfaces.

These hot composting systems take all your food waste and garden prunings when cut to size. They work best when the particle size of all ingredients is small enough to increase the speed of microbial decomposition. The faster the microbes consume the scraps, the more heat is released, and this is trapped within the system. To work most efficiently, these systems need a 'bulking agent' mixed with your usual scraps. Small, aged woodchips are ideal, as they help to capture air within the organic matter.

The good

- The walls of these products are thick and very well insulated, and this helps to retain heat. This means that even a small amount of heat generated by the microbes is captured within the system. The design helps to buffer the impact of cooler outside temperatures and creates warm conditions in which mesophilic and thermophilic microbes thrive.
- Some designs have an internal 'lung' that helps oxygen to flow easily through the organic matter. This means that you don't need to manually aerate these bins.
- They're fully enclosed systems, and this helps to keep rodents out.
- They can be positioned on hard surfaces (such as paving, decking or concrete) because they're not open at the bottom. Compost leachate is collected in a fit-for-purpose drainage system.

The bad

- They're expensive to buy new.
- They're made from component parts that clip together. If they're regularly overfilled, which places the clips under pressure, they'll eventually fall apart (after several years of use). You can help to prevent this by adding ratchet straps around the outside of the compost bin, above the harvesting hatch.
- There are lots of crevices and tiny openings in which spiders and cockroaches can hide and through which vinegar flies can enter.
- Harvesting the compost through the hatch can be tricky, especially if the bin has an internal lung. In my experience, it's awkward but not impossible to scrape out the compost. You'll need to get on your hands and knees, and use a handheld garden fork to manually extract the compost. As these bins are square, compost tends to get stuck in the corners, too.
- The lung can cause more problems than it solves. In my experience, if you don't manually aerate these systems at all, you may end up with pockets of anaerobic, smelly waste around the outside edges, and the centre of the compost around the lung might be bone dry.

The location

These insulated bins must be placed on a level hard surface, ideally a concrete pad or a number of pavers sitting on grass. They should be positioned where they'll receive full sun; however, during the summer months, you'll need to monitor the moisture content as the bins can act like ovens and quickly dry out the contents.

TOP RIGHT:
My second–hand Aerobin® has been used for many, many years and now requires a ratchet strap to hold it together – the compost microbes don't mind!

RIGHT:
You may notice condensation inside an insulated hot compost bin. As the organic matter warms up, it may produce steam that will pool and drip from the inside of the lid.

BOXES AND BAYS

You don't need to buy a fancy piece of plastic equipment to make compost. You can construct your own system out of natural materials that in time will decompose and return to the earth. In this section, I'll discuss three open composting options that take the form of boxes and bays. These are simple and cheap to construct, and they work especially well for larger gardens outside of urban areas.

COMPOST BOXES

A common design is one based on what is known as the New Zealand compost box. It's typically constructed from four walls, one of which is removable, with no top and no bottom. In the original design, the front panel has individual slats that can be inserted one by one as the bin is filled, and can all be removed to harvest the compost. You can obviously modify the design to suit your situation (for example, a lot of people in high–rainfall locations or urban areas will put a lid on top of the box).

Most systems involve two or more boxes placed side by side, which gives you the ability to fill one box, turn the contents from that box into the next to aerate them, and then start filling the first box again. If you have three boxes, then you can repeat the process and set aside the final box as your curing bay.

The best size for this sort of box is one that gives you at least 1 cubic metre of internal volume (or 1000 litres). This means that each wall panel will be a square measuring 1 metre x 1 metre. This is the ideal size to make hot compost; if you fill this box in one go, then you can safely add weeds with seeds, and diseased plant materials.

The good

- You can make a compost box yourself from recycled materials, and build it to match the size of your space.
- It's a great solution if you have large amounts of garden waste to process.
- A timber compost box is more forgiving than an enclosed plastic bin and will still produce great compost even if your mix of materials isn't quite right. This is due to the bigger capacity, the superior aeration and the large surface area that's in contact with the soil.
- It's easy to fill and harvest due to the removable slats on the front.
- It's easy to turn the compost if you have two or three boxes next to each other.

The bad

- The contents can become saturated in wet climates and dry out quickly in hot summer months. This can be solved by constructing a lid to keep the rain off and to decrease evaporation.
- If you add a lot of food waste, these boxes are very attractive to vermin and snakes. You may need to add rodent–proof, stainless-steel mesh to the bottom, to the interior of the sides and to the lid to make sure your compost boxes don't become rat hotels.
- The timber will rot eventually and need to be replaced, but this is better than the fate of plastic bins.

The location

Aim to position your compost box away from the house, in a spot that receives sun during winter but is protected from harsh afternoon rays in summer.

BLOCK OR BALE BAYS

You can make compost bays out of bales of hay or cinder blocks. These are easy to use and wonderfully insulating. I love bale bays, as the addition of plenty of carbon around the outside acts like a sponge. You'll find that if bale bays are open to the weather and get wet, then fungi will set up camp. To protect

ABOVE AND RIGHT:
This is an epic five-bay compost system designed and made by Kevin Espiritu, the founder of Epic Gardening. Each bay features a slotted front that allows you to match the height of your pile and makes harvesting the cured compost a breeze.

SALVAGE AND SAVE
Compost bays can be made from repurposed materials, such as the corrugated iron used in this beautifully simple set-up at Bend, an eco-neighbourhood in Bega on the far south coast of New South Wales.

your pile from weather extremes, place a tarp over the top. An old piece of woollen carpet works, too.

The good

- They're free or cheap to construct.
- Repurposing resources is better than buying more plastic.
- They're great for processing a lot of garden waste.

The bad

- It's almost impossible to make them rodent-proof.
- Block or bale bays take up a lot of space in your garden and can be pretty ugly as the contents are on full display.

The location

Aim to position your block or bale bay somewhere in your garden that's warm during winter but isn't hit with harsh afternoon rays in summer. These systems can be unsightly, so you might want to tuck them away in a back corner of your garden or allotment.

DIY COMPOST BAYS

Timber pallets make great compost containers, as it's easy to construct an open bay with them. Old pallets are widely available, often for free, but check that they're safe to use by examining the pallet stamps.

Look out for pallets displaying the global IPPC (International Plant Protection Convention) or EPAL (Euro Pallet) logos, plus the letters HT or KD, which indicates that the timber has been heat-treated or kiln-dried and there is no risk of toxic materials leaching into your compost.

Some pallets have been treated with a toxic pesticide called methyl bromide; they'll be stamped with the letters MB and must not be used for a compost container. Pallets stamped SF (sulfuryl fluoride) also should not be used. Although this gas was introduced as a 'safer' fumigation method than methyl bromide, I don't advise using pallets exposed to this chemical to make compost in which you'll grow food.

BOKASHI BINS

Bokashi bins harness the power of beneficial anaerobic bacteria and yeast, and they're an ace up the sleeve for space–poor gardeners. The Bokashi method originated in Japan during the 1980s and is a form of anaerobic 'pre–composting' that relies on inoculated bran or spray to ferment your kitchen waste. Bokashi bins are a gift that keeps on giving. They transform your waste into a safe soil builder and biologically active tea for your plants.

FEED your BOKASHI

WHAT IS BOKASHI?

Bokashi is an anaerobic, oxygen–free process. You're probably wondering what makes this different from decomposition in the oxygen–deprived environment of landfill. That's a good question! When placed in airtight plastic bags that are then piled on top of one another, food waste releases huge amounts of methane (a climate killer). Bokashi composting is done in a somewhat similar oxygen–free environment – a purpose–made airtight bucket – but the thing that makes Bokashi special is the inoculated bran added to the waste. The microbial inoculant that almost everyone uses is called EM, which stands for effective microorganisms. EM is a blend of primarily lactic acid bacteria, photosynthetic bacteria and yeasts. EM ferments your waste and also stops your scraps from putrefying, reeking and producing methane.

I'm not a scientist, so I can't give you a detailed explanation of what happens in a Bokashi bin (in fact, the science isn't fully worked out). But basically, the EM added to your Bokashi bin consumes a small amount of the organic matter and the energy in the starting material, and then produces various acids (lactic, butyric and acetic) as well as other compounds.

The acidic environment created by the EM is inhospitable for pathogens such as *Salmonella* and *E. coli*, so it's safe to add risky scraps to a Bokashi bin. This is a massive benefit of Bokashi: it can safely 'pre–compost' 100 per cent of the scraps you produce in your kitchen, including raw and cooked meat (and bones), slimy fish, baked goods, cooked rice, smelly cheeses, spicy curries, acidic citrus, oils, leftovers from boozy burger runs, and so on. It's a joyous thing to know that not one single sliver of food waste has to go to landfill from your house ever again.

Once the Bokashi bin is full, it must be left to ferment with the lid firmly closed for a minimum of two weeks. The fermented Bokashi material is then ready to be buried in the soil (or added to your regular compost bin). A second phase of aerobic decomposition then occurs, during which the pH stabilises, and the material further decomposes and releases nutrients. After another four weeks in the soil (or when you can no longer see any visible scraps, which can take a bit longer depending on your soil's biology and the season), the area is safe to be planted.

If you're still a bit confused about what to expect from this style of waste management, then think of it like making a batch of sauerkraut. If you fill a container with cabbage alone and let it sit, in a week or two it will stink to high heaven, and become slimy and covered in mould. But if you add salt, your cabbage will ferment, develop a sour pickle smell that is strong but not unpleasant, and look somewhat similar to what you first added.

The same is true for your food waste in your Bokashi bin, but instead of salt, the EM is the transformational ingredient. The effective microorganisms will ferment your waste and produce a strong vinegary smell. Your scraps won't look vastly different, but at a molecular level they'll have been transformed. It's important to note that the process is not 'finished' after the two weeks in the Bokashi bin, because the material at that point needs further time to fully decompose in the soil or in your compost pile before it's safe to use in the garden.

The science about whether or not Bokashi material improves soil fertility and crop growth is not clear, with some studies reporting noticeable improvements and others reporting insignificant effects. It's worth noting that whether any particular addition to the soil 'improves' it depends on what the soil was lacking before the addition, and whether what was added had that missing element. Soil is not uniform, and it changes over time. But I think that adding organic material back into the soil is never a bad thing – and if it keeps the waste from going into landfill, then that's a win!

The good

- Bokashi material is a great activator for your compost pile (see page 65).
- Bokashi bins can ferment all types of food waste, including scraps that are considered no–noes in other composting systems.

- Bokashi bins are compact and very clean, and they can be kept inside. This is a game-changer for people who don't have access to a garden. Yep, you can do it smack bang in the middle of your apartment – closet compost, anyone?
- Bokashi bins are totally sealed, so they don't attract rats or cockroaches. The fermented waste is also not attractive to rodents when you add it to your compost or bury it in the earth.
- EM prevents putrefaction, so your Bokashi bin shouldn't stink – unlike some compost bins when they're mismanaged. You won't be able to smell a thing when the lid is closed, but the fermenting scraps inside do have a funky sour–pickle odour. It's not as bad as the rotting stench usually associated with decomposing meat or dairy.
- The C:N ratio is not a concern with Bokashi, so you don't need to worry about getting enough browns.
- It's quicker to completely process your scraps – two months at most (from the start to when your fermented scraps have disappeared in the soil or in your compost) compared to four months or longer for finished compost.
- The initial process requires less labour. Unlike compost, you don't have to turn the bin.
- DIY bins can be made out of free or cheap materials.
- Bokashi bins are useful systems for community composting because the bins are small and transportable.

The bad

- You have the ongoing cost of the EM bran or spray. (If you want to cut out the middleman and make your own, then see my recipe on pages 102–3.) As a guide, I use about 10 kilograms of EM bran a year at a cost of $100 when bought in bulk.
- The quality of EM is variable depending on the brand. Inferior brands of EM will cause putrid smells.
- To have uninterrupted collection and fermentation of your kitchen waste, you really need to have at least two Bokashi bins: one that you're filling, and one that's fermenting. Bins are expensive to buy new.
- The leachate (Bokashi 'juice') can become quite whiffy if not drained regularly.

The location

It's best to keep your Bokashi bin in or near the kitchen, so it's easy to fill. However, if you keep it outside, consider bringing it inside during winter to help keep it warm. A cold Bokashi bin will ferment, but at a much slower rate. Conversely, if it's the height of summer, don't leave the bin in a position that receives direct sun. If the contents get hotter than 35 degrees Celsius, the EM will die and your food scraps will putrefy.

BOKASHI FOR BEGINNERS

You've purchased a fabulous Bokashi bin from a garden centre or hardware store, but what do you do now? Here is a step-by-step guide to filling your bin using EM bran (which can be replaced with EM spray if that's what you're using):

1. When starting a new bin, lightly sprinkle the bottom with EM bran.
2. Keep a compost caddy on your kitchen counter, and fill this before emptying the contents into your Bokashi bin. This stops you opening your Bokashi bin too frequently and letting in oxygen. If it's summer, then keep your caddy in the fridge to prevent it from developing mould or attracting flies.
3. Use an old potato masher to thoroughly squash the scraps in your Bokashi bin. This squashing step is important, as you want to create an anaerobic environment in which the bacteria can grow. Squeezing all the air out also helps to fit more food into your bin.
4. Sprinkle around ⅓ cup (roughly one handful) of EM bran on top of the layer of squashed scraps. I'm stingy with the amount of EM I use, and our waste ferments beautifully. If you're nervous about the fermentation working, then you can use more EM by following the amount listed on the packet. But remember that each handful of EM contains millions of beneficial bacteria, so a little goes a long way.
5. As you gradually fill your Bokashi bin, it's a good idea to add a layer of carbon (such as newspapers folded to size) on top of your food waste to protect the scraps from excessive oxygen exposure. Remove this carbon layer before adding the next layer of caddy scraps, squash the material, sprinkle it with EM and then place the carbon cover back on top.
6. As the dormant microbes in the EM are exposed to moisture and warmth, they gradually become active and get busy fermenting your scraps. If your scraps are too dry or left in a very cold place, the EM won't be as effective. The microbes thrive in a moist but not wet environment with a temperature of around 20 degrees Celsius.
7. Your Bokashi material is likely to produce 'juice' (or leachate, for those who like scientific words) while you're filling the bin or during the final ferment. It's essential to regularly drain your Bokashi bin via the spigot, otherwise it will start to smell. Be warned: the 'juice' is a lot more pungent than the actual fermented scraps, so you may need to hold your nose until you get used to the smell. This 'juice' sometimes develops a white, cloudy, mould-like substance on the surface. This isn't a problem, but is a sign that you haven't been draining the bin regularly enough. Also, don't be alarmed if your Bokashi bin doesn't produce much 'juice'. This can happen if you add more low-water scraps (such as rice and bread) than juicy scraps (such as watermelon rinds). The fermentation process can work without the production of much leachate, but remember that if the bin contents are too dry, the EM won't activate.
8. Once the Bokashi bin is full, the waste needs to ferment for at least two weeks. During this time, it's important to continue to drain the 'juice'. I dilute this liquid in a watering-can and use it on my garden and pots as a free and fabulous soil conditioner. (To learn more about using the 'juice', turn to page 101.)
9. It's tempting to be a peeping Tom and regularly open the Bokashi bin lid to check on the material during the final fermentation, but it's best to resist the urge. Bokashi is an anaerobic form of 'pre-composting', and the microbes that are fermenting your scraps need an oxygen-free environment to thrive. Each time you open the lid to check on the progress, you're letting in air and slowing down the fermentation.

10. After two weeks, lift the lid to see and smell the progress (the bin contents shouldn't stink, but rather have a strong pickle aroma, and you may notice a smattering of white mould growing on the surface of the scraps). If you feel that it needs a bit longer, then leave it for an additional two weeks.

BIN SOME BROWNS

It's not essential to add carbon to your Bokashi bin, as the fermenting process will work with your food waste alone. But I find that it's useful to include some household carbon if you're adding wet, sloppy scraps such as leftover muesli and milk, tea leaves and dregs, or liquid meals like stews. Carbon helps to create structure in your Bokashi bin, so it's not a pile of slops.

PROCESSING YOUR FERMENTED BOKASHI MATERIAL

You'll often see white, fluffy mould on the surface of your fermented scraps, which is fine. If you see mould that is green, blue, grey–black or pink, it's not so good. This coloured mould means that your system is probably not anaerobic, and you may have a crack in the bin lid or side – time for a replacement part or new bin! You can (and should) still bury the waste if it has gone bad, but maybe dig a slightly deeper hole than normal.

Sometimes you won't see any white mould develop on the surface of your fermented food waste. This is fine, and doesn't mean the process hasn't worked. If this is the case, you'll need to determine if the ferment is successful by using your nose. The contents of your Bokashi bin should smell pickled and sour. Well–fermented bin material will have a strong vinegary odour, but it shouldn't smell putrid.

When your Bokashi bin has finished doing its thing, you have three options to process the fermented material and complete the decomposing process:

1. If you have a large–enough yard, you can bury your Bokashi waste directly into the soil.
2. You can empty it into a slow or hot compost bin.
3. You can process it in a soil factory.

DIY BOKASHI BIN

There are enough plastic buckets kicking around in the world. Instead of rushing out and buying a new Bokashi bin, why not make your own? Here's what you'll need:

- two old buckets that are exactly the same size and make, so they sit snugly one inside the other, with a firm-fitting lid (you don't want any air leaking in) — it's important that they have a wide rim around the top, so when they're placed one inside the other there's a cavity created at the bottom that can capture the Bokashi 'juice'
- electric drill with an 8-millimetre drill bit.

Follow these instructions to create your own Bokashi bin:

1. Turn the first bucket upside down, and drill numerous holes in the base.
2. Place the first bucket inside the second bucket.
3. Start filling the first bucket with your food waste and EM bran. Make sure that you place the lid firmly on the bucket after filling it.
4. To empty the 'juice', simply remove the first (top) bucket and pour the juice out of the second (bottom) bucket.

OPPOSITE, LEFT:
It's important to drain Bokashi 'juice' regularly, so that it doesn't pool and disrupt the fermentation process.

OPPOSITE, RIGHT:
Beneficial white mould may grow on the surface of your fermented Bokashi material. This can become really fluffy like a little cloud and is a good sign that a strong ferment has occurred.

Processing directly in the soil

The fermented contents of your Bokashi bin can be buried directly into the soil in your garden or in a raised bed. When burying Bokashi material in the soil, the conditions remain relatively anaerobic. The beneficial bacteria present in EM don't need carbon to process your scraps.

1. Dig a hole that's a bit deeper than the volume of your Bokashi bin. Reserve the removed soil.
2. Empty the contents of the bin into the hole, and mix in some of the removed soil – this is important. If you leave the Bokashi material in one big lump, it will take longer to break down.
3. Add the rest of the reserved soil on top, and gently firm it down.
4. If rodents or other wildlife are an issue where you live, then place a piece of rodent–proof, stainless–steel mesh on top of the freshly covered hole. Weigh this down with a few bricks.
5. Depending on the season, your fermented scraps will take one to two months to completely decompose.
6. Plant out the area when all the food waste has been consumed by the critters in your soil.

RIGHT:
Weigh down a piece of rodent–proof, stainless–steel mesh on top of your freshly dug–in Bokashi material to keep out curious pets, wildlife and rodents.

Processing in a compost bin

The fermented contents of your Bokashi bin can be added to your slow or hot compost bins or piles. This is my preferred method, as the fermented scraps break down efficiently and it saves me from digging up my garden.

There are a couple of points I want to discuss before sharing the method:

- Bokashi material changes from an anaerobic state of fermentation to aerobic decomposition when added to your compost. This can lead to a stinky situation if not handled correctly. To prevent this from happening, it's important to mix the nitrogen–rich contents of your Bokashi bin with an equal volume of carbon (such as aged woodchips of a similar surface size, shredded paper or shredded brown leaves). This encourages the proliferation of aerobic bacteria, as mesophilic and thermophilic microbes need access to both nitrogen and carbon.
- Bokashi material is a useful compost activator, and you may find that slow composting systems heat up after you've added it. This is because the nitrogen in the fermented scraps is readily available to compost microbes, as the waste has been pre–digested.

Follow these simple steps when adding Bokashi material to your compost:

1. Empty the contents of your Bokashi bin into a wheelbarrow, tub or container, and add an equal volume of carbon. Give this a thorough mix to break up lumps of Bokashi material and to disperse the carbon throughout the fermented scraps. If you don't want to do this in a separate container, then you can mix the carbon and Bokashi material together in your compost bin (if you do this, jump to step three).
2. Now add the premixed Bokashi material to your compost bin.
3. Cover thoroughly with a layer of carbon-rich materials (such as shredded brown leaves or aged woodchips), and add a little water if conditions in your compost are dry.
4. Don't aerate your compost for five days. This will give the EM time to multiply and reactivate your compost pile by inoculating some of the surrounding organic matter.
5. After this time, give your compost a thorough aeration. It may be a bit smelly the first time you turn it, but subsequent aerations will help the stinky situation. Look closely at your pile after turning it, and you may see signs of the Bokashi bacteria at work: lots of fungal growth that resembles white, spiderweb–like roots.
6. The Bokashi material will break down quickly in your compost. If it doesn't, then cut up your scraps into smaller pieces before adding them to your next batch.

Processing in a soil factory

If you live somewhere without a yard, you can process your Bokashi material using a soil factory. This unit is easy to move, so it can be stored on a balcony, in an outdoor common area, next to the regular garbage bins or even indoors (if using a fully sealed container). Here is the equipment you'll need:

- one large garden pot, or one plastic container with a lid
- woodchips (if you're using a pot with drainage holes)
- soil (use healthy soil with lots of life in it, or finished homemade compost – the more worms and insects the better)
- gardening gloves
- garden fork or hand shovel.

Follow these simple steps when processing Bokashi material in a soil factory:

1. If you're using a pot with drainage holes, pour in enough woodchips so that they cover the holes. When the soil factory has finished processing the Bokashi material, you'll be left with nutrient–rich compost that you can scoop off the top of the woodchips (over time these will decompose beautifully, too). You can also use a pot without holes if you're worried about liquid draining onto the ground. A large, lidded, plastic container works well, too, especially if you're keeping the soil factory indoors. If you're using an enclosed container, don't add woodchips; instead, add a 5–10-centimetre foundation layer of soil or compost, and then jump to step three.

2. Cover the woodchips with soil to a depth of 5–10 centimetres.
3. Empty the fermented contents of your Bokashi bin into the pot or container, making sure to break up any large lumps of Bokashi material.
4. Add 5–10 centimetres of soil, and mix well with a garden fork or hand shovel to combine the soil and the Bokashi material.

5. Add another 5–10 centimetres of soil on top, making sure to cover all the Bokashi material. If your soil is dry, then spray a small amount of water over the surface. Your soil factory will slow down if it dries out. If using a plastic container, pop the lid on.

6. Leave the soil factory for two to four weeks. It may take slightly longer for your fermented scraps to break down if there are few worms and other creatures in the soil or compost you used. Colder temperatures will also slow things down. You can speed up the process by mixing the contents of your soil factory every week or so. Be patient: the Bokashi material will break down, and you'll have a soil factory full of great compost.

7. You can add another Bokashi bin full of fermented scraps to the top of your soil factory if there is space. Remember to add more soil and mix the contents each time after adding more Bokashi material. Remove the finished compost as needed if your soil factory is getting too full.

8. You can use the nutrient-packed compost from your factory when you no longer see the presence of food scraps. This compost can be used as a surface mulch on pot plants or anywhere else you would use regular compost.

HOW TO USE BOKASHI 'JUICE'

Bokashi 'juice' is the food–scrap leachate created during the fermentation process, and it has many useful purposes around your house and garden. Honestly, this hooch makes the best compost 'cocktail' because it's jam–packed with billions of beneficial bacteria. Once you've drained it out of your Bokashi bin and it's exposed to oxygen, it starts to lose its fertility – so, it's best to use it quickly. You can leave it for up to 24 hours in a glass jar fitted with a lid, but the bacteria won't be very active beyond that time frame.

It's a biologically active soil conditioner, but it does need to be well diluted as it's super strong. You'll need to dilute it to a ratio of 100:1 before applying it to the soil around your plants. That's approximately 1 tablespoon (20 millilitres) of Bokashi 'juice' for every 2 litres of water, or 2 teaspoons (10 millilitres) per litre. When using it as a foliar spray, increase the dilution to 500:1 – this works out to be 1 tablespoon (20 millilitres) for every 10 litres of water, or 2 teaspoons (10 millilitres) per 5 litres – to prevent it burning tender leaves. It's best to use rainwater, too, if you have it available, as chlorine can kill off the beneficial EM.

If you have a lot of Bokashi 'juice' (lucky you!) and don't have time to use it on your garden, then you can pour it straight onto your compost as an activator. Most impressively, its pure and strong form can be poured directly down the drains in your kitchen, bathroom, toilet and septic system. The EM will gobble up any hair or grease in your pipes, and they'll help to control odours and prevent algae build–up. So, say bye–bye to any toxic chemicals you may have used for this job in the past.

MAKE YOUR OWN EM BRAN FLAKES

I've adapted this recipe from one by Rebecca Louie, also known as the Compostess. She's the author of *Compost City: Practical composting know-how for small-space living.*

INGREDIENTS
- 3 cups of dechlorinated water. Rainwater is best, but town water can be left to off-gas in an open bucket for 24 hours before use.
- 2 tablespoons of EM-1 solution. This is a commercial product that you'll need to buy. You'll end up with a lot more than you need, but it won't go to waste. The solution can be used directly in your compost as an activator or mixed with water as a soil drench. Alternatively, you can attempt to capture and cultivate bacteria from everyday items, but – as Louie explains – it can be challenging to ensure that you have an optimum population of each microbe group when harvesting microorganisms from the wild. Conduct your own research if you want to give it a whirl.
- 1½ tablespoons of blackstrap molasses. This sugary substance provides the EM with energy to multiply. It can be kept for years and used in compost teas (see page 236).
- 1.5 kilograms of wheat-bran flakes. These can be purchased from animal-feed stores. Alternatively, you could freecycle untreated sawdust, coffee chaff or shredded leaves – but this is more experimental and can have an impact on the quality of the finished EM bran flakes.

EQUIPMENT
- a container that's big enough to mix the wheat bran without spillage
- a large zip-lock plastic bag or old grocery bag (make sure there are no holes)
- measuring spoons and mixing spoon
- scales

METHOD
1. Pour the water into the container.
2. Pour the EM-1 solution and blackstrap molasses into the water. Mix thoroughly until the blackstrap molasses has completely dissolved.
3. Add the wheat-bran flakes (or alternative flake material) to the container, and use clean hands to mix well.
4. Squeeze a handful of wet bran.
   - It's the correct consistency if it sticks together without dripping.
   - It's too dry if it doesn't hold its form or if it crumbles. Slowly add more water, pausing to perform the squeeze test every so often, until it achieves the correct consistency.
   - It's too wet if liquid drips from the bran. Add more dry flakes, pausing to perform the squeeze test every so often, until it achieves the correct consistency.
5. Put the damp flakes into the plastic bag. Squeeze out as much air as you can from between the flakes by pressing down on the bag.
6. Seal the bag, and store it in a warm, dark cupboard for two weeks. During this time, the microbes in the EM-1 solution will ferment the bran and multiply.
7. Open the bag after two weeks. The process has worked if the bran has developed a sweet, yeast-like odour. You may notice white mould growing on it, which is another good sign. If you see mould of any other colour, the wrong microbes have cultivated — you'll need to bury the bad batch in your garden and start again.
8. You'll need to dry your bran flakes for long-term storage. Do this by spreading the flakes out in a thin layer on trays or platters. Place the trays or platters in a warm, sunny position indoors until the flakes dry out completely. This may take a couple of days, depending on the weather.

9. Once the bran flakes are completely dry, store them in an airtight container for up to two years. Make sure they don't become moist, otherwise they'll go mouldy and won't work.

THE PROCESS HAS WORKED IF THE BRAN HAS DEVELOPED A SWEET, YEAST-LIKE ODOUR.

SOLUTIONS TO COMMON PROBLEMS

I have six Bokashi bins (a mix of commercial and DIY) at my place, and I run about 75 per cent of the food waste that my family generates in our kitchen through these bins, so I've had plenty of experience in dealing with the various issues that can arise during the process. In the table below, I've listed a number of Bokashi mistakes and how to fix them.

PROBLEM	SOLUTION
You've left your lid slightly askew and let oxygen in.	This can cause pathogenic mould to develop and prevents correct fermentation from occurring, as the EM need an oxygen–free environment to thrive. If you can see black, green, blue, brown or even pink mould growth, don't add the Bokashi material to your compost. Dig a hole and bury it, and the soil food web will sort it out.
There are maggots in your bin.	This is also likely the result of the bin not being properly sealed, and flies laying eggs. If this happens, then fill your bin to the top as quickly as you can and leave the lid closed for two weeks minimum for the final ferment. It won't be a pretty sight, but the anaerobic conditions and acidic environment will kill the maggots. You can then safely add the Bokashi material to your compost, or bury it.
You haven't filled your Bokashi bin up enough before its final ferment.	If you leave too much air space on top of your scraps, they may putrefy instead of ferment. Make sure you squeeze the waste down as much as possible so there's only a centimetre of space below the lid, and cover it all with some carbon, such as a piece of cardboard or a couple of pieces of newspaper cut to size. This will create the correct conditions for a strong ferment, and your bin won't stink.
You haven't been draining the bin regularly.	The fermenting process creates 'juice' (leachate), which you need to drain in order to allow the microbial process to continue. If you don't drain it, the bin may start to smell because of the 'juice' pooling in the bottom layer. This can also cause the contents of the bin to 'drown', and the scraps will putrefy, not ferment. Drain your Bokashi 'juice' throughout the whole process, from beginning to end. Then dilute it and use it in your garden.

PROBLEM	SOLUTION
You're not using enough EM bran flakes.	I recommend that you use ⅓ cup (roughly one handful) of EM bran per bucket of food scraps (for reference, the size of my caddy is 6 litres). That's not a lot, and it's less than what is stated on most commercial packets, but in my experience it's enough to inoculate your scraps with the beneficial bacteria. Any less and your scraps won't ferment, and they'll start to stink as they putrefy. But if you're finding that your Bokashi bin is starting to smell, then add more EM bran flakes. Experiment with the quantity until you find an amount that works for you – for example, add more if fermenting a lot of meat scraps, but add less if processing only fruit and vegie remnants.
You're using EM spray, and your bin contents are stinking.	I've reviewed several commercial EM sprays and been dissatisfied with their results. I found that my food waste started to putrefy rather than ferment. If this is happening to your Bokashi bin, then I recommend that you start using EM bran instead.

DIGESTERS

Digesters are in-ground containers that hungrily gobble up all of your food scraps and transform them into a nutrient-rich leachate (called a tea) that feeds the plants in the surrounding soil. If you're time-poor or dirt-averse, you hate creepy crawlies, or you don't need finished compost to feed your garden, then this is the perfect maintenance-free option for you.

I've kept the composting equipment listed earlier basically brand-free, but for this next section I'll be discussing the Green Cone® solar digester, which was originally developed in the United Kingdom and is now widely available in Australia, Canada and the United States.

HOW DOES IT WORK?

The Green Cone® captures heat from the sun in its double-walled cone, and then circulates warm air over the composting food for fast, aerobic, microbial decomposition. Below the cone is a perforated in-ground digestion chamber that holds the food waste and creates an ideal environment for soil microorganisms and worms to work their magic on your scraps. It's extremely simple to use: put your food waste in, and nature does the rest.

Unlike regular composting equipment that requires a balanced diet of greens and browns, this system doesn't follow a strict diet. You can (and should) load it up with all your cooked and uncooked food waste: fruits, vegies, meat, small bones, fish, seafood scraps, dairy, rice, legumes, grains, oils, even pet poo (in moderation and depending on the location – near ornamental plants only). Even if you go hard on scraps, this unit should not smell because the cone creates a hot-air vortex that allows oxygen to move through the system continually to maintain aerobic conditions.

The cone isn't designed to decompose fibrous plant materials, so keep your garden waste out of this unit. Leaves or grass clippings can clog up the cone and slow digestion. Every couple of years, you may need to empty the food chamber of any build-up of organic material that is slowing down the digestion process.

The Green Cone® doesn't produce any harvestable compost, so it's a handy solution for households that want to responsibly manage food waste but don't need compost for the garden. Depending on the season, the outdoor temperature and the mix of food waste, the Green Cone® can digest up to 5 litres of food scraps each week. This amount of food waste is the typical volume produced by a family of four.

The good

- It digests all of your food waste safely.
- It delivers microbially rich leachate to the soil.
- It can compost pet poo if the cone is positioned near ornamental plants only.
- Once it has been set up, it's very low maintenance.
- The contents don't need aeration, frequent emptying or balancing of the C:N ratio.
- The enclosed aerobic digestion holds in smells.
- It's vermin-proof.
- It's made from durable (and mostly recycled) plastic.

The bad

- It must be positioned in a sunny spot. It won't work if your garden is shady.
- It doesn't produce harvestable compost.
- Garden waste such as hedge trimmings and spent plants can't be broken down.
- It needs to be positioned in fertile, free-draining soil, otherwise decomposition will slow.
- The rate of decomposition slows down considerably in winter.

The location

The Green Cone® must be positioned in the warmest spot in your garden that receives maximum sun (six to eight hours of full sun is ideal). Choose a location with good drainage, and dig a hole in the soil that is 40–60 centimetres deep. You need to make sure that the top of the digestion chamber and the bottom of the cone both end up below ground level and covered with soil.

Ideally, you should locate the Green Cone® near your vegetable garden or flower bed to take advantage of the nutrients produced. If you live somewhere without access to soil, then you can also position the cone in a very large pot of healthy garden soil. This can be kept in a full-sun position on a deck, driveway or balcony.

TEST THE WATERS

An easy way to check your soil's drainage before installing the Green Cone® is to pour a bucket of water into the hole you dug for the cone. If the water pools and doesn't drain within 15 minutes, then the in-ground chamber will become anaerobic, will start to stink, and will slow down or stop digesting. If this happens, or you have clayey soil, increase the size of the hole and backfill with a mixture of gravel and compost around the digestion chamber to improve drainage.

PIT AND SHEET COMPOSTING

If you want to work with nature and make compost where you need it, without any fancy kit, then give pit or sheet composting a go. These on-the-spot methods of building better soil in your garden work particularly well for people who want their organic matter out of sight while it's decomposing.

PIT COMPOSTING

Pit composting is the perfect example of the KISS principle (keep it simple, stupid!). Simply dig a hole, and bury your chopped kitchen scraps and shredded household carbon. A huge benefit of hiding your waste in the soil is there are no visible compost bins that can become an eyesore or be a point of contention for fussy landlords.

Follow these instructions to compost in a pit:

1. Dig a pit directly into your garden soil. It can be any size, but if you have the space then a hole 60 centimetres deep, wide and long is ideal. Reserve the soil you've removed in a pile next to the hole.
2. Add a layer of carbon to the bottom of the hole, and then pour in your raw fruits, vegie scraps, coffee grounds, tea leaves, grass clippings, and so on.
3. Cover with another layer of carbon (such as shredded brown leaves or ripped newspaper), but don't use robust carbon sources such as woodchips. (Some people don't add any carbon to the hole and just rely on the soil biology to consume the waste, but pit composting works better with carbon.)
4. Sprinkle a little water onto the carbon, and then cover with a 2.5-centimetre layer of your reserved soil.
5. Repeat the process until the hole is full. (You can add material until the level is 30 centimetres above ground because the level will sink as the organic matter decomposes.) Cover with 10 centimetres of soil, and leave undisturbed.
6. Over six to twelve months, the life forms in the soil will consume your waste, and all of the captured nutrients will enrich your garden. You can leave the compost in situ or dig it out and use it around your garden.
7. There's no need to aerate or turn the contents of your hole in this style of composting. Because the compost is left undisturbed, it will likely develop fungi that are magnificent for the health of your soil.

DOS AND DON'TS OF PIT COMPOSTING

✓ Do chop your scraps to speed up decomposition.

✓ Do add a little water to the hole if conditions in your soil are very dry.

✓ Do dig your hole in an area where you want to add a future garden bed, or between rows of existing garden beds.

✗ Don't add vermin-attracting scraps (such as meat, bones, dairy, grains or cooked food).

✗ Don't add woodchips because they'll steal too much nitrogen from the surrounding soil; use softer carbon sources, such as shredded cardboard, paper or mowed brown leaves.

✗ Don't leave scraps uncovered with soil, otherwise they'll attract flies.

✗ Don't dig your hole in an area of your yard with bad drainage, otherwise conditions may become anaerobic.

✗ Don't dig a hole in the root zone under a tree because this can damage the tree.

SHEET COMPOSTING

Sheet composting is an in-situ horizontal composting method that's sometimes referred to as lasagne compost. It's a slow (cold) aerobic style of compost made on the earth. I think it's a wonderful style of compost creation for a number of reasons:

- It can be added to a little at a time as organic matter becomes available from your kitchen, garden or community.
- It can be used in small or large gardens and in raised beds.
- It helps to smother weeds and 'grows' soil right where you need it.
- It's a cost-effective way to expand a garden.
- It's a practical and easy way to decompose a lot of garden waste, such as grass clippings, prunings and spent plants.

As the compost pile can be positioned directly on top of your lawn, this style of composting is quite similar to no dig gardening. Where sheet composting differs is that, instead of using finished compost in the garden bed, you're actually making the compost in the bed using alternate layers of carbon-rich and nitrogen-rich materials. These layers will smother the grass and build fertility. (To learn more about no dig gardening, turn to pages 112–15.)

Follow these instructions to sheet compost:

1. It's best started at the beginning of autumn because the material can take up to six months to decompose. By spring, you should be able to plant straight into the garden bed.
2. Decide where you want your sheet compost to go. You can apply it directly onto bare soil or onto your lawn.
3. If you're sheet composting over a lawn, prepare the site by doing a short mow or removing any persistent weeds by hand.
4. Sprinkle an organic fertiliser over the area to feed any remaining weeds and grass, and water really well. (Why would you want to feed and water the weeds and grass? Well, this encourages them to grow, and then they'll rot more quickly underneath the layers of carbon.)
5. Place overlapping cardboard on the ground to prevent photosynthesis and to kill the grass and weeds below. Make sure there are no holes or plastic tape on the cardboard, otherwise the layers of cardboard won't bind together, and weeds may grow through. You can also use thick layers of newspaper (at least eight sheets). This needs to overlap by a couple of centimetres so that the weeds or grass underneath can't push through. (If you have invasive grasses such as kikuyu or couch growing in your lawn, ensure that you apply an extra generous layer of cardboard or newspaper.)
6. Thoroughly wet this foundation layer, and then cover it with a 3-centimetre deep layer of nitrogen-rich ingredients (such as manure or chopped green plant material).
7. Cover the nitrogen layer with a 3-centimetre deep layer of carbon-rich ingredients (such as brown leaves, straw, shredded newspaper, ripped paper, aged sawdust or aged woodchips).
8. Apply enough water to make the organic matter moist but not soaking.
9. Repeat this layering process as materials become available. For the juicy nitrogen layers, you can use kitchen scraps (if rodents or scavengers are not a problem in your yard), green garden waste (such as plant clippings and hedge trimmings cut or chipped into small pieces), coffee grounds, weeds without seeds, grass clippings, pelletised chicken manure, fresh animal manure or seaweed (this list is not exhaustive – get creative!). Always make sure that you top off your nitrogen with a dry, fibrous, carbon layer to prevent flies from becoming a problem.
10. The height of this bed will vary, depending on the volume of materials you have available. You do need a minimum of 50 centimetres of inputs to provide enough bulk to plant into when it has all decomposed.
11. The bed needs to be kept moist to allow for speedy microbial decomposition, but if you live in an area with a lot of rain, then

you may need to cover your bed with a tarpaulin to prevent the ingredients from getting too wet and becoming anaerobic.

12. The bed is ready for planting when there are no longer any recognisable layers, and it has all turned into crumbly compost that smells like a forest floor. You'll need to be patient as this can take up to six months, or longer if the weather is dry.

13. One final point – make sure you manage the edge of sheet-composted beds, as running grasses and creeping weeds on the periphery will want to sneak in.

JUMP-START YOUR PLANTING

If you're feeling impatient and want to start planting out the sheet-composted bed before it has finished decomposing, then you can cover the layers with a 5-centimetre layer of cured compost and plant directly into this. Alternatively, if you don't have this amount of compost available, you can dig into the top layers and add pockets of cured compost to a depth of 5 centimetres and plant into these areas. Make sure you don't puncture the carbon foundation layer, otherwise weeds will grow through.

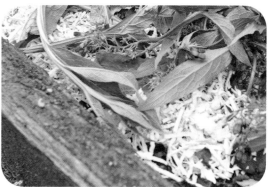

CHARLES DOWDING

THE LARGE-SCALE COMPOSTER

The promise of an abundant harvest with less weeding; less watering; no need for pesticides, herbicides, fungicides, synthetic fertilisers or crop rotation; and no backbreaking digging is extremely enticing for all gardeners. English horticulturalist, market gardener and educator CHARLES DOWDING has been championing a method of gardening known as 'no dig' since the 1980s. He teaches gardeners not to work soil, but rather to work *with* soil. As the name suggests, no dig gardening limits soil disturbance so that microbes, invertebrates, insects, fungi and ultimately plants can thrive.

What is no dig gardening, and how do you utilise it?

It's the simplest and most common–sense approach that one can imagine. You simply leave your soil undisturbed, and you feed its inhabitants with surface mulches of organic matter. What mulches you use will depend on your climate. Here at our market garden Homeacres, our climate is maritime and often damp, so I prefer to use compost because it doesn't give habitat to slugs and snails. Plus it gives rapid results of increased and healthier growth.

Why is no dig gardening so beneficial to soil biology and plant productivity?

The reason no dig gardening is so beneficial is that it favours an increase of soil biology. Soil organisms and their interactions are instrumental to the growth of all plants. The more life and activity there is in the soil, the stronger the growth above it. Therefore, it makes a lot of sense to leave all of these hardworking organisms alone, to feed those of them that thrive on organic matter, and – more than anything – to build carbon in the soil that facilitates the whole process.

Active and undisturbed organisms include networks of mycorrhizal fungi. They team up with plant roots in a mutually beneficial way that increases the rate of growth as well as the total quantity of growth. This in turn increases the quantity of carbon in the soil via photosynthesis: converting sun energy into carbon in soil. No dig gardening with a surface mulch of organic matter is a win–win process.

The compost or organic matter that you add to the surface is quickly eaten by organisms (such as earthworms), and then becomes part of the soil below. This improves structure, aeration and drainage, and in turn increases plant growth.

What are the differences between dig and no dig gardening?

A stand–out difference is that the no dig bed has a highly significant amount of carbon in its soil, compared to the soil of the bed that I dig every December. Both beds receive the same amount of compost every year. Therefore, it seems to me that no dig gardening retains, even increases, carbon in our soils. On the other side of the coin, the dug bed is losing carbon – I imagine through oxidation to CO_2 – every time I dig it.

Is compost the mainstay of no dig gardening?

This is an interesting question. Instead of 'compost is the mainstay of no dig gardening', I would say that 'compost is the mainstay of successful vegetable gardening'! All gardening, in fact, because the no dig method works equally well for ornamental plants and cut-flower market gardens.

Using quite a lot of compost at the beginning is wise because it lifts fertility to a high level. This means that you need less time and less area to grow the same amount of food.

My trial beds show that you need less compost for a no dig bed. I can't emphasise this enough! Although I talk about compost a lot, you use it more efficiently with no dig gardening and don't need so much in the end.

Can you describe your compost set-up and composting methods?

I'm making compost in three different ways: in large bays measuring 1.5 metres × 1.8 metres, in pallet beds measuring 1.1 square metres, and

in plastic Dalek-shaped structures (compost bins that are open to the ground). They all make good compost. It's important to know that whatever you can manage to do in your garden will be good. The biggest difference you'll find is the speed of decomposition and final results, according to the size of bay you use and the ingredients you have available.

My large bays get hot from mid-spring to late autumn because we add large amounts of fresh, green leaves. Any large volume of green material results in heat. To ensure that it becomes high-quality compost, we add a fair amount of brown material, which I stockpile through winter: aged woodchips (that are more than six months old and looking brown; we run the lawnmower over them first), paper and cardboard.

The pallet heaps are not as hot as the large bays because the volume is smaller. Interestingly, I find that the compost is lighter in colour, suggesting a better and/or higher balance of fungi to bacteria, and it feels beautifully soft. There are, however, a few viable weed seeds because of the reduced heat level.

We reduce the amount of rain entering our open piles by using a roof or cover. This also helps to keep our compost light and aerated. We turn our heaps just once, which gives a uniform compost and ensures a correct moisture level (occasionally we do need to water when turning the compost).

Usually, I spread out compost when it's between eight and twelve months old. It can also work when it's only four or five months old, depending on exactly how you're using it. I never sieve compost for beds, and am completely happy if there are still bits of decomposing woodchips. They sit on top of the soil and help to increase fungal activity with their decomposition.

Do you make enough compost for your highly productive market garden?

At Homeacres, we sell around 3 tonnes of vegetables every year, and in return I receive a lot of organic matter from our community (such as woodchips, coffee grounds, spent hops and any other waste that people are happy to donate). We add the urine from my compost toilet, which has soaked into straw in the urinal. After 18 months, the poo goes into flower beds and around fruit trees. I can make enough compost for about two–thirds of my needs. My homemade compost includes materials brought in (such as woodchips).

How do you ensure that these acquired inputs (especially manure) are safe?

I like using woodchips because they're a safe input without chemical contamination. Animal manures have become much more difficult to use because of pyralid weedkillers, and I use much less animal manure than ten years ago. It's an absolute disgrace that these poisons are allowed, and reveals how our legislative processes are about business and not about protecting the environment. Before spreading manure or commercial compost, I check it by sowing broad/fava/field beans in some of it.

Do you use other organic amendments or regenerative gardening practices?

I use no other amendments, feeds or fertilisers. I'm interested in the potential benefits of adding charcoal and basalt rock dust to compost heaps while we're making them, in small amounts. I'm also extremely interested in the potential of wormeries to create vermicast, in particular for potting soil and compost.

My main concern is to work most efficiently, and my most precious resource is time. I find it straightforward and effective to convert organic matter to compost and to spread that for fertility over a whole year and longer.

How does crop rotation work in a no dig garden?

No dig gardening means that plants are healthier and stronger; the soil is also healthier, with less disease and with a continuous availability of the balanced nutrients that each plant needs. I demonstrate this all the time by spreading the same amount of compost on all of my beds. It's the same whether I'm growing carrots, potatoes, cabbages, lettuce, spinach or radishes. With no dig gardening, you don't have the concept of heavy feeders and light feeders because soil organisms take care of finding enough food for all of the plants.

You don't need to rotate crops – or at least not so much – because soil stays generally healthy and disease–free. There are a few exceptions, as always, but I have no fixed rotation here, and it's working very well.

One could summarise by saying no dig gardening is an easy way to grow healthy soil for healthy plants ... for healthy people!

ELECTRIC COMPOSTERS

You may be surprised to learn that there are electric appliances that claim to compost your food waste. Manufacturers claim that these appliances save you time by only taking three to five hours to 'process' your kitchen waste. What they basically do is remove all the water from your food waste by drying it at a fairly high temperature (over 100 degrees Celsius), then grind what's left, leaving you with something that looks vaguely like brownish, crumbly compost. But the superficial resemblance of the end product is where the similarity with composting ends.

If you've been paying attention, you'll know that composting involves microbes and oxygen, and that even when it's fast, it takes weeks. Composting transforms the raw material through the activity of microbes. Something that occurs in an appliance at a temperature that would kill microbes – and that takes hours not weeks – can't be called 'composting'.

In short, these appliances dry out the kitchen waste and grind it up. That's it. What's left is pretty much what you started with, without the water. There's no transformation, and no nutrient-rich compost. If you're environmentally conscious and looking for an easy way to compost your food scraps, buying an electric composter is one of the least sustainable choices you could make.

The good

- It prevents food waste going to landfill (but only if the end product actually gets buried or composted, and not put in the rubbish!).
- If your house is solar-powered, then the energy used to run the system is not an issue.
- It's easy to use.

The bad

- The appliance requires a lot of energy to make and run.
- It costs a lot of money – apart from the initial purchase price, there's the cost of electricity and perhaps hundreds of dollars per year to replace the filters.
- It doesn't produce compost! The end product is dehydrated organic material that needs to be aged for up to 90 days before use in your garden.
- It requires ongoing replacement of filters, which will end up in landfill.
- The cradle-to-grave assessment is poor because the unit will end up in landfill, too.
- The unit is large and will take up bench space, but only accommodates waste from the meals of one or two people.

GIVE A SCRAP

If you don't have the room to create your own compost pile or bin, but also don't want to throw away all your kitchen waste, why not sign up to the free global app, ShareWaste? You can become a Compost Donor by finding a Compost Host in your local area and giving your waste to them.

TOOLS OF THE TRADE

Now that you've decided which composting system will work best for you, it's time to assemble a motley crew of bits and bobs that will help to make composting a breeze at your place. None of these tools need to be bought new: they can be repurposed, upcycled or bought second–hand.

COMPOST CADDY

A compost caddy is a lidded bucket that lives on your kitchen benchtop, so you can easily store all of the kitchen scraps left over from your cooking. Don't rush out and buy a new caddy: a repurposed 1–kilogram yoghurt tub works really well.

If you do want something a little fancier, look for a second–hand caddy with a solid lid. I dislike caddies with breathable lids that have charcoal filters, because the holes in the lid allow vinegar flies and blowflies free access to your scraps (not ideal!), and you need to regularly replace the filters, which end up in landfill.

Here are some tips that will keep the contents of your caddy smelling as fresh as a daisy:

- It's important to regularly empty your caddy into your compost bin, worm farm or Bokashi bin. This will stop the scraps from becoming mouldy and smelly, especially during summer.
- Line your caddy with a recycled piece of carbon – newspaper works well. This liner can be composted, too, and it helps to keep your caddy clean. If you're out of carbon, use the leafy top of rhubarb (or a similar leafy vegie) that you would have composted anyway.
- Use more than one caddy if you have a few different composting systems, such as Bokashi bins, worm farms or chickens. Label or colour code the caddies so your household knows what to put in each one.

- In the height of summer, you may want to put your caddy in the fridge overnight to stop stinky smells or mould developing.
- Make sure to always close the lid of your caddy firmly to stop flies feasting on your tasty scraps.
- If you don't want to use a caddy, you can always keep your scraps in a plastic bag, bowl or container in the fridge or freezer.

COMPOST TURNER

Turning your compost requires a bit of muscle. However, one of my favourite pieces of compost equipment, the corkscrew compost aerator, makes the job far easier. As the name suggests, it looks like a giant corkscrew. It works by manually screwing through the organic matter in your bin and pulling the bottom scraps up to the top.

This aerator helps to create holes in your heap, into which you can throw your fresh bucket of scraps. All you then need to do is cover the heap with carbon, and your compost will be happy and well oxygenated. If you've decided to compost in an enclosed bin, then this is the ideal tool for you; if you're working with an open pile, a garden fork is a more useful tool for the same job. Corkscrew aerators can also be used in worm farms because they aerate via a twisting rather than a slicing action that won't hurt your worms.

GARDEN FORK

A large garden fork is the perfect tool to use for turning large, open piles of compost, or moving organic matter between open compost bays. A small handheld fork (with rounded tines) is a handy tool for digging food scraps into worm farms.

COMPOST THERMOMETER

A compost thermometer is a handy piece of kit if you want to get some direct data about the heat your hot compost is packing. Compost thermometers are helpful throughout the whole composting process because, even after the steamy thermophilic stage has finished, it's useful to be able to measure the temperature of your compost to find out when it has fully cooled.

PH TEST

This isn't an essential tool, but is useful if you're into data. You can use these kits to test not only your compost but also your soil. (To learn more about the importance of soil pH, turn to pages 194–5.)

N95 MASK

This may not be a sexy accessory, but I highly recommend that you wear an N95 mask when aerating your compost, handling dry manure or spreading dust with fine particles (such as rock dusts, diatomaceous earth or garden lime). This is especially important if you are pregnant or have an autoimmune disorder. Wearing a mask prevents you from breathing in airborne particles, which can become dangerous lung irritants. Keeping the organic matter in your compost moist will help to reduce the risk of very small particles becoming airborne and entering your lungs.

GARDENING GLOVES

Pop on some gloves when handling compost, castings or manure, and always remember to cover cuts and grazes with bandaids, too. This helps to prevent the risk of getting tetanus.

5.

THE
WORMS

LET'S GET WIGGLY!

I think everyone should have a worm farm (called a wormery in the United Kingdom). Worm composting (or vermicomposting) is a fantastic compost solution for a lot of reasons:

- It's a superb small-space alternative to backyard composting that can be done indoors or on a balcony.
- When managed correctly, it's basically odour-free.
- It's low maintenance.
- You can process a lot of waste in a small space.
- You can make a worm farm out of repurposed materials for free.
- You can move the bin around easily as the seasons change.
- You get rich castings (the fancy name for worm poo) to use as a soil conditioner.

But the main benefit – as with all of the compost options in this book – is that you'll divert kitchen waste from landfill, and you'll be putting the nutrients back into your garden to get better, healthier plants and food in return. You'll soon fall in love with your little red wigglers, and this relationship will connect you with your environment and your waste cycle, and enrich both your life and your garden. Seriously, worm farming is rad!

WHAT IS WORM FARMING?

A worm farm is a composting system with optimised conditions for special worms (see pages 132–3), which become the chief composters. Let's start at the end (both metaphorically and physically): what you get out of a worm farm is decomposed food waste and bedding material, as well as precious worm poo (known as worm castings or vermicast). Together, they form vermicompost, which contains nutrients in plant-accessible forms, humus (with all of the benefits we've already discussed), and a flourishing community of beneficial bacteria, fungi and other microorganisms.

Something magical happens inside the gut of a worm: what comes out their rear end packs a higher nutrient punch than what went in. Worm castings are jam-packed with nitrogen, potassium, phosphorus, micronutrients, beneficial soil microbes (such as nitrogen-fixing bacteria), plant-growth hormones and mycorrhizal fungi. Impressive, right? So, even if worm farming is not your primary composting method, it's definitely worth having it as a complementary system to feed your soil.

HOW IT WORKS

Worm farming in its most basic terms is simple: microorganisms (aerobically) decompose the bedding and food waste, and then worms continue to digest the organic matter. The final result is lots of luscious poo.

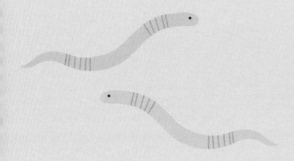

I find the relationship between compost worms and bacteria fascinating. They work hand-in-hand and have a healthy co-dependency. Worms get all our attention in vermicomposting systems, as they're the organisms we can see; however, worms only have a rudimentary digestive system. It's actually bacteria that do most of the hard work, consuming and breaking down the organic matter before worms then finish off the process. In exchange for their services, worms create an aerobic environment rich with castings that allows the bacteria to thrive, and the nutrient-recycling loop continues.

Now, be prepared to have your understanding of what worms eat flipped on its head. Worms get most of their nutrition from eating the bacteria rather than the food waste in your worm farm. Worms only eat your scraps once they've become colonised with bacteria.

What happens is this: the microbes use enzymes to break down your scraps and turn them into a soupy slurry on all exposed surface areas. As the scraps decompose, more of the surface area is then exposed to bacteria, which results in their population booming. You now have many billions of tiny microbial mouths dining on your scraps. Worms then enter the party and start sucking up the bacteria-rich scrap slurry. Delicious!

Worms don't have teeth, so they can't bite into chunky scraps; rather, they suck soft and decomposing scraps into their mouths. By understanding this characteristic, we can optimise their scraps by chopping them up, freezing/thawing them (this helps them to decompose more quickly) or, even better, blitzing them in a food processor to create lots of surface area for both bacteria and worms to easily consume.

As bacteria enter the worm's digestive tract, they're exposed to the flora in the worm's gut – and this is when the magic happens. The bacterial populations continue to party in the gut of the worm and form a condensed mucus around the digested organic matter. This is then deposited out of the worm's backside as rich castings. The release of poo triggers bacteria to bloom in your worm farm, and this in turn forms an important part of your worm's next meal. What a beautiful, closed–loop system worm farms are!

CROWD CONTROL

Worms are smarter than they look: they prevent their pooey paradise from becoming overcrowded by regulating their population. Their breeding cycles are based on the available space, temperature, moisture, pH, bedding material and amount of food you provide them. If you nail the conditions of their home, then there'll be a lot of worm sex and a wriggly baby boom (don't blush – this is what we want: more worms means more waste is consumed and more poo is pumped out!). Your farm's worm population can double every 90 days if there is room and the conditions are right.

BELOW:
Red wigglers (Eisenia fetida) are happiest when conditions in a worm farm are temperate and moist.

LIFE CYCLE OF A WORM

Some may argue that worms are more advanced than us simpletons when it comes to making babies. Worms have thrown gender roles out the window. They're hermaphrodites, so there are no 'boy' or 'girl' worms, but they do require a lover with which to exchange genetic material.

WORM SEX

All worms have both male and female reproductive organs, as well as a ring–like section of glandular tissue called a clitellum, which is found on the outside of the worm's body. Worms don't need to roll over and say, 'Not tonight, honey,' if they're not in the mood. This is because the clitellum signals fertility: this bulbous gland glows orange when the worm is ready to get it on.

Now, I'm going to describe the actual act of worm sex in simple terms, so you understand the process and don't feel too shy about it. The worm parents–to–be snuggle next to each other, positioned nose to tail, and bring their sex organs in contact. They then exchange sperm, plus some secretions of mucus and albumin – sexy! The sperm from each worm contains male cells that fertilise the other's female cells.

When the act is complete – it's a marathon that can take up to 24 hours – the two worms wiggle apart. If the act was a success, then each fertilised worm secretes a mucus ring that passes over the worm's upper body; it then hardens and forms a cocoon filled with eggs.

COSY COCOONS

You've probably seen worm cocoons in your worm farm or compost bin and not realised it, as they're small and easy to overlook. When cocoons are first formed, they're about the size of a grape seed or a match head, pearly white in colour and shaped like a lemon. The cocoons become more noticeable when they mature and turn yellow. Worm cocoons are extremely durable and can survive in your farm, soil or compost for up to a year until conditions are right, and then the eggs will hatch.

We all know that the human gestation period lasts nine months. In comparison, worm egg incubation occurs in a flash – it only takes around three weeks. Each cocoon contains an average of six baby worms, but usually only two or three hatchlings emerge. When the baby worms are ready to enter the world, the cocoon turns dark maroon.

The worms in your farm typically prefer to reproduce in mild temperatures and are happiest at around 12–25 degrees Celsius. If all of the variables in your farm are on point (space, food, pH, moisture) and the weather is pleasantly warm, each worm can mate and produce a cocoon every seven to ten days. Consequently, they can produce about 50 cocoons a year, from which 100–150 baby worms will hatch. Remember, they'll only reproduce if there is enough space and food, so their population won't get out of hand.

A BABY TO A BREEDER

Baby worms might look very pale pink and tiny, but they're born with big appetites. Immediately after hatching, they'll start consuming your scraps. In around two to three months, they'll grow from their birth size – the thickness of a piece of cotton and about 1 centimetre long – to their mature size.

Baby worms don't have any functioning reproductive organs. They reach adulthood when their sex organs fully develop at around three months old, and they themselves are then ready to make babies. If you're a good worm parent, some of the worms will live a long and happy life in your farm for up to five years.

CHOOSING THE RIGHT WORM SYSTEM FOR YOUR SPACE

When you first start a worm farm, you'll become a parent to thousands of worm babies. It's a big responsibility! If you follow my tips, you'll receive an A in 'worm parenting 101' and will be rewarded with plenty of their precious poo.

The first question is what sort of worm farm do you want? There are two basic choices:

1. **In-ground worm farm** – This could be a bin or a bucket.
2. **Above-ground worm farm** – This could be a simple box, a tiered structure or a continuous-flow system.

I have both an in-ground bin and an above-ground continuous-flow system, and each one has both good and bad aspects.

IN-GROUND WORM FARM

The biggest benefit of an in-ground worm farm (sometimes referred to as a worm tower) is that it connects the system to the soil food web. There's an 'open-door policy' for all soil microorganisms (such as beneficial bacteria, fungi and composting invertebrates). These microbial mates and composting critters move in when there are scraps to gobble up, and they work with the worms to help cycle nutrients. This allows you to be more free-wheeling and adventurous with your in-ground farm.

In my experience, you can be more heavy-handed with scraps that worms don't love (such as small amounts of citrus, onions, garlic and spicy food) because, if conditions are off, your worms can find refuge in the surrounding soil. They can also move out if you've been on holiday or forgotten to feed them. Your worms will leave the farm and let the compost microbes do their thing, then come back when conditions have settled down. This escape route is clearly not available for above-ground worm farms, so if you're time-poor or disorganised (I'm often both!), then an in-ground worm farm is the best option for you.

There are many other benefits of an in-ground worm farm:

- Worm tea (liquid that leaches from the worm farm), castings and compost will naturally enrich the garden in which the worm farm sits.
- The temperature and moisture in the bin will be regulated by the surrounding soil. So, the bin is unlikely to dry out or get saturated, and is less likely to overheat.
- The worms can cope with less attention. They can travel out of the farm and into the surrounding soil to find food. They'll return to your farm once conditions have improved.
- If you stop feeding the worms altogether, they'll just leave. The organic material that is already in the worm farm will slowly decompose without much bother.

There are some drawbacks to an in-ground worm farm. Obviously, you need a garden with enough space. Harvesting the compost can also be a little more physically difficult than with an above-ground worm farm, and you can't harvest the worm tea at all. To be frank, this is no biggie. The liquid that is created in worm farms and often marketed as 'worm wee' is not produced by worms – as they don't urinate! It's leachate that forms as your food scraps decompose and that drains through the worm castings. This liquid is variable in nutrient quantity and quality, as it hasn't been processed in the gut of worms. For this reason, worm tea is massively overrated.

DIY in-ground worm farm

If you have a small space, or love upcycling things around the house, then you can easily build your own in-ground worm farm using an old bucket or PVC pipe. This small worm farm is great for apartment dwellers, as the whole unit can live in a large pot placed on your balcony or in a common area next to the garbage bins.

1. Get a plastic bucket with a secure lid. Alternatively, you can also use a piece of PVC pipe cut about 5 centimetres taller than the depth of your pot or bed, with a push-on cap to secure the top.
2. Drill lots of holes in the sides and base of the bucket (or the PVC pipe) using an 8-millimetre drill bit. Be warned that this will create lots of small fragments of plastic, so do the drilling where you can easily sweep them all up.
3. If you have a garden, this worm farm can be dug-in exactly where you want the nutrients to go (such as in the middle of a vegie bed). For people without gardens, it can be placed inside a large pot. If you're using it in a pot, then add a 10-centimetre layer of woodchips to the base of the pot first. This isn't an essential step, but it does help with drainage.
4. Place your worm farm in the hole in the ground or on top of the woodchips in the pot, and then backfill with compost or soil.
5. Fill the worm farm with your carbon bedding materials (decaying leaf litter – or leaf mould – is my favourite, but shredded cardboard will work, too) and food scraps. Add a handful of healthy garden soil or compost to introduce beneficial biology.
6. Add a handful of compost worms. These will multiply quickly, so you can use a handful from a friend's farm if you don't want to buy your own.
7. You can plant herbs and flowers around the perimeter of the worm farm. These will grow abundantly as they're fed by the castings.
8. Monitor how quickly your worms are eating the scraps, and then feed them accordingly. Don't load up your farm with more scraps until they've almost finished their last meal. Make sure you add carbon each time you feed them, too, to keep the conditions aerobic.
9. Gently aerate the worm farm each time you add food waste, using a gloved hand, a corkscrew compost aerator or a handheld garden fork with rounded tines.
10. It's a good idea to cover the worm farm with a worm blanket cut to size (this can be made from old natural-fibre clothing or a hessian coffee sack) to help insulate the worms.
11. When the worm farm is completely full of vermicompost, a lot of the worms will move out to the edges. If you used a bucket with a handle, you could pull it out of the ground or pot and harvest your finished vermicompost following the methods on pages 139–40.

BELOW:
A commercial in-ground worm farm sits next to a homemade version. Both work equally well.

ABOVE-GROUND WORM FARM

What about above-ground options? As mentioned earlier, there are three types:

1. a simple box
2. a tiered structure
3. a continuous-flow system.

Simple box

The simplest system is just a box, but it must be aerated! If air can't get in (and leachate can't drain out, or at least drain away from the bedding), then you'll end up with a mess of anaerobic sludge.

Any box that can be modified so that air can get in and leachate can drain out will be fine. (This can be done by adding gravel with geofabric on top to the base of the box.) Ideally, the box should have a lid; if it doesn't, then you can use an old woollen blanket or coffee sack to cover the contents (but be aware that this will be attractive to flies). As long as the worms can get to work in the dark, and you can keep some moisture in, then any type of cover will work.

Pros – It's simple; a box is unlikely to break; there are no legs to fall off.

Cons – A commercial box may have a system to collect and harvest worm tea, but a DIY box will probably leak some worm tea and therefore may not be ideal for use on a balcony (and definitely not indoors). Harvesting the compost can be a bit more fiddly (see pages 139–40).

Tiered structure

The tiered design with trays is intended to solve a few problems. The worm farm has a bottom tray with a spigot that allows for easy collection and harvesting of the worm tea. It has multiple food-waste trays that are progressively filled from the bottom up, and the worms will (usually) follow the food and migrate upwards, leaving finished compost in the lowest tray. This can then be easily harvested by lifting the tray out (and then putting the tray back at the top of the farm when it's empty).

Pros – It's a fully enclosed system (usually on legs) that can work indoors or on a hard surface. Harvesting the worm tea and worm castings is easy, and you can move the unit to suit your life and the seasons.

Cons – The commercial ones are typically small in size (probably because they're intended for balcony or indoor use), and so they won't process a large amount of waste. They can also require more maintenance to ensure that the moisture and temperature remain suitable because they're not naturally insulated by the soil.

Continuous-flow system

This is a big bin that is usually tapered (so it's larger at the top and smaller at the bottom). You add food at the top where the worms hang out, and you harvest finished compost from the bottom. Commercial models usually have a method for retrieving the compost from the bottom, such as a harvesting hatch or trapdoor.

Pros – It's efficient and simple, and typically larger in volume than a tiered structure. It's fully enclosed and can be used on a balcony or patio.

Cons – It takes a bit of maintenance to ensure that the material inside keeps moving 'through' the system. In my experience, once the original bedding has decomposed, the material in the bin may not allow enough air circulation; it can then become too moist and get stuck. This means that you will need to stick your hand into the guts of the bin to scrape out the worm castings occasionally.

WORMS ARE HAPPIEST WHEN THE OUTDOOR TEMPERATURE IS 12–25 DEGREES CELSIUS.

WHERE TO POSITION YOUR WORM FARM

Placing your farm in the right spot is a crucial step in creating a happy home for your worms to work efficiently. Temperature extremes are one of the biggest worm killers, so you need to consider your climate and the season before you choose the farm's final resting place (unless it's one you can move easily).

Worms are happiest when the outdoor temperature is 12–25 degrees Celsius. So, in most areas of Australia, protecting worm farms from hot temperatures is a more important consideration than shielding them from the cold. In hot climates, position your farm on the southern side of your house in summer, where it will receive the least amount of direct sun. If this isn't possible, then place it where it will receive morning sun only and is shaded from hot afternoon rays.

In winter, if your farm is freestanding, then you may want to move it inside (into a laundry or garage, for instance) to keep your worms cosy. This will help your worms to consume your scraps right through the chilly months. If you have an in-ground worm farm, then you obviously can't bring that inside – but you can insulate it. Make a simple cold frame to place over the top, or buy a mini greenhouse and secure it over the worm farm. Alternatively, you could simply place thick layers of carbon (such as straw) on top of the worm farm. Although worms can't survive freezing temperatures, their cocoons can, and baby worms will emerge from a dormant winter farm in spring.

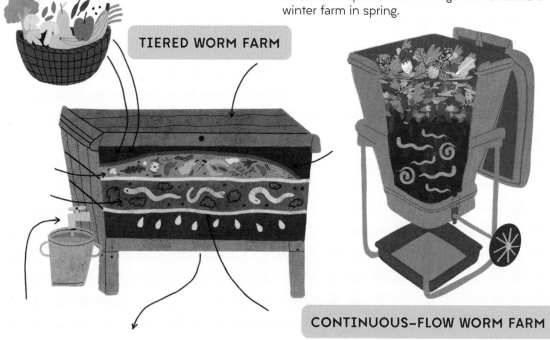

TIERED WORM FARM

CONTINUOUS-FLOW WORM FARM

HOW TO USE YOUR WORM FARM

After you've sorted out the type of worm farm and where it's going to live, the next question is what do you put in it? The answer is four things:

1. compost worms (red wigglers or red tiger worms)
2. scraps (juicy, nitrogen–rich greens)
3. bedding (dry, carbon–rich browns)
4. grit (abrasive particles that help worms to grind food in their gizzard).

COMPOST WORMS

A common misconception is that all worms are the same. Compost worms are surface dwellers that have evolved to live in the leaf litter on forest floors. They're classified as epigeic, which comes from the ancient Greek term for 'upon the earth'. As their classification suggests, they thrive in decaying matter that sits upon the surface of the soil (such as piles of manure, decomposing leaves or the contents of your composting system).

The most suitable species of compost worms to purchase from a store or to obtain from a friend are *Eisenia fetida* (red wiggler) and *Eisenia andrei* (red tiger worm). It's really important to get the correct species of worms, as others are invasive (such as *Amynthas agrestis*, the Asian jumping worm).

These two composting worms are reddish brown and small, but looks can be deceiving. They have huge appetites and, with the help of compost bacteria, they'll make short work of large amounts of organic matter in your farm. These worms are really accommodating and will reproduce quickly within the confines of a farm, too. They don't need a lot of space, as they don't burrow in the same way that earthworms do. Compost worms will also put up with you disturbing their feast by gently digging in their bedding to add scraps. What little legends they are!

ABOVE:
A powerfully muscular earthworm, which has evolved to burrow deeply into the soil, sits next to a diminutive compost worm. Looks can be deceiving, though, as the compost worm can eat half its weight in scraps every day.

Earthworms are very different characters altogether. Think of them as 'free rangers' that are wild at heart. Their powerful bodies have evolved to burrow deep within the soil, and they play an important role in aerating and draining the soil. They're classified as endogeic, which comes from the ancient Greek term for 'within the earth'. Earthworms will go on strike in your worm farm because they:

- need an expanse of soil to roam in
- dislike having their burrow system disturbed
- hate mating in close quarters.

They won't power through your waste, either; instead, they pick up dead organic material from the surface of the soil and carry it underground. Don't put earthworms from your garden in your worm farm or compost bin – they'll simply move out or die due to incorrect environmental factors and a lack of suitable food.

SCRAPS

There are three things to keep in mind when feeding your worms: balance, moderation and diversity. Adding too much of one particular food item can disrupt the microbiome and pH of your farm. Worms thrive in an environment with a neutral pH, so you do need to be careful not to add lots of acidic scraps (such as onions, tomatoes, pineapples and citrus) all at once. If you provide your worms with a balanced diet of diverse greens and browns, while adding the occasional acidic scrap in moderation, your worm community will thrive.

The table on page 135 will help you balance the inputs in your worm farm. Worms love the 'more please' scraps, so add as many as you like to your worm farm. They'll tolerate the 'just a little taste' scraps, but adding too many can overload your system and make it stink. Worms loathe the 'no thank you' scraps, so don't add them at all.

Citrus and salt

Citrus contains a chemical compound called limonene that is toxic to worms. Your worms may cope with an occasional bit of lemon peel or half a squeezed orange every now and again, but it's best to chop up citrus to create a greater surface area for the microbes to get to work on it before the worms come near it. If you have an abundance of citrus scraps, composting them is best. (For other creative ways to use up leftover citrus, turn to page 164.)

Processed food that is high in salt can be a disastrous input for your worm colony, as salt draws moisture from their bodies. If worms dry out, then they can't breathe and will quickly die. So, err on the side of caution when it comes to salt.

Meat and dairy

It may surprise you to know that you can feed small amounts of dairy, meat and bones to your worms because they're omnivores. However, before you chuck a steak or half a tub of yoghurt into your farm, there are two concerns I'll flag: the odours that these protein–rich scraps produce as they decompose, and the fact that they're attractive to vermin.

Small amounts of protein–rich scraps do regularly end up in my worm farms, and I haven't had any issues with this, as I always bury my scraps and add plenty of carbon. When it's time to harvest my castings, I pull out the well–picked–over bones and turn them into biochar. (To learn more about this magical stuff, turn to pages 230–3.)

If you've accidentally added too many protein–rich scraps and things have become a bit whiffy, simply add a bit more carbon on top and don't disturb the worm farm for a week or so (as turning it will release the odour). Within that time, the stench should have settled down. If not, give the farm a thorough aeration, add more carbon and fresh scraps, and don't disturb it for another week. It should come up smelling like roses.

If you have a small worm farm that you keep indoors, use common sense about the amount of meat and dairy you add. I can't emphasise strongly enough that diversity of scraps and moderation when it comes to any one input are key to a healthy worm farm.

WORMS

SCRAPS

GRIT

BEDDING

MORE PLEASE	JUST A LITTLE TASTE	NO THANK YOU
Most fruit and vegie scraps, especially water–rich scraps with a neutral pH (such as watermelon, banana peels and apple cores)	Cooked leftovers (too much oily food will coat the organic matter, and worms won't be able to breathe, so go easy with these scraps)	Anything high in salt
Cooked salt–free vegies (such as baked pumpkin, skin and all)	Crushed eggshells	Acidic food (such as citrus and pineapple)
Plastic–free tea bags, loose–leaf tea and coffee grounds	Onion, garlic (worms don't really mind these scraps – especially the papery outsides or when cooked – but too much of the flesh can cause odours and increase acidity)	Highly processed fast food (if high in salt, sugar or preservatives)
Grains, rice, bread, pasta, pizza crusts	Dairy	Spicy food
Ripped newspaper, torn–up egg cartons and toilet–paper rolls	Meat and fish	Anything inorganic (such as plastic, foil or glass)
Shredded brown leaves, leaf mould, small amounts of aged sawdust, lucerne (alfalfa) mulch, pea mulch and nitrogen–rich garden refuse (such as seedless weeds, prunings and herbaceous green leaves)	Grass clippings (adding small amounts at a time is okay, but large amounts will heat up your worm farm and cause problems)	Fats or oils (large amounts of olive, vegetable or canola oil will cause disastrous anaerobic conditions in your worm farm)

Overfeeding

You can kill your worms with kindness, and overfeeding is often the main reason why worm farms fail. Adding more food than your worms can happily consume will result in it rotting and giving off toxic gases, and the conditions in your farm will become acidic and anaerobic. This will cause your very stressed worms to either attempt to escape the farm or die.

It's easy to get overly enthusiastic about the amount of food that you think your worms will consume, especially when you hear that worms can consume half their body weight in food and bedding per day. With this thinking, if you bought 1 kilogram of worms, surely they could munch through 500 grams of food waste per day, right? Sorry to be the bearer of bad news, but generally that's not the case. Your worm farm would have to be operating at optimum efficiency for this to happen (perfect pH, ideal outdoor temperature, a farm with a large surface area, and an acclimatised and hungry adult worm population).

Instead of focusing on weight, it's actually best to be guided by observation and direct feedback from the worms when it comes to the quantity and frequency of feedings. Always eyeball what's left in your farm before you add more scraps – and give it a sniff, too. If there's a lot of their last meal left, then hold off giving them more. If it's a bit smelly, then this can be a sign that you've added too much food, and anaerobic conditions are taking over. Don't add more food scraps if this is the case, and instead add dry carbon and give the contents a turn to rebalance conditions.

MOULD OR GOLD?

Let's talk about mould for a minute. Feeding mouldy scraps to your worms is fine for the most part. Mould cells are just one of the many different types of microorganisms that are breaking down your scraps. The only real problem is if the food scraps in your wormery are becoming mouldy before they have finished decomposing – this can be a sign that you're overfeeding your worm colony.

As I explained earlier, scraps with more surface area will be consumed more quickly because the microbes will get to work faster. So, chop or blend your scraps to supercharge the amount of waste your worms consume.

BEDDING

Worm bedding is a misnomer that sometimes trips people up because they misinterpret it as something that you only need to apply once when setting up a worm farm. This isn't the case: carbon–rich bedding materials need to be added regularly to your worm farm to keep it functioning aerobically. I like to add carbon every time I feed my worms, not only for the sake of the worms but also for the compost microbes and bacteria that need carbon sources for energy and to help them reproduce.

I love adding leaf mould or shredded brown leaves to my worm farms as a natural source of carbon. I mow over the leaves a few times first to break down their size. Worms love ripped–up egg cartons and shredded corrugated cardboard (you'll see them hanging out in the folds); torn paper works well, too. Lots of what you put in your recycling can instead be processed by your worms and returned to the earth (make sure you read the tips on page 168 to learn how to safely compost manufactured carbon). I give my worms the occasional treat of moist lucerne (alfalfa) mulch or pea mulch, and they also enjoy coconut coir – but this commercial product is not a particularly sustainable choice because of the emissions from global shipping, as well as the chemicals and large volumes of water used to wash and process the pith into coir.

It's always a good idea to cover your scraps with carbon, such as brown leaf litter, to replicate what happens on forest floors. This also stops flies and other pests being attracted to the food waste.

GRIT

Worm farms benefit from the addition of grit because worms don't have teeth to chew their food (bless 'em and their gummy little mouths!). Interestingly, worms have a gizzard similar to birds, and they need grit to help break up food particles. Good sources of grit include:

- crushed eggshells (these are my favourite as they are free and add calcium to your farm that helps worms to reproduce)
- crushed mussel, clam or oyster shells
- crushed bones (see page 228)
- rock minerals (such as Azomite®)
- fine, washed river sand (from a garden centre or hardware store)
- biochar (see pages 231–233).

You don't need to add grit all the time, as the coarse particles you add are cycled through your farm many times until you harvest your worm castings. So, the best practice is to add about ½ cup to an average–sized farm when you first set it up, to aid digestion. Then, each time you harvest your castings, add another handful and mix the grit in with the bedding and scraps. You can add more grit at other times if you've recently overfed your worms or you've noticed the farm becoming a bit whiffy. The sources of grit listed above are naturally very alkaline and will help to restore a neutral pH in a worm farm that has become acidic. But it's important to be mindful of the quantity of grit you add. If you add a lot of grit to try to rectify an acidic farm, then the pH level may rise above the optimal range for worms to thrive. For this reason, it's best to do a pH test of your worm farm before adding extra grit.

DIY WORM FARM GRIT

Here's exactly what you need to do to turn eggshells and mussel, clam or oyster shells into a worm–farm conditioner.

1. **Dry them out –** To make them brittle enough to pulverise, I bake mussel, clam or oyster shells in an oven set to low (150 degrees Celsius) for 20 minutes. I do this at the same time as cooking a stew, but on a separate tray. With eggshells, I give them a rinse and then leave them to air-dry on a windowsill, or I bake them in an oven on low (150 degrees Celsius) for 20 minutes.

2. **Smash them up –** I love to use a mortar and pestle to crunch and crush my grit by hand. If you don't have a mortar and pestle, then use a bowl and glass jar.

3. **Store them –** This is a shelf-stable worm-farm amendment that can be kept in an airtight, labelled jar for years.

ADVICE FOR EVERY STEP OF THE WAY

In this section, I'll outline how to set up and use a worm farm in general terms. You can confidently follow this advice regardless of the system you choose to use.

SET UP AND SEED

The set–up is important: you need to lay down plenty of slightly moist bedding materials (such as leaf mould, ripped paper and cardboard, or partially decomposed or shredded brown leaves you've raked up from your garden or street). Try to use free sources of carbon that you have readily available. This bedding ensures that the worm farm doesn't become anaerobic (and smelly!), by allowing air to move through it.

Seed your farm with a handful of healthy garden soil, finished compost or worm castings from a friend's worm farm. This isn't essential, but in my experience it helps to kickstart the microbial conditions in your farm – and this will allow your worms to eat more quickly.

SETTLE IN THE WORMS

Leave the worms in the bedding for a couple of days to settle in, perhaps with a mini snack of food waste (such as a banana peel or two). Your worms will be happy adjusting and eating the bedding if you don't give them anything else.

Then start feeding them small amounts of your food waste. Monitor how quickly it's being eaten by your worm colony, and feed them again when it's almost all gone. This helps to prevent overfeeding when you're first getting the hang of it.

DON'T HESITATE – AERATE!

Just like us, your worms need oxygen to survive. Worm farming is an aerobic process, and oxygen is necessary for all of the microorganisms living in your farm. Thankfully, the worms themselves

do a lot of the work to keep their home well aerated by burrowing through the organic matter. But we can give our worms a helping hand by manually turning over the farm to increase airflow.

A well–maintained, oxygen–rich environment will stop your worm farm from stinking and allow you to keep it inside in your kitchen or laundry, on a balcony or in your basement. Here are some tips for increasing the ventilation in your farm:

* Use a box or bucket with plenty of air holes and good drainage. If your worm farm doesn't drain well, overly wet conditions can quickly lead to an anaerobic environment and mass worm deaths – eek!
* Regularly add carbon, which creates open pore spaces that capture air within the castings and organic matter.
* Gently aerate your worm farm by raking over it with a gloved hand or using a round–tined garden fork or a corkscrew compost turner to ensure that it's gentle for your worms. Don't worry, the compost turner won't harm your worm babies, as it's a twisting (rather than slicing) motion that opens up the castings.
* Bury your scraps. The simple action of digging with a gloved hand into the organic matter in your worm farm to bury scraps often provides enough oxygen for your farm to function efficiently.

ADD MOISTURE

To survive and thrive, worms must have moist skin to allow dissolved oxygen to pass through into their bloodstream. Worms don't have noses, and they don't use their mouths to breathe, either. Lucky for them, they don't need to catch their breath while eating, as they breathe through their skin. It's for this reason

that your worm farm needs to be kept moist – but not wet – at all times.

There's no need to get trigger–happy and hose down your worm farm. For most of the year, the food scraps are juicy and provide enough moisture. If you notice your farm drying out, the best way to maintain correct hydration is to use a spray bottle or watering–can and wet the bedding by hand before adding it to the farm. This allows any excess water to drain away.

I don't recommend pouring water directly into the farm itself because this can quickly lead to overly wet and anaerobic conditions. However, during very hot seasons, it may be necessary to place a moist blanket (made from hessian sacks, old natural–fibre clothing or coconut husk) over the farm to stop excessive evaporation.

TUCK IN THE WORMS

It's always a great idea to tuck in your babies with a blanket and a generous amount of carbon (such as brown leaves) that covers the surface of your farm. We know that compost worms are surface feeders, and protecting the top layer of your worm farm with a cover helps to replicate the natural conditions in which they thrive – breeding and feeding under leaf litter on forest floors.

Blankets keep farms dark, moist and cool; they provide a steady source of carbon; and they help to prevent flies from laying their eggs on exposed food scraps. Over time, the worms and microbes will consume these blankets, so they'll need to be replaced every few months. You can repurpose hessian coffee sacks or old

woollen, cotton, silk or linen clothes as DIY blankets, or buy a commercial blanket made from coconut husk.

FEED THE WORMS

Work out a feeding frequency that matches the size of your worm farm and its current worm population. Remember, their numbers can double every 90 days if conditions are right, so as time passes the amount of waste you feed your worms should increase. After three to six months of feeding the worms scraps and household carbon, your farm will have enough worm castings and vermicompost to harvest.

HARVEST THE CASTINGS

When the farm/tray/bucket is full, it's time to harvest the castings. Well–processed castings should have a crumbly texture similar to the biscuit base of a cheesecake. Castings shouldn't be sloppy or smelly. If yours are, then add more dry carbon to help absorb excess moisture, give your farm a thorough aeration, and leave the lid off for a day or two to help dry the castings. You may need to wait a few weeks before harvesting them, as wet castings are a nightmare to gather.

Harvesting well–processed castings is an exciting job, and you can do it in lots of different ways. I'm going to describe the three simplest methods that work best for me, and I think you'll find them easy, too.

1.   Dump and sort – Remove the blanket, any surface covering of carbon and any unprocessed food scraps, and then

empty the contents of your worm farm – worms and all – onto a few sheets of newspaper or a tarpaulin, or into a large plastic container, in bright, direct sunlight. Separate the castings into sections, making little cone–shaped piles. Worms hate being exposed to sunlight, so they'll wriggle down deeper into the castings to escape. Scoop the poop by removing the top layer of castings from each pile, until you start to see worms. Wait about 20 minutes for the worms to move to the bottom of the pile, and repeat this process, however many times over, until you're left with piles that are mostly worms in a small amount of castings. Now you can use the harvested worm–free castings on your garden and add the worms and small amount of castings remaining back into the (now empty) farm, along with the carbon and food scraps you removed earlier and the blanket.

2. Segregate and sort – When your farm is getting close to full, divide it into two halves and pick a side to feed and a side to ignore. Only add scraps to one side, and most of your worms will hang out on this side. After two weeks, you can scoop the poop from the side you haven't been feeding and then follow method one above. There'll be a few naughty worms that have strayed into these castings, but their numbers will be low.

3. Sieve and sort – This method works well if you don't want to wait until your worm farm is full before harvesting the castings. You'll need to buy a gardening sieve or make your own. Pull back the top layers of carbon and food scraps, grab handfuls of the castings, and place them into the sieve. Gently tap this over a bucket; the poo will fall through, while most of the worms will stay in the sieve.

4. Sun and sort – I've left the easiest harvesting method until last, as it works best for harvesting a small amount of castings, rather than a full load from a worm farm or tray. If you want to add a scoop of worm poop to your garden, then simply open your farm on a sunny day, and remove the worm blanket and any scraps sitting on the surface. Give the worms a couple of minutes to escape the sunlight; they'll naturally burrow deeper into the farm. Now you can scoop the poop from the top of the farm without also evicting too many of your wriggly inhabitants.

It's worth mentioning that it's impossible to harvest castings that are completely worm–free. Worm cocoons will be present, too. These stray worms and cocoons can survive in your garden if you've covered your soil with mulch and there's plenty of organic matter for them to consume. So please don't stress about them!

USE THE POO

So, you've got a luscious load of worm poo … now what do you do? One of the great things about worm castings is that you don't need to leave them to cure. They can be applied directly to your garden once they've been harvested. You can use them in a number of ways:

- Put a handful in your pot plants, and your potting mix will buzz with beneficial bacteria and retain more moisture.
- Sprinkle some into planting holes to encourage root growth.
- Scatter castings across the surface of your soil before adding a layer of mulch.
- Steep a few handfuls in dechlorinated water, and pour the nutrient–rich liquid over seedlings and pot plants. Or brew it into casting tea (see pages 235–7).
- Boost your DIY potting–mix recipe with some castings (see page 203).

TROUBLESHOOTING

Here are some common worm–farm problems, and what to do about them.

MY WORMS ARE TRYING TO ESCAPE

Composting worms are sometimes attracted to the lid of your worm farm (and compost bin) by the condensation that forms when organic matter heats up through microbial activity. Or sometimes, just before a major rain event, worms naturally migrate higher into your farm to find drier ground. Both of these situations are natural occurrences and nothing to worry about. Your worms should settle down in a day or so.

On the other hand, escaping worms can also indicate that conditions in your farm are becoming unfavourable to worms. The pH level may be off; the contents may be too dry, too wet or too hot; or the organic matter may be anaerobic.

To correct these things, add more carbon, give the farm a turn, check the moisture level (worm farms should not be soaking wet or bone dry, but rather moist at all times), and check the pH (using a pH monitor from a hardware store). If the contents are acidic, increase the pH by adding alkaline inputs (such as ground eggshells, DIY bonemeal or shell meal, or a small sprinkle of garden lime). If it's the height of summer and your worms are trying to escape a hot farm, move it to a shady spot if possible, and freeze your scraps before giving them to your worms; as the scraps defrost, they'll help to cool down the farm.

MY WORM FARM IS WET AND SLOPPY

A well–functioning worm farm will have crumbly castings and airy bedding. If your farm is wet and sloppy, then it's likely that anaerobic bacteria are taking hold. You need to move fast to correct these conditions.

There are three main reasons why your worm farm may have become too wet:

1. You've been adding only food scraps and no carbon.
2. You've forgotten to drain your farm, and the worm tea is pooling in the bottom layer and saturating the castings.
3. You left the lid open in a downpour, and the farm got saturated.

The quickest way to safely dry out a wet worm farm is to add dry carbon (such as shredded newspaper or mowed brown leaves) that will suck up excessive moisture like a sponge. You can also leave the lid off your farm on a warm and sunny day to temporarily increase evaporation. Adding moist but not soaking coconut coir helps, too, as it acts like a bulking agent for your sloppy castings and increases airflow.

MY WORM FARM STINKS

Nine times out of ten, this is due to overfeeding. Remove some of the excess food waste from the surface of your worm farm, and replace this with fresh carbon–rich materials. Give your farm a gentle but thorough aeration to fluff up the bedding and castings, and to introduce more oxygen. Hold off feeding your worms any food scraps for a week, and the farm should no longer be pongy.

MY WORM FARM IS ATTRACTING BAD BUGS

Turn to pages 154–6 to learn how to stop flies, cockroaches and ants from becoming pests.

HOW TO SAVE A NEGLECTED FARM

Your worm farm may look lifeless if you've forgotten about it for a period of time. But did you know that worm eggs can remain dormant for at least a year, until conditions are good enough to support baby worms? That's remarkably reassuring as a new worm parent. So, if you improve the environmental factors – moisture and bedding – and provide a slow and steady food source, the remaining eggs will hatch and restart your worm colony.

6.

THE
WHO

COMPOST CRITTERS

Your backyard compost bin and worm farm aren't monocultures – you'll find bugs galore, and without them these complex systems won't work. Try not to let these composting critters worry you. They're an important part of the compost ecosystem and true recyclers: they serve as food for each other, transform organic matter into forms that others can use, clean up each other's messes, and manage each other's populations.

This chapter's main purpose is to help you to resist the urge to squash unsuspecting critters. A little knowledge goes a long way, and the identification information will stop you from having a compost–side conniption

the next time you see a swathe of multi–legged inhabitants in your heap – I promise!

Before you dive into the bug festival, I want to reassure you that your finished compost won't be a banquet for bigger bugs (such as slaters, grubs or millipedes) when it's applied to your garden. It's true that a treasure trove of microbiology will hitch a ride from your cured compost; will survive and live in soil, on leaf surfaces and around roots; and will help to improve the functioning of your garden's ecosystem. But once all sources of food have decomposed in your cured compost, a lot of your bug buddies will move on to more fertile ground.

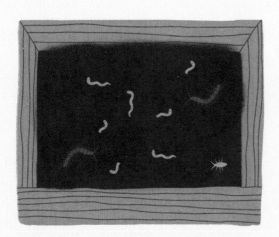

SURE CURE

Don't forget to cure your compost for up to six months before applying it to your garden. This maturation period allows any snackable scraps time to become stable humus that won't attract unwanted critters to your garden.

THE FOOD WEB OF YOUR COMPOST

A well-managed compost heap or worm farm is alive with a seething and heaving mass of life. There are bugs that you can see (such as worms, beetles and ants) as well as a wealth of microorganisms that are invisible to the naked eye (such as bacteria, nematodes and protozoa). This community of critters works together in a food web to consume your scraps. A food web is the term used to describe all of the food chains in the compost ecosystem. Energy flows from one organism to another in a natural recycling system, as one critter is eaten by another higher up the food chain. The compost food web is divided into three tiers of consumers:

1. First-level consumers – These are some of the most important minibeasts of the compost food web because they directly consume organic materials. They turn your spoil into soil, and make the organic matter readily digestible for many other composting critters.
2. Second-level consumers – These eat first-level consumers directly or consume their waste products. Yummy!
3. Third-level consumers – They're the predators of your pile. As the highest critters on the food chain, they gobble up first- and second-level consumers.

Some organisms (such as composting worms, pot worms, snails, slugs, slaters, millipedes and black soldier fly larvae) can appear in more than one camp. They're considered first-level consumers when directly eating raw materials, and second-level consumers when they eat the bacteria that are breaking down your scraps.

Why do you need to know all this? Long story short: it helps to illustrate the fact that without bugs working together, you won't be able to make nutrient-packed compost. So, no pesticides please – if you kill the creatures in your compost pile, then there'll be no finished black gold to use in your garden.

FIRST-LEVEL CONSUMERS

Bacteria, actinomycetes and fungi are the three main workers in this tier, and they do the bulk of the decomposition. For the most part, these hardworking and hungry critters work incognito, as they're invisible to the naked eye (aside from fungi at the fruiting stage, when they've developed into mushrooms, moulds or mycelia). If you peek through a microscope, you'll see these greedy gourmands feasting on your greens and browns. These first-level consumers are essential players in the compost food web, so let's take a moment to get acquainted with them.

Bacteria

Bacteria are the most numerous organisms in your compost. Despite their microscopic size, they pack the biggest punch – they're responsible for most of the decomposition and heat generation in your heap. Bacteria have a composting superpower, which provides a distinct advantage over other microorganisms: their ability to make a range of different enzymes to chemically break down whatever material they find.

You don't need to introduce bacteria into your pile. They're everywhere. Humans are walking petri dishes, and all of our scraps and plant material are covered in them, too. You can encourage the good aerobic bacteria into action by actively aerating your pile, so that anaerobic bacteria (the stinky ones) don't take over.

Actinomycetes

Have you ever noticed a greyish white, cobwebby growth on top of your compost and wondered if you've done something wrong? It may not look like it, but this is a great sign – so don't freak out!

These thin filaments indicate that actinomycetes are actively digesting and breaking down woody plant material. Actinomycetes are a fungus-like bacteria, and are one of my favourite microorganisms found in compost because they produce compounds that give compost its luscious earthy odour.

Fungi

You may not realise it yet, but it's cause for celebration if you see alien-looking fungi blooming in your compost or worm farm. Fungi comprise mushrooms, moulds, mycelia and yeasts, and they're responsible for breaking down tough, woody organic matter and plant polymers in your compost.

Fungal species grow and spread quite prolifically during the initial mesophilic phase of composting and also when your compost is curing. They help to consume organic matter that's too acidic, dry or low in nitrogen for bacterial decomposition. Fungi enable bacteria to join the feast and continue the decomposition once most of the cellulose has been consumed.

Bacteria

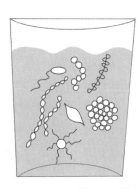

Actinomycetes

Fungi

SECOND- AND THIRD-LEVEL CONSUMERS

Once bacteria have done the bulk of the chemical decomposition, along with help from actinomycetes and fungi, bigger bug buddies move in and feast. They continue to chew, grind and suck your scraps – I can almost hear the slurps and burps from here! Below are some of the most common invertebrates (animal species with no backbone) you may find in your worm farm or compost (aside from worms, which are discussed in Chapter 5). This is not an exhaustive list, but rather a helpful guide to the who's who of most composting systems.

Beetles

Beetles are a group of insects that are really efficient decomposers, but their role in compost or a worm farm is often overlooked by the home gardener. You will likely notice a number of different varieties and their larvae, with three of the most common being the ground, feather-winged and rove beetles. They're most active at night, when they become stealthy nocturnal hunters looking for their next meal of slugs, insect larvae, fungal spores or decaying plant matter. You should encourage a diverse range of predators in your pile to keep the population of other insects in check.

People sometimes freak out when they see white C-shaped grubs in their compost. These beetle larvae are nothing to worry about. They help with the process of decomposition by feeding on the roots of plants placed in the compost pile. If you feel that their population is too large and are concerned about their presence in your garden, fish out a few and feed them to your chickens or local native birds as a treat. But please be mindful, as these grubs may, in fact, be the larvae of the gorgeously glossy Christmas beetle, which is becoming a rare sight due to pesticide use.

Black soldier fly larvae

For too long, black soldier fly larvae (BSFL from here on) have copped a bad rap, as many gardeners assume that they're maggots. True maggots – the young of several species from the Brachycera suborder of dipterid flies (such as houseflies and blowflies) – can be unwelcome pests, as the adult flies can transmit pathogens and spread diseases. BSFL superstars are an entirely different matter, as the adult fly from the Orthorrhapha suborder of dipterid flies doesn't have a mouth, so it can't bite or transmit diseases. Adult black soldier flies only live for a handful of days, just long enough to reproduce. They aren't scavengers or an annoyance, as they aren't attracted to humans, manure or food.

Black soldier flies are global composting critters and can be found on every single continent except Antarctica. Depending on the climate, they can breed year-round, but you're more likely to see them active in the warmer spring and summer months. The adult black soldier fly looks like a long, bluish black wasp, but don't worry – it doesn't sting. Its larvae are easily distinguishable from squishy-bodied maggots: they're noticeably bigger and visibly segmented, with distinct black pinprick heads. The larvae start off white, but they become darker as they mature.

There's no doubt that the appearance of these omnivorous larvae in a compost heap or worm farm can make a squeamish gardener want to run for the hills. But let's move beyond their looks and instead focus on their insatiable appetites and the beneficial role they play.

- BSFL plough through your scraps in the blink of an eye. What would take a compost worm colony a month to get through would be consumed by the larvae in as little as three days. They also love munching on tricky-to-compost scraps such as meat, citrus and spicy or oily food.
- When you have BSFL, you have a closed-loop poop system – this larvae produces black, nutrient-rich sludge called frass that the biology in your soil will gobble up.
- They survive in high temperatures in hot compost, and they help to prevent housefly and blowfly infestations around compost bins by outcompeting maggots. Yay!
- A well-managed compost pile has room for a diversity of waste eaters. Worms and BSFL can happily shack up together and feast on your waste as long as you provide enough scraps to sustain both groups of composting critters.

LIQUID GOLD

If you have a lot of black soldier fly larvae in your compost or worm farm, then your finished compost or worm castings will have a liquid texture. This is totally fine, but does take getting used to as it's quite different from the crumbly compost or castings produced by worms and other microorganisms.

Earwigs

Looks can be deceiving when it comes to the insect world. The aggressive pincers on their rear end make earwigs look like ferocious pests, but they're actually useful soil workers and nocturnal pollinators. During the day you may occasionally see an earwig or two in your compost or worm farm, but they're busiest at night eating organic matter and feasting on pests in your patch (such as aphids, baby snails and codling moth larvae). They also consume pollen and, in doing so, help to pollinate your productive plants. Yes, they may also occasionally chew a tasty seedling, but they're not particularly destructive – so, let them be.

Millipedes and centipedes

Millipedes might look a little unsightly, with their long, round body covered in legs, but they're actually helpful critters in the composting process. They perform important functions in your heap and worm farm, such as aerating the material by tunnelling as they eat, and breaking down leaf litter to an extent that allows springtails and mites to skeletonise it. For the most part, millipedes are vegetarian and won't harm your worms. Instead, they feed on all the moist, dead plant matter you've set out for them, as well as insect poo and the occasional carcass of a dead bug.

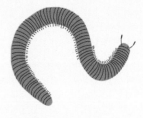

Mostly found in the top 5 centimetres of organic matter, centipedes are fast-moving predators that prey upon worms, spiders, slugs and larvae. Even though they don't actively aid the composting process because they don't eat decaying plant matter, I personally don't remove them from my compost as they play a part in crowd control. I do move them out of my worm farms, though, as I don't want my worm colony to be decimated by this stealthy predator. Make sure you wear gloves when handling centipedes, as they can move like lightning and give you a nasty sting.

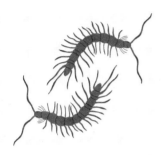

Mites

Seeing masses of tiny mites crawling on the surface of your compost or worm farm might make you recoil, but they're just another member of the interdependent critter community. There are thousands of different mite species; some eat decaying plants or wood, while others hoover up mould or the soft tissues of leaves. There are also mites that choose to feast upon the faeces of other critters.

Most mites are beneficial to the composting process, but they can breed prolifically and outcompete worms for food, so you'll need to monitor their numbers. If their population explodes, or if you see red mites that are parasitic and may harm your compost worms, then action is needed. Bait them with a piece of white bread moistened with milk. Place the bread on the surface of your compost or worm farm, then remove and dispose of it when it's covered in mites.

Pot worms

If your compost or worm farm is too wet, then you may see a boom of small, white worms breeding in your soggy scraps. These harmless critters are commonly known as pot worms (from the Enchytraeidae family) and can sometimes be mistaken for baby composting worms.

Pot worms eat decaying organic matter in the same way that compost worms do, but they prefer moist compost conditions with a low, acidic pH. There is no need to get rid of these worms, but they can be a sign that your worm farm or compost bin is too wet or acidic and may become anaerobic. Add some dry carbon to soak up the excess moisture, give the pile or farm a thorough aeration to introduce more oxygen, and sprinkle the surface with ground eggshells to increase the pH.

Protozoa and nematodes

You won't spy protozoa or nematodes without using a microscope, as they're tiny. However, they're unsung heroes of the compost pile and worm farm, so let's give them a moment in the spotlight.

Wherever you see a thin film of water covering organic matter in your composting system, you can be certain that bucketloads of one–celled protozoa are rocketing around. Nematodes are free–ranging microscopic worms and will be found all through your compost, too; some nematodes are considered garden pests, but the types found in your compost are an important part of the compost food web.

Protozoa and nematodes help to mineralise the nutrients held by the bacteria and fungi into more available forms for plant roots and other organisms. Nematodes in particular are prolific eaters: they'll chow down directly on organic matter and feast upon bacteria, fungi and parasites in your pile.

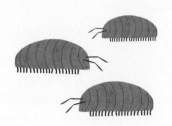

Slaters

These compost creatures have many different names: roly–polies, pill bugs (these roll into a tight ball when disturbed) or sow bugs (these remain flat). Where I live in Australia, we call them slaters; in some parts of Melbourne, they're affectionately known as butchy boys. In the United Kingdom, they're called woodlice, cheeselogs, granny greys or cheesy bugs, and in some parts of the United States they're referred to as potato bugs. Regardless of their name, these critters are easy to identify. They're usually grey or brown with flattened plates on their bodies.

Slaters aren't insects, but rather land–dwelling crustaceans. They're commonly found in dark nooks and crannies with plenty of decaying plant material (such as rotting leaves or wood). These critters have got a bad rap, as they can eat seedlings in your garden, but they're actually beneficial in your compost and worm farm because they're able to shred tough cellulose fibres in woody materials. Slaters make these materials more accessible for worms and other insects to feast on. If their population explodes, it can be a sign that your compost or worm farm is too dry. Add more juicy nitrogen–rich scraps or a splash of water to balance conditions.

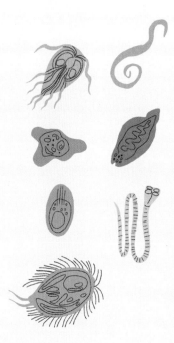

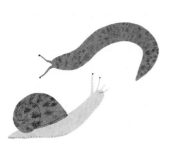

Slugs and snails

Slimy slugs and snails love hanging out in damp, dark environments with access to plenty of rotting plant matter, so your compost bin and worm farm may become their ideal home. They're likely to appear in the early stages of decomposition when organic matter is plentiful and the temperature is cool. Slugs and snails can be a bother in your edible garden, but they're generally beneficial to the composting process, so don't despair if you see them there.

I should note that there are some species of slugs that like to gobble up worms, so observation is key when it comes to sussing out what's going on in your farm. If there's a large number of slugs, then it may be a sign that your worm farm or compost bin is too wet. Add dry carbon, and leave the lid off your composting system for a day or two.

Springtails

If you notice very small, six–legged insects flicking into the air when disturbed, then you've got yourself a mob of hardworking compost cleaners known as springtails. These critters are common in composting systems and are beneficial, as they help to 'cleanse' the pile by eating organic matter and the droppings from other compost invertebrates.

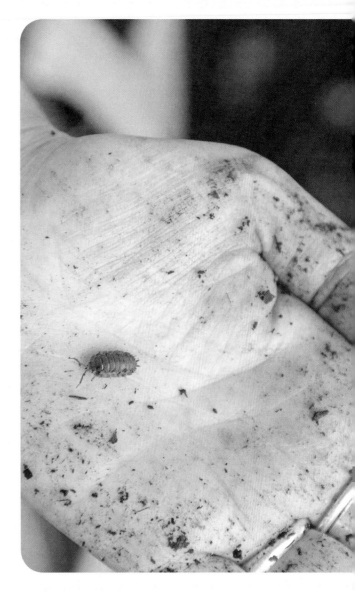

SAVE YOUR PLANT BABIES
To stop slaters from becoming a problem in your garden, provide them with plenty of mulch and leaf litter to dine on. This way, they'll leave your seedlings alone.

FROM GUEST TO PEST

As a general rule, I encourage you to take a pacifist's approach to the bugs in your compost and worm farms, as they play an important role in consuming your waste and cycling nutrients. This may be challenging for insect-averse folks, but it pays to remember that nine times out of ten they're doing more good than harm.

If your compost pile or worm farm has been mismanaged, then the population of one particular species can explode and become a nuisance. At this point, certain critters transform from guest to pest, and it's time to act. Below I provide management – not eradication – strategies for a number of critters that can quickly overrun your heap or worm farm: ants, flies and cockroaches. Note that these bugs are totally fine if you only see them occasionally. You only need to act if they're overwhelming your composting system or worm farm. I've also outlined management strategies for rats and mice.

STOP THE ANTS FROM MARCHING

Opening the lid of your compost bin, tumbler or worm farm and seeing an army of ants charging about can be annoying, but it's not always bad news. Ants are beneficial to the composting process and can often live harmoniously with worms, as they shred food into smaller particles for worms to eat, their tunnels increase aeration, they help to attract fungi to your heap or worm farm, and they can enrich your compost with phosphorus and potassium.

Here are some tips to keep their population in check if they start to overrun the material in your compost or worm farm, or if they're aggressive varieties (such as fire ants, termites, carpenter ants and army ants):

- Turn the contents of your compost pile and worm farm regularly (at least once a week) to stop ants from forming colonies. If you see numerous clusters of very small, white, oval-shaped ant eggs, then use a long-handled shovel (to prevent angry ant parents crawling up your arms) to scoop as many of them out as you can, and move them to another part of your garden. You may by chance scoop up the queen ant; consequently, all of the worker ants will leave the compost or worm farm to join her. (Like bees, ants are organised in a caste system, with the queen at the top of the pecking order.)
- Ants love hanging out in dry worm farms and compost piles. So, the easiest way to

BE CAREFUL IN THE KITCHEN

Prevent flies from landing on food scraps left on chopping boards, or zooming in and out of your kitchen caddy. If you leave your cooking scraps or the remains of your meals out in the open for too long, then flies will come in hot to feed and lay their eggs on this delicious feast. The eggs will hitch a ride to your compost or worm farm, and the cycle will start all over again.

manage them is to increase the moisture level of the farm or pile by adding a moderate splash of water.

- Bury your scraps – always dig your scraps into the core of your compost or underneath worm castings, rather than leaving them exposed on the surface of your pile. Ants are attracted to the smell of food scraps, so burying them helps to reduce the release of delicious ant–attracting odours.
- If you've been heavy–handed with fresh fruit and vegie scraps, then this will likely increase the acidity of your system, which is a perfect environment for ants. Add a sprinkle of ground eggshells, bonemeal, shell meal or wood ash to raise the pH.
- Ants don't like hot temperatures, so add some compost activators to increase the core temperature of your heap to encourage the ants to move on. This isn't an appropriate measure for worm farms, as worms don't like the heat, either.

HASTA LA VISTA, ANTY

If you want to reduce a rapidly growing ant population, then get your hands on some diatomaceous earth (DE). It comprises the fossilised remains of ancient aquatic microorganisms that have been mined from sedimentary rock. DE has many uses and comes in different grades. It's important to buy food–grade DE for use in the garden, as it's the gentlest and safest form. DE is effective against any insect that has an exoskeleton (ants, fleas, mites, millipedes, earwigs, cockroaches, centipedes, isopods, most beetles, and so on), and therefore it won't harm worms.

Wear an N95 mask when handling this dust, and sprinkle it where you see the most ant activity. Don't get DE wet, otherwise it will stop working. The sharp particles in DE pierce the ant's exoskeleton, and the ant will desiccate, dehydrate and die. Even though DE is a natural pesticide, please be aware that it can also kill beneficial insects – so, don't use it liberally. Also, bear in mind that there are sustainability issues with anything mined from the earth.

SHOO FLY, DON'T BOTHER ME

Nothing signals the start of the sweaty summer months more than opening up your compost bin or worm farm and being greeted by a cloud of small black flies buzzing around your face, up your nose and into your eyes. There are many different names for these annoying flies. They're sometimes referred to as 'small fruit flies' or, more scientifically, as *Drosophila* flies, but I'll be calling them vinegar flies. These aren't to be confused with the flies in the Tephritidae family – the true fruit flies – that feed on fruits and are usually not attracted to compost.

Vinegar flies are extremely annoying but won't harm your plants, produce, worms or compost. Houseflies and blowflies can spread pathogens, so it's worth managing both these and vinegar flies, otherwise you won't want to go near your compost or worm farm during the warmer months of the year. The tips below will help to stop fruit flies, gnats, vinegar flies, blowflies and houseflies from becoming a problem in your compost bin and worm farm:

- Bury food scraps under the organic matter in your compost and worm farm, as flies lay their eggs on exposed decomposing food.
- Every time you add food scraps, make sure you cover them with carbon.
- Keep your compost and worm farm moist but not too wet. Soaking conditions encourage the proliferation of flies. Add dry carbon if necessary.
- Flies prefer a low–pH (acidic) environment. If you've been adding a lot of acidic inputs (such as Bokashi material) to your heap or worm farm, then raise the pH by adding a modest handful of ground eggshells, wood ash or garden lime to neutralise excessively acidic conditions.
- A bowl of apple cider vinegar with a drop of dish detergent, placed near the compost bin or worm farm, will attract and kill flies. Change the liquid regularly to keep the fly trap working.

KICK COCKROACHES TO THE KERB

I love seeing bugs hanging out in my compost or worm farm, but no one – not even me – wants to see a hoard of hungry cockroaches chowing down on their scraps. If your compost bin or worm farm is close to your home, then it's understandable that you'd be concerned about a cockroach infestation. Thankfully, most cockroach species found in composting systems don't invade homes, and they're efficient and safe decomposers. But if roaches give you the willies, then follow these steps to rid your compost and worm farm of them:

- Cockroaches can turn from guests to pests if you've been overloading your system with too much food waste and not enough carbon. The best course of action is to remove some of the food waste, add plenty of carbon, and stop feeding the system for a week. This should lead to cockroaches moving on to find their next meal elsewhere.
- You can sprinkle the surface of your system with diatomaceous earth (DE). This natural pesticide will kill cockroaches but not harm your worms. Or you can add sticky traps to the top of your worm farm. Both of these methods may also kill beneficial insects, so use them with caution.
- Cockroaches are attracted to rotten stenches, so don't add meat, dairy or fish scraps to your system without processing them in a Bokashi bin first.
- Increase the temperature of your compost bin (but not your worm farm), as roaches can't make nests or breed once organic matter heats to 55 degrees Celsius. To increase the heat, add an activator such as coffee grounds, manure or blood and bone.
- Turn your system regularly to displace and disperse cockroach nests.
- Cockroaches prefer dry conditions, so increase the hydration of your system to move them along.

USE YOUR RAT CUNNING

No one wants to see a fat rat or family of mice living in their compost. Thankfully, it's pretty easy to get rid of these vermin. The most common-sense strategy for evicting rodents is to think like a rat. Alys Fowler shares some useful rat psychology in her book, *The Thrifty Gardener*. She explains that rats are commensal (live primarily by eating our food), neophobic (wary of new things) and thigmophilic (rely primarily on touch to navigate). So, if you never turn your compost bin, then you're unintentionally creating a very comfortable rat hotel – an unchanging shelter packed with food. The more you aerate and turn your compost, the less enticing it will be for a rat to visit, because it's a changing environment, and rats won't want to nest there.

The same principles apply to mice, too, but if you want to be sure that vermin won't enter your compost in the first place, then add a piece of rodent-proof, stainless-steel mesh to the bottom of your compost bin. This mesh works best with enclosed bins, as it's almost impossible to rodent-proof open piles.

We need to be careful with how we manage rat and mice populations in our gardens. Seeking to eliminate rodents via the use of poisons can do serious damage to the biodiversity of our patch and wider local environment. If a bird of prey (such as an owl) eats a poisoned rodent, then it can also become poisoned and die. Instead of poison, use old-style manual mice and rat traps, live cage traps or modern electric traps. If you do need to use poison, then look for First Generation baits with the active ingredients warfarin, coumatetralyl or sodium chloride because native birds and animals (and your pets) can cope with these when taken in through secondary poisoning.

To prevent rodent numbers from booming, it's essential to restrict the amount of free food on offer in your garden by:

- using rodent-proof chicken feeders that can only be accessed by your chooks
- collecting rotting orchard fruits and adding them to your rodent-proof compost bins
- not leaving pet food (or your dirty dishes!) out in the open.

HOW TO USE RODENT-PROOF MESH

With the right equipment and know-how, you can banish rats and mice from your enclosed compost bin forever.

EQUIPMENT
* a roll of heavy-duty, rodent-proof, stainless-steel mesh with a hole size no bigger than 6.5 × 6.5 millimetres, and a length that matches the diameter of the bottom of your compost bin
* gloves
* wire-cutters

METHOD
1. Unroll the rodent-proof, stainless-steel mesh, and place it underneath your compost bin.
2. Wearing gloves and using wire-cutters, cut a piece of mesh that's larger than your bin's diameter.
3. Trim this mesh to the shape of your bin (circular or square), leaving 10 centimetres of wire around the base of the bin.
4. Still wearing gloves (as the mesh can be spiky), fold up the mesh edges over the bottom edge of the compost bin, crimping them slightly with your fingers, and then gently press down with your shoe to close any large gaps. Be mindful that you'll be re-using this piece of mesh for each batch of compost you make, so ensure that you can easily remove it.
5. When it comes time to harvest your compost, pull back the mesh edges from the bottom rim of your compost bin, then lift up the bin to expose the compost.
6. Repeat Step 4 before filling your compost bin again.

Another simple (and almost as effective) method for making a compost bin relatively rodent-proof is to bury the bottom 10–15 centimetres of the bin and then backfill around it with soil.

STEEL YOURSELF

When deciding on the sort of rodent-proof mesh to use, look for stainless-steel products instead of galvanised mesh. This is because in some instances the lead content in galvanised mesh or wire can be high, and over time this can leach into the soil.

THIS MESH WORKS BEST WITH ENCLOSED BINS, AS IT'S ALMOST IMPOSSIBLE TO RODENT-PROOF OPEN PILES.

OPPOSITE:
Rodent-proof, stainless-steel mesh has been applied to the bottom of my enclosed compost bin. This not only keeps rodents at bay, but also stops snakes (and moles and voles in the United Kingdom) from entering the bin.

7.

THE SCRAPS

A-Z OF COMPOSTABLE MATERIALS

Use this information as a 'cheat sheet' for when you have a question about the compostability of a particular item. The items have been listed alphabetically, so it's easy to find what you're looking for.

It includes all of the things that are usually considered composting and worm-farming no-noes: weeds, meat, bones, dairy, citrus, pet and human poo, oily food, onions and garlic – because, with care, this organic matter can (and should) be composted. I personally find strict compost rules problematic. Saying no to so many nutrient-dense materials means that they'll end up in landfill, and home composters will miss out on returning this fertility to their soil.

I've also included some suggestions for relevant food scraps that can help you to make the most of your edible bits before composting them. We need to remember that the most sustainable thing to do with our food scraps and leftovers is to eat as many of them as we can before we compost the rest.

FEED
your
COMPOST

ASH AND CHARCOAL

Don't add coal ash from barbecues or fires to your compost. It contains chemicals that shouldn't end up in your soil, especially around edible plants. It's only safe to add ash and charcoal from untreated timber to your compost (in moderation).

Ash from untreated timber is full of valuable minerals (potash, phosphorus and calcium), but it's very alkaline so only add it to your compost a little at a time. Don't go overboard, as it will disrupt the natural pH of your pile – which should be slightly acidic for compost bacteria to thrive – and it will slow the composting process. Another way to use wood ash in the garden (depending on your soil's pH) is to make a nutrient–rich slurry from ash and urine that can be applied around your heavy–feeding plants (such as tomatoes).

BONES

If you're getting your Bokashi groove on by adding meat with bones to this system and then processing them in your compost or soil factory, you'll end up with piles of well–picked bones in your cured compost. Sure, you can add these to your garden beds whole, but they'll take an age to decompose – and minerals such as phosphorus won't be in plant–available forms. To get the most bang for your buck, turn the bones into bonemeal (see page 228) or biochar (see pages 230–3.)

STOCK UP

Before you add that chicken carcass to your Bokashi bin, why not get all of the goodness and flavour out of it by turning it into stock? If you add in your leftover vegie peelings and scraps (such as carrot tops, spinach stems and celery leaves), then you'll make a tasty mix.

BREAD

Bread can be added to any composting system once the bin has been rodent–proofed. (To find out how to do this, turn to pages 156–9.) If you leave bread in big chunks, it will go mouldy. This is fine for the compost, but not something to which you should be exposed. To speed up decomposition, soak larger pieces in water before breaking them down into smaller pieces.

CITRUS

You can compost citrus, but the thick skins of lemons, limes, grapefruits and oranges contain oils that repel water, and this slows their decomposition. Also, citrus contains a chemical compound called limonene that in large quantities is toxic to worms. So always make sure you cut up citrus into small pieces to increase the surface area before adding it in moderation to your composting systems.

COFFEE GROUNDS

These tips will help you to transform coffee grounds into stunning compost:

- It's not a good idea to apply coffee grounds directly to your soil without composting them first because caffeine can suppress seed germination and root growth. Add the grounds to your compost bin, and allow the microorganisms to break them down first.
- Despite their colour, coffee grounds are a green addition to your compost, as they're high in nitrogen. Their fine particle size results in speedy decomposition, and they can boost the temperature of a slow compost bin.
- Coffee grounds have antibacterial properties. If you add too many to your compost, they can impede your system's thriving microbiome. The volume of coffee grounds added at any one time should be no more than 20 per cent of the total volume of your compost. Otherwise, they can overwhelm the compost critters in your pile.
- To balance the C:N ratio, make sure you add lots of carbon–rich materials (such as shredded brown leaves, aged woodchips, shredded office paper or ripped newspaper) mixed in with the coffee grounds.
- It's important to manually aerate your pile on a regular basis if you're composting a lot of coffee grounds. The small, dense particle size of the grounds can suppress the flow of oxygen in your compost. This can result in the grounds going mouldy and the conditions in your compost becoming anaerobic.

CAKES AND PASTRIES

First, why have you got any of these left over? But if you do, just like bread, these can be added to all composting systems that have been rodent–proofed. If ants are a terrible bother in your garden, it's worth being conservative with the amount of sugary scraps you add to your compost or worm farm.

WHEN LIFE GIVES YOU LEMONS

Before you compost your squeezed citrus skins, why not give them a new lease of life first? You can:

- turn them into a natural cleaner by soaking them in vinegar
- preserve them in salt with some tasty Mediterranean spices, and after a few weeks you can use this mix in cooking, dressings and marinades
- zest them, and add this to fruit salads or mix it with salt to make a tasty condiment
- dry your mandarin and orange skins, and use them as fire starters.

- It's safe to feed compost worms small but regular amounts of coffee grounds, which contain potassium – something that worms love.

COMPOSTABLE PACKAGING

There's a grey area around these purportedly green products. While plastics are largely disastrous materials for our planet, some compostable alternatives aren't much better, especially if they end up in landfill.

In Australia, there's a standard for biodegradable plastics suitable for home composting (AS 5810). If packaging has this standard, it should break down and turn into biomass, water and carbon dioxide in your home compost bin within 180 days. Such products are typically made from a combination of cornflour, PLA (renewable bio–based plant material) and PBAT (a biodegradable polymer that isn't fully renewable as it's partly derived from petrochemicals). Testing has shown that these certified 'bioplastics' should break down in your compost or worm farm, but 'emerging research shows that the impact of increasing compostable plastic content in compost may impact its safe application to land'.

Industrially compostable products come with the certification AS 4736 for Australia and EN 1342 for Europe, and can only be composted in large facilities where the items are spun and kept at high temperatures. Many local governments in Australia have recently banned industrially compostable items from being added to your green waste bins, though.

So, what's the verdict? Compostable packaging is superior to traditional plastic, but is by no means a perfect solution. If it ends up in landfill, it will release methane as it slowly decomposes; if it enters the soil, it will contribute to environmental pollution. And only time will tell if these products are actually safe for our soil.

CONDIMENTS

Have you discovered a mouldy jar of relish hidden in the back of your fridge, and you're not sure what to do with it? Binning it is the worst option; you should compost it instead (with a few caveats). Most condiments contain salt, and compost with a high level of salinity isn't good for your soil. Add old condiments in moderation so you don't end up with overly salty compost. Don't add condiments to your worm farm, as salt is a worm killer.

COOKED FOOD (FISH AND MEAT)

You can compost cooked food containing meat, fish and oil using a Green Cone® (see pages 106–7). Or add it to a Bokashi bin and – once fermented – place it in your regular compost bin or bury it directly in the ground.

You can also add cooked food to worm farms and compost bins as long as they're vermin–proof. These ingredients are attractive to flies, so always bury these scraps and cover the surface with a generous amount of carbon. This also helps to reduce odours.

CORN

The cobs, stalks and husks of corn take a long time to decompose because they're made from cellulose, but don't be impatient as it's worth the wait. Use a sharp knife or kitchen scissors to cut up husks before composting, and use a cleaver to break down the cobs into smaller bits. If you want to take the lazy route and add the cobs whole, then you'll need to cycle them through your composting system a couple of times, but while they're hanging around they're servicing your wriggling friends as comfortable worm hotels.

DAIRY

Small amounts of milk, butter, yoghurt, cream and cheese can be added to all composting systems if they're vermin-proof and animal-proof. Be aware that dairy products can be quite stinky as they break down. So, it's best to chop up cheese into small pieces, disperse liquids throughout the organic matter in your compost, and cover the surface with plenty of dry carbon.

DISEASED PLANT MATERIAL

You need to be a confident hot compost cook to tackle diseased plants. Pathogens are destroyed once temperatures reach 55–60 degrees Celsius for a minimum of three days. To ensure that you've eradicated diseases, it's important to cure your compost to allow 'hygienisers' (such as worms) that attack pathogens to colonise your heap. Don't add diseased plant material to slow compost bins/piles or worm farms, otherwise pathogens will spread into your garden via the finished compost or castings.

DRYER LINT

If some of your clothes are made from synthetic materials, then lint from your dryer can contain millions of microplastics. My advice: bin the lint, as you clearly don't want these microplastics ending up in your soil. Only compost lint if you know that it's from clothes made from natural fibres (such as cotton, wool, linen or silk).

EGGSHELLS

You can add eggshells to all composting systems. If you don't crush them up, they'll hang around in your finished compost or castings; however, when added to your soil, they'll break down over time. There are lots of uses for eggshells in the garden:

- Dry and smash them up into small pieces, and feed them to chickens to help the girls lay strong eggs.

- Sprinkle eggshell powder into worm farms as grit, and add it to your compost if conditions are becoming too acidic (eggshells are alkaline).
- Use vinegar extraction to make a regenerative gardening amendment that's rich in calcium. (To learn how, turn to pages 227–8.)

EUCALYPTUS LEAVES

You can compost eucalyptus leaves (either fresh and green, or brown and dried) but there are a couple of things to keep in mind. These leaves contain volatile oils and allelopathic compounds that make them quite resistant to decomposition. To speed things up, mow or shred them and mix with pelletised or fresh chicken manure, or blood and bone. (To learn more turn to pages 200–201.)

FRUIT AND VEGIE SCRAPS

Fruit and vegie skins, stems, leafy tops, peels, seeds and cores will make up a significant volume of what you add to your kitchen caddy. These scraps are full of water (around 90 per cent), nitrogen and minerals, and they break down quickly in worm farms and compost bins once chopped into smaller pieces. It's worth making the effort to chop these scraps before composting them, as this creates more surface area for compost microbes to access – which results in efficient decomposition without odours or mould.

GARDEN WASTE

I encourage you to think twice before throwing any organic matter that your garden generates into your green–waste bin. The most fertile and bountiful gardens cycle plant matter back into their ecosystem to feed their soil. See Chapter 8 to learn how to transform your garden waste into valuable soil–building and soil–feeding amendments.

GRAINS, LEGUMES AND RICE

These are often described as compost no–noes because they're attractive to rodents and wildlife, and cooked rice can breed unwanted bacteria in a mismanaged slow compost bin. Don't let this deter you: they can be safely composted if you follow these tips:

- Process them in a Bokashi bin before adding them to your slow compost. The EM will prevent *Salmonella* from developing, and the fermentation process speeds up the decomposition that occurs after the finished Bokashi material is added to your compost.
- Feed them to your worms, which will consume them before they can develop pathogens or attract vermin. If they're covered in salty or spicy sauces, then don't add them to worm farms. Worms dislike strong or salty scraps – compost the scraps instead.
- Hot compost them. High temperatures in hot composting systems will prevent pathogens from proliferating.

HAIR AND FUR

Did you know that you can compost human hair and pet fur? Whether it's blond, ginger or black hair, it doesn't matter; due to the low level of available carbon, hair is considered a green material in your compost. It's often overlooked as a potential input in a compost pile, but it's a great source of slow–release nitrogen.

One thing to note is that hair and fur can take up to two years to decompose in a slow compost pile. Even before it has fully broken down, it will help your compost pile to retain water (which is useful if you're composting in hot, dry climates). You can add small amounts of hair and fur to worm farms as bedding materials, too, but they'll take quite a while to fully decompose.

If you plan to compost hair, try not to leave it in clumps or long strands. It will break down much faster if it's chopped and mixed with other organic matter. Compost microbes have

WASTE NOT, WANT NOT

Before you compost your fruit and vegie scraps, why not try one of these ideas:

- Store vegie scraps in an airtight container in the fridge or freezer, and boil them up into a delicious, waste-free stock.
- Make tasty pesto from the leafy ends of homegrown carrots, or a salsa verde from the stems of herbs (such as coriander, mint and parsley).
- Create kimchi from vegie stems, peels and tops.
- Make the most of apple cores and peels by turning them into homemade apple cider vinegar.
- Transform watermelon rinds into a pickled condiment that is seriously yummy.
- Add whole strawberries (edible green tops and all) to smoothies.

an amazing ability to remediate chemicals and render them safe, so it's okay to compost dyed hair if it's added in moderation.

An alternative idea is to use hair or fur as a surface mulch around fruit trees and ornamental shrubs. Lay it down on your soil and top with woodchips to stop it from blowing away. The combination of the nitrogen–rich hair and the carbon–rich woodchips creates a moisture–retentive mulch that has a balanced C:N ratio.

HUMANURE

If you think that flushing your poo down the loo is an absurd way to use fresh water – especially when you consider that normal flushing toilets use 30,000–40,000 litres of water per person per year – then let me introduce you to humanure. Here's the scoop on poop: human faeces are completely compostable, but they do need to be 'handled with care' in a dedicated composting system, as they can contain pathogens and diseases.

Just like other manure, humanure is rich in nitrogen and must be balanced with plenty of carbon (aged sawdust, wood shavings or woodchips are best, as they help to neutralise odours). Composting toilets work a charm, as do in situ compost bins, so there's no need to handle the compost until it's well processed. Composting toilets need not be fancy. Turn to page 183 to learn Hannah Moloney's simple method. Finally, well–cured humanure <u>must not</u> be used on your herb and vegie gardens; it should only be applied to ornamental plants and established fruit trees.

If you're interested in learning how to use humanure, then I recommend that you read *The Humanure Handbook* by Joseph Jenkins. It has become a compost cult classic since it was published in 1994.

MANUFACTURED CARBON

Cardboard and paper products are handy materials to use around your garden to add carbon to your compost, to smother weeds in sheet composting, or to establish a no dig bed. But unfortunately, not all of these products are created equal.

I'm not a scientist, so in this section I'll provide information from credible sources that shines a light on some of the issues that you need to think about when choosing what sort of cardboard and paper products to use in your garden or compost. Ultimately, it's your decision, but here's my advice: if in doubt, leave it out. Alternatively, focus on using natural sources of carbon in your garden (such as brown leaves, organic mulches, aged sawdust or woodchips).

I hope this discussion encourages you to use fewer manufactured carbon products in your life. Instead of accepting single–use paper bags and cardboard containers, why not bring your own re–usable fabric bags and airtight containers?

<u>Dioxins</u>

Chlorine bleaching of both pulp and paper produces dioxins. The World Health Organization classifies dioxins as persistent organic pollutants, as they accumulate in the food chain. They're highly toxic, and 90 per cent of our exposure is through food. Because

<u>MY TAKE ON MANUFACTURED CARBON</u>

There's no doubt that manufactured carbon has compounds and chemicals that I would prefer weren't there. To minimise exposure, I focus on using natural sources of carbon in my compost (such as brown leaves and woodchips), and use newspaper and brown cardboard with small amounts of printing as my main sources of manufactured carbon. So, I suggest that you go hard in autumn and collect enough brown leaves to use as carbon for the next year.

we're at the top of the food chain, we accumulate dioxins from eating other animals.

People became concerned about the contamination of paper products with dioxins in the 1980s. Today, chlorine bleaching has been replaced by Elemental Chlorine Free (ECF) bleaching, which significantly reduces – but doesn't completely eliminate – the production of dioxins. Safer methods for whitening paper use oxygen, peroxide (used for newspapers) or ozone, which eliminate chlorine altogether. Look out for the terms Totally Chlorine Free (TCF) or Processed Chlorine Free (PCF – this includes recycled material, which may contain trace levels of dioxins) when buying office paper, if you want to use it in your compost.

Dyes

I recommend that you don't add heavily coloured or dyed cardboard or paper to your compost. However, if it's not glossy then it's probably safe in small portions, as most modern inks and dyes are vegetable–based. I'm personally not worried about composting white paper and cardboard with some black printing on it, or single–colour cardboard such as yellow or pink egg cartons.

Gloss

I don't recommend using cardboard or paper that is coated, waxed, shiny or glossy (such as magazine paper) in your garden or compost. This coating can be made from a number of things, including a fine clay pigment that is safe to compost, but it can also be made with a plastic coating. It can be hard to tell the difference, so I recommend recycling glossy items instead.

Glue

Cardboard uses adhesives, and while some of these are starch–based – one particular manufacturer claims that they're 'eco-friendly' because they're made from natural carbohydrates – many contain mineral oil aromatic hydrocarbons, to which you should limit your exposure. These bad hydrocarbons are in most of the cardboard food packaging in our supermarkets, and they can migrate to food, but thankfully the incidence of this is relatively low.

Lots of gardeners have used corrugated cardboard as mulch and in compost for years (me included), and the amounts of hydrocarbons that ultimately make it into food are likely very small. But it's something to think about.

In better news, at least one study suggests that compost seriously reduces the levels of heavy mineral oils in soil. The authors suggest that 'the enhanced degradation of heavy mineral oil in compost–amended soil may be a result of the significantly higher microbial activity in this soil'.

Newspaper

Newspaper is a useful source of carbon if you don't have natural sources on hand. The ink no longer contains heavy metals and is instead vegetable–based. Newspaper is also chlorine–free (which means that it's less likely to be contaminated with dioxins). As with any manufactured paper product, there'll be small amounts of trace chemicals in newspapers, but this is not of significant toxicological concern and is at a level that is safe to use in your compost and edible garden.

Be aware that newspaper decomposes slowly in compost bins and worm farms because it has a high lignin content. Lignin is a substance found in the woody cell walls of plants, and it's highly resistant to decomposition. So, make sure you rip and shred the newspaper into small pieces to speed up its decay.

PFAS

A very concerning problem is the presence of Perfluoroalkyl and Polyfluoroalkyl Substances (PFAS), which are harmful to human health, in many cardboard and paper food packages. The main reason PFAS are used in cardboard and paper is that they're very resistant to heat, stains, grease and water, so they stop food fats and liquids from soaking into the packaging.

Since the 1950s, there has been increasing evidence of the negative effects on health, the environment and the food chain of at least some PFAS. The Australian government has set up a taskforce to coordinate its response to PFAS contamination. According to the government, 'the PFAS of greatest concern are highly mobile in water, which means they travel long distances from their source–point; they do not fully break down naturally in the environment; and they are toxic to a range of animals'. Humans included!

Thankfully, you can conduct a simple test using olive oil (a non–polar oil) that will show whether there are PFAS in your cardboard or paper packaging (see the box on the next page).

The results of a study of 92 samples of cardboard and paper packaging from UK supermarkets and fast–food outlets, using this olive–oil test, found strong indications of PFAS in 30 per cent of the samples. The highest concentrations of PFAS were found in moulded–fibre takeaway boxes (all three of the sugarcane or bagasse moulded–fibre boxes tested had been promoted as compostable). According to the Australian Packaging Covenant Organisation, 'If composted, most of these chemicals will not break down, and those that do will form other fluorochemicals. Composting packaging containing PFAS will therefore result in contaminated compost.'

Due to the widespread use of PFAS in paper and cardboard food packaging, I can't say which types of packaging are safe to use. I encourage you to conduct a quick olive–oil test on each piece of manufactured carbon before using it in your garden. You only need to conduct the test once per item; for instance, test the cardboard carton of a particular brand of eggs you regularly buy. Once you've determined that it's safe, then you can confidently add this to your compost time and time again.

TEST FOR THE PRESENCE OF PFAS

Drop a small amount of olive oil onto the cardboard or paper product (don't substitute vegetable or mineral oil, otherwise the test won't work). Observe what happens.

- If the olive oil soaks into the material, then it's highly likely that no waterproof or greaseproof barrier is present. In other words, there are no PFAS.

- If the olive oil doesn't soak in, but instead spreads, then this indicates the presence of a greaseproof barrier. This material is most likely sealed with a non-fluorinated finish that is not PFAS.

- If the olive oil forms a bead, then it's very likely that the material contains PFAS. So, don't use this material in your compost or garden.

Soaking   Spreading   Beading

Recycled paper products and BPA

We're all used to seeing 'BPA–free' on plastic bottles and containers. But did you know that many recycled paper and cardboard products contain trace amounts of bisphenol A (BPA), too? This is because thermal shop receipts – which are notoriously full of BPA – end up in mixed paper recycling and get turned into new paper products.

BPA is a chemical that has been linked to a number of serious health issues. According to Food Standards Australia New Zealand, however, the overwhelming weight of scientific opinion is that there is no health or safety issue at the levels to which people are exposed. The US Food & Drug Administration came to the same conclusion in its 2014 safety assessment.

Nevertheless, I want to limit the amount of BPA in my compost and garden because it doesn't belong in the environment. I don't put thermal receipts in the compost, but I'm happy to add other paper and cardboard even though they may contain small amounts of BPA.

MANURE

Manure from cows, sheep, horses and chickens can be added to your composting systems as a nitrogen-rich input (yep, they're a green even though they're coloured brown). There are a few things you should know:

- It's a misconception that manure is acidic. It can actually be quite alkaline, with a pH typically between 8 and 12.
- The amount of nitrogen in manure varies depending on the animal and their diet. Chicken manure is the 'hottest', as it has a significant amount of organic nitrogen. This is because chickens don't wee, and all the nitrogen is captured in their poo – so, it must be composted before being applied to your garden.
- Don't add any fresh manure to your garden without composting it first, as it can stunt plant growth.
- Avoid using manure if you don't know what has been sprayed on the grass or feed eaten by the animal. Manure contaminated with aminopyralid is unfortunately common, as this is the active ingredient in broad-leaf weedkillers. (To get up to speed with this, turn to page 198.)
- Animal worm medications can persist in manure for 45 days or more. But compost microbes (especially thermophilic ones) can decrease the concentration of ivermectin (the active ingredient in the medications) to a level that is safe for beneficial insects and worms.
- If you have access to a lot of safe manure, then it's best to age it in a separate pile under a tarpaulin for up to a year, or mix it with carbon and compost it (in a separate bin or pile to your usual one) before using it on your garden.
- Horse manure is often full of weed seeds that can germinate in your garden, so it's best to hot compost it.
- Be wary of using pig manure, as it can contain *Salmonella, E. coli* and parasitic worms. It must be hot composted before use on the garden.

NAIL CLIPPINGS

Are we going to stop the climate crisis by composting rather than binning our nail clippings? No. But they're a useful addition to composts and worm farms, as they're high in slow-release nitrogen. Don't add painted nail clippings or fake nails, as they contain plastics and chemicals that you don't want in your soil.

NATURAL FIBRES AND FABRICS

The best way to keep fabrics out of landfill is to buy less and wear what you have. Clothes made from natural fibres (such as cotton, silk, wool, cashmere, hemp, bamboo and linen) can be composted at the end of their life – but don't forget about repairing them first. Once a garment is beyond repair and you've got enough rags in your life, follow these tips to return it to the earth:

- Cut off anything that won't biodegrade (such as elastic waistbands, polyester threads and tags, and metal/plastic zips or buttons), and keep anything that is useful for repairs.
- Keep garments whole, and use them as a worm blanket. Alternatively, rip them

into strips or cut them into small squares if you're adding them to compost bins (otherwise they'll get tangled up when you're aerating the compost).

- Keep fibres moist to speed up their decay. The fibres will become food for the biology in the soil.
- Use fabric in your garden as a weed suppression blanket by putting it on the soil then covering it with a layer of mulch.
- Non-biodegradable fabric – basically anything that is synthetic (such as polyester, spandex, nylon and rayon) – can't be composted.
- Dyed fabric is safe to compost, as our clever little composting critters can remediate the chemicals present and render them safe.

OIL

Small amounts of oil (olive, vegetable, peanut, rice bran, and so on) can be composted, as long as they're dispersed throughout the organic matter and balanced with dry carbon. Oil is resistant to decomposition; if you add large volumes to your compost, the oil will coat organic matter and reduce airflow, leading to an unhappy heap. An oily compost heap will start to rot, attract pests and stink. Be cautious with the amount of oil you add to a worm farm, too, as it can prevent worms from being able to breathe through their skin.

THE GOOD OIL

Where possible, re-use cooking oils and animal fats in your cooking, if they haven't gone over the 'smoking point' (started to smoke). To do this, allow the oil or fat to cool, strain it into an airtight jar, and store it in the fridge for a week (or the freezer for long-term storage). It may solidify, but that's fine – it will melt when heat is applied. It can then be used for cooking (animal fat makes the crispiest baked potatoes). You can also mix small amounts of fats and oils with chicken feed or dog food (it helps to make dogs' coats shiny).

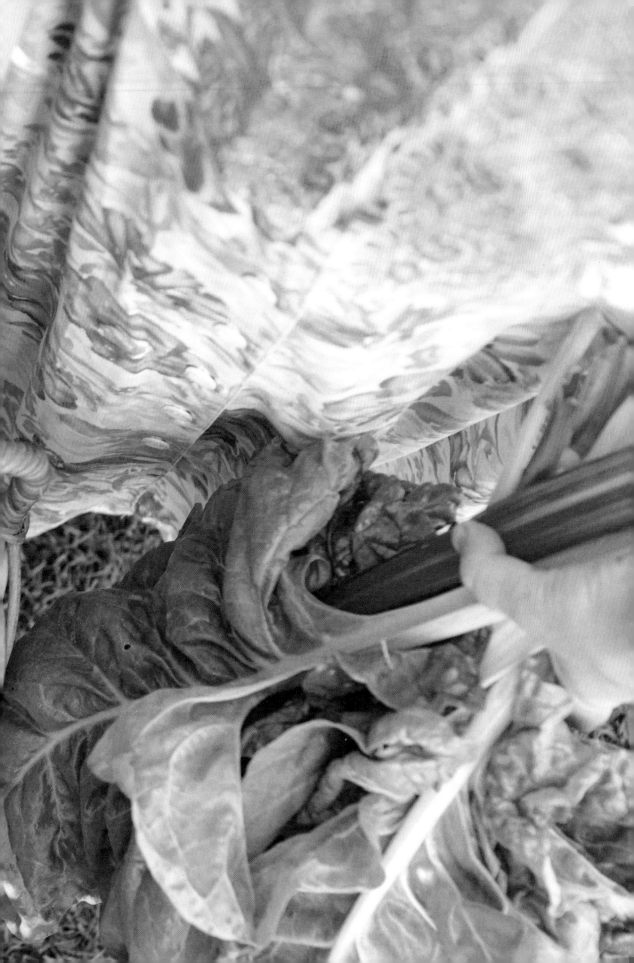

ONIONS AND GARLIC

These are often listed as compost no-noes, but they can be composted with care. One of the issues with these scraps is that new plants can sprout from the tops of onions and garlic cloves. To prevent this from happening, just chop and squash these scraps before composting them. The other issue with the flesh (not the skin) of onions and garlic is that it's acidic and whiffy when decomposing. Go easy on adding raw onions and garlic to worm farms, and bury these scraps under organic matter in your other composting systems.

PALM FRONDS

Palm fronds can be a pain to dispose of, as they take an age to break down. Don't despair – they can serve several useful purposes in your compost and around your garden.

- Place them down as the first layer of your new compost bin or pile to create air pockets and allow good airflow. They'll keep their structure for a long time and help to move air throughout the organic matter in your compost.
- Transform them into a 'lung' to allow air to flow through compost. Do this by tying a couple of palm fronds together and placing them vertically in the centre of your compost bin or pile.
- Use them as an organic cover on top of hot compost piles, compost bays or chicken–wire cages filled with leaves making leaf mould. This helps to prevent moisture loss in warm weather.
- Remove the tough central stem, and then the fibrous leaves can be added directly to your compost. It's wise to run a lawnmower over the leaves to cut them up – this will speed up their decomposition.
- Use them as a sturdy base layer in your Hügelkultur beds (see pages 204–5).

PESTICIDE RESIDUES

If you're getting your organic groove on, you may start questioning whether you should add fruit and vegie scraps from conventionally grown produce to your compost, due to the presence of pesticide residues. To put your mind at ease, studies on pesticide biodegradation have concluded that composting accelerates the breakdown of most modern pesticides (not DDT and aminopyralid – but it's unlikely that these chemicals would be on shop–bought produce), and any trace concentrations remaining in compost don't appear to affect human health or plant growth.

PET POO

Poo from your vegetarian pets (such as hamsters, guinea pigs and rabbits) can be safely composted, and the finished product can be used on your edible garden. Dog and cat poo can be composted, too, but the finished compost must not be used anywhere near your edible garden. Only apply it to your ornamental plants where there is no risk of run–off into your vegie patch. You need to be hyper–vigilant because cat and dog poo can contain parasitic worms that can cause blindness in humans, and cat faeces can contain pathogens that cause diseases such as toxoplasmosis (which is very dangerous for pregnant women).

Being a sustainable pet owner isn't easy, and our pets' environmental footprint is bigger than we'd like to think, but returning cat and dog poo to the soil is worth the effort and helps to lessen their impact. Bagged and binned poo releases methane in landfill and becomes climate poison, so here are some methods you can use to manage it safely:

- Dog and cat poo may be brown, but it's full of nitrogen, so it's considered a green input into your compost. If you're planning on creating a separate compost bin to process your pet poo, then make sure you balance it with carbon (such as shredded brown leaves, aged woodchips or sawdust).
- Create a worm farm just for this job; your worms won't know any better! It's best to

use an in-ground worm farm positioned away from your edible garden, so the poo becomes part of the soil without the need for regular removal (the less you handle it, the better). I advise not to add poo to a worm farm for at least a week after your pet has received a worming treatment.

- You can use an in-ground Bokashi bin specially designed for pet poo called an EnsoPet®. Like in regular Bokashi systems, you need to sprinkle the cat or dog poo with inoculated bran flakes. The microorganisms in the bran accelerate the breakdown of the poo, help to eliminate the smell, remediate pathogens in your pet waste, and ultimately contribute to healthier soil in your garden. Purr-fect! You don't need to empty this in-ground bin, as worms and microbes will do the work for you. When it's full, the bin can be moved to another area in your garden, but it <u>must not</u> be near edible plants.
- Even more simply, you can dig a hole in your soil away from any edible plants and bury pet poo. The life in the soil will sort it out.

Please note that not all kitty litter is compostable. Make sure you use a litter that is made from timber or paper only. If you're using 'Home Compostable' pet-poo bags, then ensure that you empty the poo out of the bag and add the bag and the poo separately to your pet-poo composting system of choice. This might seem counterintuitive, but it will speed up the decomposition of the poo.

PINE CONES AND GUMNUTS

Fallen pine cones, gumnuts and other woody seed pods that are brown, aged and dry are little nuggets of carbon, but they're resistant to decomposition due to their tough, protective exterior. Before adding them to any of your composting systems, it's best to break them down by smashing them with a hammer, running them through a high-powered shredder or mowing over them.

ROOT VEGETABLES

Have you ever noticed that the peels from carrots, potatoes and parsnips take ages to decompose in your compost or worm farm? The skins of root vegies are actually quite resistant to decomposition, as they have evolved to grow – rather than rot – in soil.

It's best to chop up the peel, top and flesh of the root vegetable into small pieces to help speed up microbial decomposition. Or better yet, process them in a Bokashi bin first, as fermentation softens them.

Be aware that the eyes of potatoes can sprout in your compost, so it's a good idea to squash and bury them in the core of your compost where it's hotter and away from the light needed for germination. One final point: potato tubers that have been affected by blight shouldn't be composted.

SAWDUST

Untreated sawdust made from hard or soft wood is a useful source of carbon for your composting systems. It can be collected for free from timber workshops and furniture makers. Be mindful that fresh sawdust needs to be mixed with plenty of nitrogen and water for it to decompose successfully.

Even though sawdust has a fine particle size, it can take up to a year to fully decompose. To speed this up, I suggest that you age sawdust in a bin or pile under a tarpaulin for up to a year before putting it in your compost (if you have room to do this). The ageing sawdust needs to be kept moist during this time, otherwise the maturation will stop. Fungi will slowly decay the sawdust, and after a year you'll notice that it has darkened and softened. Using aged sawdust in your compost is a joy, as it breaks down at a rapid rate.

SEEDS, PIPS AND STONES

Who has time to remove all of the seeds, pips and stones from their kitchen scraps before composting them? It's inevitable that some will germinate in your compost. You can work around this by applying your finished compost one month before planting out seeds, so these volunteer plants have time to emerge. They can then be worked back into the soil as a free source of green manure.

If volunteer seedlings are a constant bugbear, then turn up the heat and make a hot compost pile or bin. Seeds, pips and stones won't be able to germinate once thermophilic microbes have worked their steamy magic on them. Remember, your hot compost needs to reach 55–60 degrees Celsius and stay at that temperature for a minimum of three days to render the seeds, pips and stones non-viable and to prevent germination.

SHELLS FROM MUSSELS, OYSTERS AND CLAMS

The hard shells from seafood (such as oysters, mussels and clams) can be dried out, ground down and added to your composting systems, or fed to your worms or chickens. Shells are full of minerals that plants need to grow, such as calcium carbonate, chitin (a slow-release form of nitrogen) and the trace minerals magnesium, manganese, boron and iron. (To learn how to make the most of shells, turn to pages 227–8.)

TEA BAGS AND TEA LEAVES

Read this before you sling your next tea bag into your compost. Many tea bags are sealed with glue that contains a small amount of plastic material called polypropylene. This is 'biodegradable' but takes a long time to decompose, and the end result is microplastic contamination of your compost and soil. The netting material of many popular tea bags is also made from plastic, so check the labels before adding them to your compost.

The most sustainable way to make tea is to use loose-leaf products. Tea leaves are packed with nitrogen and can be added to composting systems, worm farms or Bokashi bins.

THORNY VINES, BRAMBLES AND ROSE PRUNINGS

Prunings from plants that are covered in thorns (such as those from roses or blackberries) are a pain to handle, but they can be composted. This plant material is often quite woody, so it's best to cut it down into small pieces before composting it. Like all organic matter, it will decompose in time. To speed up this process, it's a good idea to hot compost it (especially if the rose has been affected with the fungal disease called black spot).

URINE

If you want to capture fertility from weird and wild sources, then consider adding 'liquid gold' to your compost. Historically, the use of urine in agriculture was commonplace before the invention of the modern sewer system.

Urine is full of nitrogen (N), phosphorus (P) and potassium (K), which are the three key nutrients used in inorganic fertilisers made from fossil fuels. Global reserves of phosphorus are quickly running out, so urine may become

A DROP IN THE BUCKET

Capturing urine can be a bit tricky for women. However, a relatively civilised way to do this is by placing a small bucket inside your toilet.

a sustainable substitute. It seems crazy to flush away wee instead of using it to fertilise our gardens, especially because the urine that a family produces would provide enough NPK to sustain a home garden.

Undiluted urine can be added directly to compost as an activator, but be mindful of balancing this nitrogen–rich input with carbon, and don't add it to a compost bin that is overly wet. It can also be used as a soil drench (not a foliar spray) by diluting one part wee with 10–15 parts water.

It's true that there will be some bacteria present in urine; however, if you're healthy, then the biology in your soil can sort them out. The pH of urine for most people is around 6.2, so it's relatively neutral, but it does contain salts. Don't use it near salt–sensitive plants (such as onions or potatoes). In addition, avoid using urine if you've just taken antibiotics or other medications.

USED TISSUES AND PAPER TOWELS

I used to compost used tissues and dirty paper towels, believing that this was the most sustainable thing to do, as these items can't be recycled. However, I've since learned that most of these products have been treated with 'wet strength' chemicals to make them more robust. This treatment often involves formaldehyde resin, and clearly you don't want to contaminate your compost and soil with this synthetic polymer. In an ideal world, we would all replace these single–use items with hankies and cotton cleaning cloths (which can be composted safely when worn through).

VACUUM CLEANER DUST

Err on the side of caution when considering whether or not to add vacuum cleaner dust to your compost or worm farm because it can contain harmful chemicals. According to the NSW Environment Protection Authority, 'Studies show that vacuum cleaner dust derived from furniture, textiles and electronic devices is a potential source of polybrominated diphenyl ethers (PBDEs) chemicals'. Vacuum cleaner dust can also be contaminated with microplastics if your carpet or rugs are made from synthetic fibres.

WEEDS

All parts of weeds – including the roots – contain valuable nutrients. However, if the weeds are pernicious or invasive (such as kikuyu, nettle, couch grass, bindweed and ground elder) and spread by runners, root fragments, bulbs or seeds, then it's best to hot compost them in a pile that's at least 1 cubic metre in volume, solarise them in heavy–duty plastic bags or make weed tea from them. Don't add them to slow composting systems.

WOODEN PICKS AND STICKS

Lots of household items that are made from wood can be composted, including matches, iceblock sticks, chopsticks and toothpicks. Use your hands to snap thinner items (such as toothpicks and matches) into smaller pieces, but chunky items (such as chopsticks) may need to be sawed or shredded. Over time, the bits of wood will decompose.

MATCH POINT

Used matches are safe to compost. The match heads are made from phosphorus sulphide and potassium chlorate, which are two common ingredients in inorganic fertilisers. Once burned, they turn into carbon.

HANNAH MOLONEY

THE PERMACULTURE COMPOSTER

HANNAH MOLONEY is helping to build a resilient world by revitalising her urban life. Her approach to living is centred on the concept of radical homemaking. Hannah's home, family, community and local economy are at the core of her everyday existence.

Like every human on this planet, Hannah and her family are nurtured and strengthened by food. Hannah has rebelled against the big, broken and wasteful industrial food system by growing her own productive and edible patch. Growing, preserving and sharing food may seem like radical ideas in this modern world, but Hannah believes that they are, in fact, empowering and simple tasks that we can all perform to have a positive impact on our planet. Here, Hannah and I talk about how food, soil and compost are three ingredients for living a good life.

What is radical homemaking?

Radical homemaking is a concept from Shannon Hayes in the United States (see her book, *Radical Homemakers*) that flips the modern view of home on its head. Rather than homemaking being something you only get to do on the weekend, radical homemaking invites you to explore how much you can activate your home by embracing frugality, growing your own produce, working from home (if feasible) and turning your home into a place of production instead of only consumption.

What is permaculture, and how do you apply it to your garden?

Permaculture is a holistic design framework that can create sustainable human settlements. I was drawn to it for the gardening/agriculture practices, but stayed for its holistic overview and application. I realised that I could use it as a proactive and positive form of activism to help advocate for and shape a just and climate-safe world for all.

In our garden, permaculture has helped us to design a system that has no waste – just resources that we cycle from one section to another. We don't have a closed-loop system just within our property; rather, we have one in our community. For example, we send all of our big branches from our goat fodder to the local council's mulcher down the road. They mulch up the branches, turn them into compost and provide the compost to the community. We love embracing NOT doing everything ourselves, instead fostering the concept of community sufficiency, whereby we can meet all of our needs by working alongside one another.

How does growing your own food help to mitigate the climate crisis?

Our mainstream food system is broken and contributes to the climate emergency. As I wrote in my book, *The Good Life* (which was published in 2021): 'Agriculture in Australia is responsible for approximately 13% of our annual emissions. This does not include emissions from deforestation, which is a common part of the livestock industry to clear bush for grazing. It also doesn't include food transportation, which plays a central role in moving food across the country. So it's safe to say this is a conservative figure.'

Growing your own food might seem insignificant, but every lettuce, carrot or parsley bush that you plant is a step towards becoming more connected to where your food comes from. It can bolster food security and helps to craft a food culture that celebrates you being part of it.

RIGHT:
A repurposed bathtub makes a wonderfully effective worm farm.

OPPOSITE:
Hannah applies rodent- and snake-proof mesh to the bottom of her compost bins to keep uninvited critters out.

What would you say to novice gardeners hoping to grow their own food?

First up – just start. Don't feel like you need a big garden – there are plenty of opportunities to grow in pots on a balcony or even on your kitchen bench. Secondly, start small and choose the easier crops to grow (all the leafy greens and herbs). Also, grow what thrives in your climate and season – this will set you up for success.

How do you manage your kitchen and garden to eliminate waste?

We have really simple systems to channel organic waste to the right area on our property. When it comes to food scraps, it all comes down to our kitchen set–up. We have three buckets in one of our kitchen drawers: one for the bunnies, another for the chickens and the last for the compost worms or compost bin.

What is your daily and weekly composting routine?

We use the three buckets in our kitchen to divide up where the scraps go, and they're emptied as needed. We collect a range of carbon from around our property and opportunistically from our neighbourhood, so we have it on tap as needed to add to the compost bins or worm farms.

How do you work with animals to regenerate your landscape and soil?

Our animals are key to generating the bulk of the compost on our property. We're big fans of large–scale slow (cold) composting as the primary method of composting. For us, this is centred on our deep–litter system in our goat and chicken yard. It's around 80 square metres and consists of lots of woodchips dumped on the ground; this means that there's no exposed earth, no mud and no bad smells. Instead, the deep layer of woodchips (around 20 centimetres deep) absorbs all the manure and rain.

Over a few months, it starts to compost into beautiful crumbly matter – I add fresh woodchips on top as needed so it never smells. Then once or twice a year we scrape out the whole run and pile it up in the compost bays for another six months to finish the composting process. Eventually, it all ends up on our edible gardens, and the cycle continues again.

What other regenerative practices do you use in your garden?

We grow green-manure crops through our annual vegie beds, and make liquid fertiliser from plants and mature worm castings. The other major thing is that at least 80 per cent of our property consists of perennial plants. These are better for overall soil health, as growing them involves minimal soil disturbance by us – this fosters a healthy soil food web and improves water and nutrient retention. Overall, you have better ecosystem stability and health with a perennial-based garden.

How do you use humanure and pee in your garden?

We have a simple yet powerful compost-loo system made from a 20-litre bucket hidden beneath a standard toilet seat. Once the bin is full (with sawdust and humanure), we empty it into a wheelie bin, add compost worms and let it sit for six to twelve months. The bin contents are then applied to our orchard as gorgeous compost. All the urine is included in this blend, or we harvest it in a separate bucket then dilute it 10:1 and use it as a liquid fertiliser across our gardens. Urine is high in nitrogen – an essential growing input for healthy plants – and is perfectly safe to use.

How does radical hope stop you from despairing about the future?

Radical hope is about having hope in the face of huge uncertainty, such as the climate emergency. Where – despite the trajectory not looking overly promising – you do everything you can to help turn the ship around, knowing that it might not work. But you do it anyway because there's a chance that it just might. This is not naive optimism; this is love and courage in action. Importantly, it's acting from a place of love instead of fear – something I think is crucial in navigating these times. We need to foster joy and fun among all the big work to be done. I also remind myself that this is generational work; we're not going to solve everything in our lifetime. But we can do our best to progress things towards a better world for all.

SCRAP HIERARCHY

If you have more than one composting system, you may be wondering what scraps are best to add to each system. This is where my scrap hierarchy comes into play. Below are short, itemised lists for reference so you can determine the best use of your organic matter.

WORM FARMS

If you have a worm farm along with another composting system, then aim to feed your worms these three groups of scraps:

1. Water-rich fruit and vegie scraps – These include melon skins, strawberry tops, lettuce, celery, cucumber and zucchini. The scraps can be raw or cooked, but if they're cooked then they mustn't contain too much salt, oil or spice.
2. Carbohydrate-rich scraps – Worms love chowing down on rice, grains, pulses and noodles without spicy or salty sauces, and they also like bread and leftover cereal and muesli. Make sure you moisten dried bread crusts first, and rip them into smaller pieces to speed up their consumption.
3. Coffee grounds and tea leaves – Worms like these nitrogen-rich scraps and are not adversely affected by the caffeine.

BOKASHI BINS AND GREEN CONES®

If you have a Bokashi bin or Green Cone® composter along with another system, then focus on adding tricky scraps such as:

* citrus
* meat and bones (either raw or cooked)
* spicy- and/or strong-flavoured food
* dairy
* cooked food
* oily or salty food.

ENCLOSED COMPOST BINS

These freestanding composting systems will take all your food waste (including rodent-attracting scraps, such as meat or bones, once you've fitted a piece of stainless-steel mesh to the bottom – see pages 156–9). Aim to use your enclosed bin primarily for:

* food scraps
* household manufactured carbon
* herbaceous and tender garden waste (such as hand-pulled weeds), or small amounts of grass clippings added in thin layers
* shredded brown leaves
* aged woodchips.

OPEN PILES, BOXES OR BAYS

Open composting systems can be extremely hard to rodent-proof. If you have both an enclosed system and an open system, then use the enclosed one for your food waste and your open one primarily for your green and brown garden waste:

* fibrous plants (such as cornstalks, brassicas or sunflowers)
* robust hedge trimmings

- lopped and chopped fruit–tree branches from an annual prune
- vine or rose clippings cut down to size
- bulk amounts of spent plants at the end of the season
- large amounts of grass clippings added in thin layers
- weeds or plants that have gone to seed (hot compost them).

CHICKENS

It can be tempting to view chickens as the ultimate composting companions because they'll eat just about anything you sling their way. I'm a new chook mum, but I've quickly learned that it's important to use some tough love when deciding on which leftovers you give to your hens. Many of the scraps generated in your kitchen – especially those high in carbohydrates (such as bread, rice and oats) – are nothing but empty calories for your chooks, and they really should be viewed as treats rather than the bulk of their diet.

Chickens are omnivores. Their diet should be based on a balance of protein and fresh greens, along with a good–quality, commercial, organic poultry feed that provides them with plenty of calcium. However, I know a number of backyard chicken keepers who feed their chooks all of their kitchen and table scraps with no ill effects, as their chooks also forage for fresh greens and bugs, and have access to commercial feed. Having said this, if you can process scraps that are less healthy for chickens via a worm farm, Bokashi bin or compost pile, then I recommend doing that instead.

On the next page is a table that shows what you should and shouldn't give to your chickens. There is quite a long list of no–noes, but don't be discouraged from composting with chickens because backyard hens will lay the most delicious eggs if they have access to a wide variety of safe scraps, plants and bugs along with their regular commercial grains, pellets or mash.

DO FEED YOUR CHICKENS ...		DON'T FEED YOUR CHICKENS ...
Good food from the garden	**Good scraps from the kitchen**	**Items for the compost**
Weeds – chickweed (it's called this for a reason!), clover, dandelion, purslane, stinging nettle	Most fruit and vegie scraps – cucumbers, grated broccoli stems, watermelon, carrot peels and tops, banana (not the peel), apple peels and flesh, berries (freeze them as treats on hot days), corn on the cob, spinach and silverbeet (don't overdo these leaves, as they contain oxalic acid), raw or cooked pumpkin (and the seeds, too)	Processed or cooked foods high in salt or sugar
Spent edible plants – let the chooks pick over them for a day or two, and then compost what's left	Cooked meat or seafood (without salt); small amounts of fatty meat trimmings (as treats)	Avocado skins and stones (the flesh is fine)
Worms, black soldier fly larvae and other beetles, grubs and bugs from your compost	Cooked eggs – sounds crazy but they're a good source of protein, as long as they're not recognisable so chooks don't steal eggs from nesting boxes; scrambling the eggs is best	Leaves of rhubarb, warrigal greens, apricot (also the pits) and iceberg lettuce
Fresh leafy greens – chooks love the leaves from broccoli, pumpkin vines, zucchini, beetroot, comfrey and borage	Ground eggshells or oyster shells – chooks can also eat these when the shells have been turned into biochar	Raw green tomatoes or green potatoes – ripe red tomatoes are fine in small quantities
Cabbage leaves – or even a head of cabbage tied up with a string; chooks will peck at it for hours	Small amounts of cooked beans and pulses, pasta, noodles, bread ripped into small pieces	Onion and citrus fruits – small amounts are okay but this can result in reduced egg production
Garlic – add a whole fresh clove to the chooks' water as it has many medicinal qualities	Small amounts of dairy products (as treats; chickens struggle to process large amounts of dairy)	Uncooked rice or beans
Sunflower heads that have gone to seed	Nuts (as treats)	Chocolate – but why would you have any to spare?
A mix of sprouted green-manure seeds – they're an excellent source of nutrition	Cooked (or fermented) grains: barley, wheat, oats, rice	Coffee and tea

Safely composting with chickens can be done in three ways:

1. Safe scraps from your garden and kitchen can be fed to your chickens, and what remains can become compost as part of a deep-litter system. To set this up, you'll need to spread woodchips or other carbon-rich organic matter (such as brown leaves, hay, straw or wood shavings) thickly over the base of the chicken run. Any leftover scraps and the chooks' nitrogen-rich poo will compost down into this litter. After about a year, this will all become beautiful compost that can be dug out of the run and used in your garden.

2. Chickens' foraging habits can be used to your advantage if you give them access to your open compost piles whenever they need turning. Your chooks will have a brilliant time scratching at the organic matter to find worms, bugs and seeds, and will make short work of aerating your pile. In addition, your chooks will provide your pile with plenty of droppings, which are a fabulous and free compost activator. It's safest to allow them to do this only when all of the food scraps have broken down (so the chooks don't get sick from eating unsafe scraps).

3. Contain your chickens in a chook tractor, and allow them into your garden beds at the end of the season to help with the clean-up. They'll eat any bugs, spent plants or weeds, turn over the soil and feed it with their manure. Once the chook poo has aged in the soil for a few months, your patch will be ready for planting out the next crop.

YOUR CHOOKS WILL HAVE A BRILLIANT TIME SCRATCHING AT THE ORGANIC MATTER TO FIND WORMS, BUGS AND SEEDS.

TOXIC SHOCK!

Don't feed chickens any plant material from the nightshade family (such as tomatoes, potatoes and chillies), as the leaves and stems contain solanine. If eaten raw and in a large volume, this can be toxic to chooks. Apple seeds can also be toxic, so put apple cores in the compost. Don't give chooks iceberg lettuce, as it can cause diarrhoea. Avoid food that has become mouldy, rancid or rotten – if you wouldn't eat it in case it makes you sick, then your chickens shouldn't, either.

8.

THE SOIL

THE GOOD STUFF

I'm really excited for you to read this next part.
I go beyond compost to share simple – and
often free – regenerative gardening practices
that you can use in your own backyard to restore
and rejuvenate your soil.

Regenerative gardening is a holistic approach
to creating a self–sustaining garden ecosystem
using either homegrown or locally sourced raw
ingredients that improve soil health. It's about
giving back to the soil just as much as we take,
so that your plants thrive and your produce
grows abundantly and is nutrient dense.

With simple forms of organic matter, many
of which you can grow yourself or that come
package–free, you'll be able to enliven and
replenish your soil with bucketloads of biology
and plant–accessible minerals. These techniques
will allow you to work towards creating a truly
sustainable patch.

NOT SO FANTASTIC PLASTIC

Before you jump into this chapter, take
a moment to consider how much plastic
your garden produces. Do you buy plastic–
wrapped compost, manure, mulch or potting
mix? Fertiliser in single–use tubs and bottles?
Seedlings in plastic pots? Within this chapter,
I'll outline some exciting sustainable practices
that will help you to reduce – or remove –
your reliance on commercial products that
have been packaged in plastic.

GET TO KNOW YOUR SOIL

Before you can work out what amendments your soil needs, you need to get up close and personal with it. Healthy soil is made up of:

- 45 per cent mineral components (sand, silt and clay in differing ratios)
- 25 per cent oxygen (and other gases)
- 25 per cent water
- 5 per cent organic matter (anything that has lived before, that's slowly being consumed by the life in your soil and becoming humus).

To be perfectly frank, it's unlikely that the soil in your backyard will contain this much organic matter (unless you've been feeding it compost for a couple of years). Overworked or compacted soil can contain as little as 2 per cent organic matter, and not much air and water, which leads to both a poor habitat for soil biology and unhappy plants. Biologically dead soil has no organic matter left in it (33 per cent of global soils are moderately or strongly degraded). Globally, soils are under massive threat from erosion, overworking, depletion, contamination, compaction and sealing over with hard surfaces (such as roads).

Don't get anxious about this, get active! Above all else, organic matter is the most useful addition when transitioning poor soil to healthy soil. The volume of organic matter in your soil has the biggest impact on plants' ability to grow in it, so this chapter will show you simple ways to capture fertility by reclaiming organic matter in your garden.

TESTING FOR ORGANIC MATTER

Life begets life! The number and diversity of critters in your soil are good indications of its organic matter content. As a general rule, the more life you see, the more organic matter there is. Dig into the topsoil of your garden (about 20 centimetres deep), and scoop a few handfuls into a bucket. Rake over this soil with your fingers, and say hello to any hardworking creatures that you spot. Seeing worms, slaters, millipedes, beetles, ants, grubs, springtails, earwigs, spiders and mites is a great sign, as this indicates that your soil ecosystem is thriving and your soil is rich in organic matter.

Healthy soil will also be teeming with life forms that are invisible to the naked eye, but for this simple test we don't need to worry about our microscopic mates. If you don't see anything wiggling, crawling or scuttling around in your soil, then it's a clear indication that more organic matter is needed.

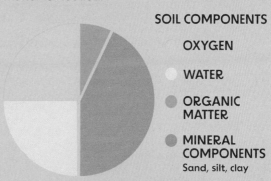

SOIL COMPONENTS

OXYGEN

WATER

ORGANIC MATTER

MINERAL COMPONENTS
Sand, silt, clay

TESTING FOR SOIL MINERALS

You can use a jar test or a squeeze test to determine if the minerals in your soil are mostly made of clay, sand or silt. These soil tests are adapted from Costa Georgiadis' wonderful book, *Costa's World*.

Jar test

Follow these instructions to perform the jar test:

1. On a dry day, dig out a small shovel-full of soil. Pick over it or sieve it using an old colander to remove any larger debris, rocks and organic matter (leaves, sticks, roots).
2. Using a glass jar with straight edges and a lid, fill around one-third of it with the soil to be tested.
3. Add water to the jar, leaving a 3-centimetre gap at the top.
4. Pop the lid on, and give the jar a vigorous shake. Leave the mixture to settle for 24 hours. Don't touch the jar during this time.
5. The soil will settle into three separate layers. Sand has the largest particles and will be at the bottom, silt will be in the middle, and clay will be on top.
6. If one layer is bigger than the other two, then that is the predominant mineral content of your soil.

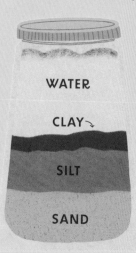

WATER

CLAY

SILT

SAND

If you have equal amounts of sand and silt, and a little less clay (a ratio of around 40 per cent each of sand and silt, and 20 per cent of clay), then this is ideal. It means that you have loam soil, which is magical for growing vegies. Don't despair if your soil is higher in either clay or sand – it will just need lots more organic matter added to it over time to improve it.

Squeeze test

An even simpler soil test is the squeeze test, which involves feeling the texture of your soil. With bare hands, grab a small amount of damp soil and rub it between your palms to try to form a ball. If it doesn't easily hold its form and you can feel rough particles, then it's likely to be sandy soil. This soil won't hold water well unless it's amended with plenty of additional organic matter (such as compost, aged manure and mulch).

If your soil forms a ball easily and has lots of fine particles that feel smooth or slippery, then it's mainly clay-based. Heavy, clayey soil doesn't have much oxygen in it and is not free-draining, so you need to add plenty of organic matter (and some gypsum powder) to open it up.

If your soil can be shaped into a ball that holds its form, then you may also be able to roll it into a noodle shape. If this noodle breaks when you try to pick it up or bend it, then you most likely have loamy soil. Hurrah! This sort of soil is made from a balance of sand, silt and fine clay, and it's a joy to work with. But you'll still need to feed it regularly with compost to keep your plants bountiful.

TESTING YOUR SOIL'S PH

Now it's time to test your soil's chemistry by determining its pH. Soil pH varies depending on where you live because it's influenced by the underlying bedrock, agricultural use and rainfall.

Available from garden centres and hardware stores, soil pH testing kits have a scale that ranges between 1 (acidic) and 14 (alkaline). The sweet spot on this scale is in the middle, with a neutral pH of 7. When soil has a neutral pH, your productive patch will be most bountiful, as heavy-feeding edible plants can readily access nutrients (such as nitrogen, potassium and phosphorus). If the pH is too high or low, plants will struggle to take up the nutrients they need, and weak plants will be more susceptible to pests and diseases.

Understanding whether your soil is acidic, alkaline or neutral will help you to pick suitable plants for your soil. Blueberries love acidic conditions and thrive in a soil pH of 5, while carrots, potatoes, pumpkins, cucumbers and tomatoes can tolerate only mildly acidic soil. Garlic, spinach, brassicas and olive trees can tolerate alkaline soil with a pH up to 8.

To get an accurate pH reading, take samples from multiple locations in your garden on a dry day (before you've added any compost or other minerals to the soil). Follow the instructions in your pH test kit. Depending on the results, you may need to amend your soil to alter its pH.

How to safely change your soil's pH

Altering the pH of your soil is a balancing act. I personally prefer to do it slowly and steadily with natural organic matter and by growing green manure, before using shop-bought mineral amendments, because if you're too heavy-handed with these it can be a battle to bring things back.

If your soil is too acidic (a low pH), then it tends to lock up some nutrients. First, add a gentle amendment (such as aged chicken manure), or a modest amount of wood ash from untreated timber, homemade biochar (see pages 230–3) or rock minerals (such as rock dusts; see pages 229–30), and grow a green-manure crop to work into the soil (see pages 215–16). Retest your soil after three months, as these naturally alkaline inputs and the extra organic matter work gradually (which helps to prevent plant stress).

If you decide to use some faster-acting amendments (such as dolomite or garden lime), then follow the instructions closely with regard to the appropriate amount to apply to your soil. It's important not to go overboard with lime because it increases the pH of your soil quickly. Biodynamic gardeners warn that

this sudden jump can 'burn out' the humus complex by overstimulating soil. Always incorporate lime into the top few centimetres of moist soil, rather than simply sprinkling it on the surface. Make sure you do this two or three months prior to planting out the area.

It's trickier, but not impossible, to lower the pH of alkaline soil. Do this by feeding your soil as much homemade compost as you can and, where appropriate, mulch with pine woodchips and pine needles, and grow a green-manure crop. Compost, woodchips and green manure won't dramatically alter soil pH, but rather act as a biological buffer so plants can more readily access nutrients.

The commercial mineral amendments that improve an alkaline pH are iron chelates and powdered sulphur (applied no more than once a year, at a rate of one handful per square metre). This is not a quick fix, so don't expect your pH to bounce back straight away – there will be no noticeable change in your soil's pH for about six months.

TAKING TESTING ONE STEP FURTHER

If you want a detailed understanding of your soil's macronutrients and micronutrients, then you can send samples off to be tested in a lab. For a new gardener, this isn't essential information. But if you've embraced your inner soil nerd and want to dive headfirst into regenerative gardening, then go for it.

These tests will tell you which nutrients and minerals you need more or less of, and – importantly – the amount of organic matter available. The results of these tests can be surprising, as soil that has been fed a lot of commercial fertilisers in the past often has excessive amounts of macronutrients, which are not beneficial to plants.

What these tests don't tell you is the amount of biology that's in your soil. You may find out that your soil has a good level of a particular nutrient or mineral, but without beneficial bacteria, nematodes, fungi, mycorrhizal colonies, protozoa and other soil-dwelling microorganisms that are part of the soil food web, your plants won't be able to access these

FUEL INJECTION

Adding compost to both acidic and alkaline soils is an absolute must, as it helps to buffer the extremes of pH. In addition, the biology that compost injects into your soil helps to unlock nutrients and make them available to plants.

food sources. To get detailed information about what is living in your soil, you can send samples to the Soil Foodweb Institute run by leading soil microbiologist Dr Elaine Ingham.

Is your soil safe?

Before growing food at your place, I highly recommend that you get your soil checked by a laboratory (such as VegeSafe) to see if it's contaminated. This is especially important if you're planning on growing a large amount of food on a suburban block or in an urban garden. Professor Mark Taylor, the lead researcher and developer of VegeSafe, notes that '50 per cent of Australians grow some food in their gardens and these soils contain legacy contaminants that come from industrial activity'.

The presence of heavy metals in our soils follows the movement of people. They have been spread wherever people have lived and worked. In Australia, lead was used in paints until the mid–1970s and in petrol until 2002. Unfortunately, urban soils are still often contaminated with metals, toxins and persistent chemicals. So, discover what you're working with by sending off some soil samples to be tested, taken from different spots in your garden.

Thankfully, there are two solutions to soil contamination, so don't freak out!

1. Grow produce in raised beds lined with geofabric or compacted gravel (or both) to completely separate the produce from your backyard soil.
2. Grow produce in pots and containers.

Don't forget that even when growing plants in raised beds or containers, toxic particles from other areas of your garden can be blown on them (particularly if your soil is dry and dusty). Always wash your herbs and vegies before eating them, especially produce with large leaves (such as lettuce or spinach).

Here are some strategies for soil that is contaminated with lead:

- If lead is a trace contaminant and not at an unsafe level (the test results will tell you), adding plenty of organic matter (such as homemade compost) on top of your soil will help. Organic matter helps to lock up heavy metals in the soil, so plants are less likely to take them up. Organic matter can't remove lead, but it will reduce the likelihood of you eating it in the produce you grow.
- Lead is much more available to plants if your soil has an acidic pH. Monitor the pH, and aim to maintain a neutral to slightly alkaline range of 7–7.5.
- Plants, vines and trees that produce fruits (such as tomatoes, pumpkins and citrus trees) tend to have the lowest concentration of lead. If you've moved into a home with established fruiting plants that are growing in contaminated soil, then it's likely that their fruits are safe to eat.

DISCOVER WHAT YOU'RE WORKING WITH BY SENDING OFF SOME SOIL SAMPLES TO BE TESTED.

COMMERCIAL COMPOST: A CAUTIONARY TALE

If you've conducted some (or all) of the tests mentioned above and have worked out that your soil is lacking organic matter, please read this cautionary tale before rushing out to the shops. Buying compost, potting mix, manure and mulch may seem like a convenient and reasonably cheap thing to do, but weaning yourself off commercial products has far–reaching benefits. Homegrown organic matter is the most transparent and trustworthy amendment you can use on your plants. Let me explain why ...

In Australia during 2020, there was widespread use of toxic commercial compost that contaminated the soil of thousands of home gardens with aminopyralid, a hormone–based herbicide that's commonly used on broadleaf weeds in agricultural settings. Aminopyralid is a problematic persistent herbicide, as it remains in the organic matter throughout the composting cycle and doesn't easily disappear in soil. Unfortunately, product contamination has been regularly reported in the United Kingdom and United States, too.

Hay and straw harvested from paddocks where aminopyralid has been used will still have the herbicide on it because it binds to the grasses. Cows, horses and sheep that feed on grasses in contaminated pastures eat the herbicide, and it then passes into their manure. Commercial compost, manure, mulches, potting mix and mushroom substrate that have been made from these manures or grasses can be contaminated.

Aminopyralid is released from these products as they decompose, so you only discover that there is a problem after several weeks of plant growth. You can tell if your soil has been contaminated if you notice damage to sensitive broadleaf plants (such as tomatoes, beans and peas). Red flags are poor seed germination, the cupping of leaves, twisted and elongated growth, and distorted fruits. Plants growing in compost or mulch with aminopyralid residues usually won't die, but your harvest will significantly suffer.

WHAT CAN YOU DO?

Buying certified organic compost, manure, mulch or potting mix helps, but you still can't guarantee that it won't be contaminated, as there is limited regulation of the supply chain for the raw materials used in these products. It's always best to sow seeds of plants with a high sensitivity to aminopyralid (such as broad beans, tomatoes or peas) in small pots filled with the compost or a mixture of bagged manure and potting mix. Monitor plant growth before applying these products to your garden.

Testing mulch is a little more challenging, as the effects are only visible once the mulch decomposes – and this can take several months to happen. So, aim to buy safe commercial mulches (such as lucerne [alfalfa] or pea straw) – aminopyralid can't be used near these plants, as it will kill them.

So, with this cautionary tale front of mind, let's talk about ways you can cycle nutrients to safely feed your soil. These nutrients will come from resources generated in your kitchen, grown in your garden or foraged from your local area.

NUTRIENT CYCLING

There is no doubt that the best way to improve your soil is to increase the amount of organic matter in it. Resources rich in nutrients are all around us – you just need to get creative and be a little greedy! Instead of sending away weeds, plant prunings, grass clippings, brown leaves and dead plant material in your green-waste bin every week, keep them and cycle the nutrients back into your garden. This stops you from paying out money twice: once in rates for using the bin, and then again to buy organic matter in the form of commercial compost, mulch and fertiliser.

I encourage you to 'shop' in your house and garden for resources that increase soil fertility, rather than running to your local gardening megastore to purchase organic matter. Grass clippings are packed with nitrogen. Brown leaves build soil biology. Woody materials attract fungi to your soil.

Bones and eggshells are full of calcium and phosphorus. Homemade biochar has near-magical soil-improving qualities.

Sourcing organic matter from your own patch, your neighbour's garden and your local streets and beaches also helps to prevent persistent chemicals being introduced to your yard. Perhaps more significantly, it allows you to capture and reproduce indigenous microorganisms that have adapted to your local ecosystem.

I've divided the resources found over the following pages into four main groups:

1. browns
2. greens
3. whites, grey and black
4. teas.

Within these groups, each commonly found (and often overlooked) natural resource comes with actionable methods and practical guidelines that explain how you can utilise them to regenerate your soil.

TIME HEALS ALL WOUNDS

Unfortunately, it's commonplace for cheaply made commercial compost and potting mix to contain microplastics, other pollutants and persistent chemicals such as aminopyralid and PFAS (see pages 170–1). Many of these products are made from municipal waste and industrial by-products, and it's almost impossible to police pollutants from such a large-scale waste stream. In Australia, poor-quality commercial potting mix has been found to contain decomposed timber pallets treated with methyl bromide.

Using products contaminated with aminopyralid on your garden may result in damage to your soil. Thankfully, with care and time – and the help of microorganisms – your soil can heal itself. Contaminated soil can be restored with additional homemade compost, cultivation (forking over the ground) and regular watering. The microbiology in your soil will render the chemicals relatively neutral in around one year, and it will be safe to grow edible plants in your soil again.

FERTILISER FACT

Did you know that nitrogen-based inorganic fertilisers are made using huge amounts of fossil fuels, and that only about 40 per cent of fertiliser is absorbed by plants? The rest of the material pollutes our atmosphere, rivers, lakes and oceans.

BROWNS

Look around, and you'll see plenty of useful carbon! From autumn leaves and wood waste to woodchips and logs, these sources are abundant – and often free.

BROWN LEAVES

Collecting and using fallen brown leaves is one of the most worthwhile things you can do for your garden. If you're an avid compost creator, then autumn is your peak carbon–collection period for the year. You'll be constantly monitoring the leaves on your street trees as they turn from green to red to brown, and scanning the roads, footpaths and gutters for this fallen bounty.

Here are my tips for safely and sustainably collecting street leaves ('gutter gold'):

- Check with local authorities before removing any leaf litter from streets and parks. Many local governments actively remove and dispose of fallen leaves, so you need to get in quick. Gathering street leaves as soon as they fall also helps to prevent contamination from pollutants.
- Don't touch the leaves in areas where authorities won't remove them until spring, as many beneficial pollinators overwinter in piles of fallen leaves. This leaf litter provides natural protection and nesting areas for many bees and butterflies during the winter months.
- Introduced deciduous trees are a big problem near waterways. The leaves are washed into drains, accumulate in lakes and rivers and then contribute to algal blooms. So, many local governments actively encourage leaf collecting from public spaces (but do check first).
- Aim to collect leaves from hard surfaces only, or at least away from the drip line of trees (because trees use these leaves as root protection, and food when they naturally compost).
- Avoid collecting leaves from gutters and stormwater drains after heavy rain, as these leaves will have absorbed pollutants from

run–off. Collecting wet leaves from other areas won't pose a problem, as they're still a great source of carbon.
- If you're planning on slow composting your leaves, it's best to avoid collecting leaf litter filled with seeds, otherwise some may germinate. Also, make sure you shred them first (mowing over them works well) to speed up decomposition.
- Be mindful of aminopyralid contamination of leaves collected from parks, sports grounds, golf courses or council–managed grass verges. This persistent herbicide is often applied to turf in amenity situations, so avoid collecting leaf litter if you can see that the grass has been recently mowed, and a lot of the grass clippings have been mixed with the leaves.

Leaf management

People can get hung up about the tannins or oils in some leaves, or the robust texture of others, but it's important to remember that every type of leaf will break down in time. Here are some pointers for dealing with the 'trickier' sorts of leaves, so you can get the most out of them.

- Three common trees that produce leaves with volatile oils and allelopathic compounds are eucalyptus, camphor laurel and black walnut. When these green or brown leaves are used on your garden beds, they can suppress the growth of other plants. Thankfully, an active slow or hot compost will break down the toxins in the leaves through exposure to air, water and bacteria, and over time render them neutral.
- Leaves with an oily texture (such as those of eucalyptus) or large surface area can become hydrophobic (repel water) if they're added to your compost when green (or in thick layers when brown). It's best to shred these leaves before using them in your compost or garden. This speeds up their decomposition and stops them from matting together.

- You can also denature fibrous, waxy or oily leaves before using them in your compost or as mulch. Add your brown leaves, 1–2 cups of well-cured compost, 2 cups of urine (yep – it's a stinky but safe activator) and ½ cup of blackstrap molasses to a large bucket, barrel or wheelbarrow. Cover with dechlorinated water (see page 236), and leave uncovered in the shade for three to seven days. Give the mixture a stir a couple of times every day to help it to stay aerobic. The combination of bacteria and nitrogen helps to soften and microbially colonise the carbon of the dead leaves, and this allows for more efficient decomposition. Simply drain the leaves when they're soft, and use them in your compost or as mulch.
- To denature pine needles, Moreton Bay fig leaves or large magnolia leaves, you can inoculate them with fungi. Place whole leaves into a thick black–plastic bag. Mix in two large handfuls of compost or aged manure, and pour in enough aerated compost tea (see pages 234–6) to moisten the leaves. Poke some holes in the bag to encourage airflow and drainage. Leave the bag in the shade, and in around one month the leaves will be soft and covered in fungal spores. They can now be applied directly to garden beds as mulch or used in your compost.
- You can deploy a team of scratching chooks to break down brown leaves to a more usable size. I add mountains of deciduous leaves to the bottom of our chicken run throughout autumn as part of our deep–litter system (see page 188). Come spring, our hardworking ladies have shredded the leaves and mixed them with their nitrogen–rich manure, and the leaves are ready to be raked up and added to a compost pile.

GET SHREDDED!

Large, thick, whole leaves can take years to decompose. If you have a shredder or mulcher, use that to knock them down to size, or run a lawnmower over the top of them a few times. Add shredded leaves to your compost in thin layers, mixed with a compost activator (such as chicken manure). The smaller the leaf particles, the quicker they'll degrade.

Leaf mulch

Stop buying mulch – use brown leaves instead! Let's replicate what happens in nature and use brown leaves as a natural ground cover to suppress weeds and add fertility to the soil. Here are three tips to nail their use in your patch:

1. You can apply small leaves directly to your garden bed as a surface mulch without shredding them, but it's useful to shred or mow over large leaves. Otherwise they'll matt together and stop water from penetrating into the soil.
2. If you have the space, it's a great idea to compost leaves down a little in a separate pile before using them as mulch. This stops them from blowing away.
3. Don't use waxy leaves for mulch (such as frangipani or eucalyptus leaves) – shred and compost them instead.

It's worth noting that if slugs and snails are a big issue in your patch, then this isn't the best mulch for you – they'll hide in the leaf litter.

LEAVE THE LEAVES

Leave your leaves where they fall in your garden over autumn and winter. Only collect, mow and use them in other areas of your garden in spring. This leaf litter provides a crucial habitat in which many beneficial pollinators, reptiles and insects overwinter. It also protects the biology in the soil from the freeze–thaw cycle and provides insulation for tree roots.

Leaf mould

I think that every gardener should have a pile of leaf mould on the go, as it's the most simple yet versatile compost you can make. All you need is a mountain of brown leaves, a cool shady spot to store them, water and time.

Making leaf mould is an easy, hands–off composting process. Unlike traditional composts that are bacterially driven processes fuelled with nitrogen, leaf mould is carbon–heavy. This attracts fungi, which do the hard work of breaking down the leaf structure into crumbly, dark, delicious–smelling compost. Leaf mould has little available nitrogen and is not nutrient–rich, but is high in cellulose and lignin. Its structure and moisture–retaining ability mean that it's a fabulous soil conditioner, mulch, bedding material for worms and growing medium for seedlings.

Depending on the variety of leaves you use (oak leaves are some of the best), you'll have finished leaf mould in one to two years using these simple methods adapted from *Gardening Australia*:

*   Bag them – Fill robust plastic bags with moist brown leaves (don't use flimsy plastic shopping bags, as they'll break down). Punch a few holes in the bags, as the leaves need to be kept moist in an airy environment for fungi to thrive. Store the bags in a shady spot or in a garage, checking occasionally to see if the leaves are still damp; add water if necessary.
*   Roll them – This method is the same as bagging up the leaves, but on a larger scale. Lay a tarpaulin out flat, and make a big pile of brown leaves in the centre. Dampen the leaves, and then roll up the tarpaulin so that you create a bonbon shape. Tie off both ends with twine, and leave the leafy bonbon in a shady spot in your garden.
*   Cage them – Make an upright tube out of chicken wire, secure it to the ground with a garden stake, and fill it with damp brown leaves. Pack them in tight. The leaves must be kept moist during this process, so line the cage with cardboard or hessian to help minimise water loss. Cover the cage with hessian or shadecloth.
*   Bin them – If you have the luxury of an empty compost bin on hand, fill it with damp brown leaves and let the fungi do their thing.

LEAF MOULD TEA

You can supercharge your leaf mould and spread its goodness over a larger patch in your garden by brewing it into a biologically active soil amendment. See the full recipe on page 240.

DIY potting mixes

Once you have a batch of leaf mould, you can make your own seed–raising mix and general–purpose potting mix for free. For the seed–raising mix, you'll need:

- one part leaf mould
- one part coarse river sand (from a garden centre or hardware store)
- one part worm castings or well–cured compost.

Make sure the castings and leaf mould are well sifted, so that your mix will be light and airy, and then combine all inputs thoroughly. Seeds don't like growing in a rich mix, so this low–nutrient recipe works well. It has just enough nutrients to allow seeds to germinate and grow their first set of 'true' leaves. When your seedlings have reached this stage, they need to be planted into the garden or repotted in general–purpose potting mix. For this, you'll need:

- two parts leaf mould
- two parts coarse river sand (from a garden centre or hardware store)
- one part worm castings
- one part compost
- half part organic slow–release fertiliser.

Use a soil sieve to sift the leaf mould, castings and compost to help remove the chunks (add these back into your next batch of compost). Then mix all inputs thoroughly to combine.

CRITTER ALERT

It's likely that you'll find a lot of composting critters in your leaf mould piles. Spiders might make you jump, but they're important predators in the compost ecosystem, so live and let live. Also be mindful of snakes taking up residence in your leaf piles. If you're concerned about snakes, the best method for making leaf mould is using an enclosed compost bin with rodent- and snake–proof, stainless-steel mesh on the bottom.

WOOD WASTE

We need to rewild our suburban blocks and urban yards to help make the gardens of our future look more like the natural landscapes from our past. Gardens can operate just like miniature forest ecosystems if we embrace the mess and reclaim carbon–rich organic matter (such as leaf litter, dead branches, logs, twigs and sticks).

This climate–resilient approach to gardening means that you stop endlessly cleaning up after nature. Shelve your leaf blower, chainsaw and secateurs, and stop throwing away your garden's carbon–rich goodness in your council green–waste bin. Our soils are yearning for more organic matter, our climate benefits massively when we sequester carbon in our soils, and our insect populations are always looking for more habitat.

Create a Hügelkultur bed

Old branches and rotting logs are full of fertility and can be used in a layered soil–building technique called Hügelkultur (this German term translates to 'mound culture' or 'hill culture'). It allows you to make a productive and moisture–retentive garden bed with free resources that you may otherwise throw away. The benefits of this technique include increased:

- soil aeration (you create a long–term no dig bed)
- fertility (ideal for gardens with poor soil or heavy clay, as the wood releases nutrients slowly)
- water–holding capacity (the decomposing wood acts like a sponge)
- fungal activity (fungi thrive in carbon–rich soils)

- bacterial activity (the heat generated by bacteria helps fungi to break down the wood, and this can extend your growing season)
- worm activity (they love setting up camp in soil rich with organic matter)
- biodiversity (an ideal habitat in which frogs and pollinators can overwinter)
- carbon sequestration in the soil (helps to battle climate change).

Traditionally, this type of garden bed was built in the shape of a small hill about 1 metre high, as this offered a larger surface area for growing plants (twice its footprint). However, it's an inappropriate shape for hot, dry and windy climates like those in Australia. Here, it's more common to see this technique used in raised garden beds or trenches (where the material only rises slightly above ground level).

Follow these instructions to make a Hügelkultur bed:

1. Mark out your garden bed, and dig out a shallow trench about 30 centimetres deep. (For raised beds, start at Step 2.)
2. Fill the trench with aged, decaying or even rotten wood. Pile dead branches on top of one another so that they reach the top of the trench (or exceed this level to form a small mound). If using a raised bed, aim to fill the bottom third with aged wood. Water this layer well.
3. To help kickstart the composting process and counteract nitrogen deficiencies, place a layer of nitrogen–rich inputs (such as weed–free grass clippings, seaweed, manure or compost) directly on top of the woody material. This should be at least 5 centimetres thick.
4. Add alternate layers of browns and greens (such as seaweed, shredded brown leaves, grass clippings, shredded cardboard, and so on). Aim to build these layers 5–10 centimetres thick and tuck them in, as large air pockets around the wood will lead to dry conditions and slower decomposition. These brown and green layers should make up another third of the total depth of the new bed. Water them well.

5. Finally, on top of this add healthy garden soil (this can be the soil that was removed from the trench) or more compost. It's important that this is at least as deep as the wood base if you're filling a raised bed.

You can now plant directly into the top layer, but I recommend that the first crop you grow is food for the soil: nitrogen–fixing green manure. One month before you plan to plant out an edible crop, cut down the green–manure crop to the ground. Leave the slashed plant matter on the soil and the roots in place, water well, and cover with a piece of cardboard weighed down with bricks. In around four weeks, the soil food web will have consumed this juicy green organic matter, and you'll have beautiful soil to grow in.

HÜGELKULTUR HINT

Over time, your Hügelkultur bed will naturally hold a lot of moisture, but in the first year of use it's important to keep it moist (not saturated) to help the organic matter decompose. If the bed dries out in the first year, the process will be significantly slower and less successful.

WORKING WITH WOOD

A bird's nest bin (see page 210) is being made next to a dead hedge (see page 208). These carbon–rich structures can be left to compost passively or can be used as growing frames for food and flowers.

Erect a dead hedge

If the thought of messy piles of dead wood lying around your garden offends your sense of order, then build a neat and tidy dead hedge (also known as a dry hedge or Benjes hedge). This technique involves building a vertical structure that acts like a rustic fence, using carbon–rich waste materials (such as branches, hedge trimmings, saplings, twigs and rotting logs). You can use dead hedges to:

- slowly decompose carbon–rich organic matter (that you would have otherwise thrown away or burned) into humus
- contain open compost piles
- hide away your stashes of garden rubbish
- serve as a border between properties, urban patches or allotments
- help prevent erosion
- act as a windbreak, which can help to create a microclimate ideal for growing edibles
- attract fungal organisms to your patch
- create a refuge and ecological corridor for wildlife.

This technique is a much more sustainable alternative to using a bonfire to get rid of garden waste. Instead of burning wood and releasing the carbon into the atmosphere, you can sequester carbon by returning it to the soil. If you live in a bushfire–prone area, then ensure that your dead hedge isn't close to your house. However, for those in an official 'Flame Zone', dead hedges are not suitable for your garden. Also, if termites or snakes are active in your garden, then you should think twice about building a dead hedge, or at least erect it away from your house.

Follow these instructions to make a dead hedge:

1. Using pegs and string (or just eyeballing it!), mark out where you want your dead hedge to go.
2. Gather together larger branches (around 4 centimetres in diameter) or timber/metal garden posts, which will be used to create the formwork for the hedge structure. If you're using branches, then cut these 30 centimetres longer than needed, and sharpen the ends into a point so you can drive them into the ground.
3. Dig or hammer the branches or posts into the soil at regular intervals in two parallel lines. The size and shape of your dead hedge will depend on what it's being used for, the amount of garden waste you have and the space in your garden. The posts in the formwork should be close together if you're using short lengths of woody waste, or up to 1 metre apart if you're using long logs of decaying wood.
4. Fill the hedge framework in one of two ways. Pile all of your woody materials in between the posts, or – if you want a more ordered look – weave flexible branches between the posts first before filling the hedge with woody materials.
5. Top up your dead hedge as the materials slowly rot down and sink. This can be done when it's hedge–trimming season, when you prune your fruit trees or at any other point when you have plenty of green or brown woody materials from your garden maintenance.

Build a bird's nest bin

At the end of every growing season, you're likely to have lots of spent plants that are big and chunky. Your green–waste bin can quickly fill to the brim with hedge prunings, stalks from sunflowers or corn, brassica stems and more. These plants are often too fibrous or coarse to be put directly into your compost bin without shredding or mulching them down to size first. If you don't own a high–powered shredder, then why not manage this fibrous waste by weaving the stems together to form a bird's nest bin? Also called a 'binless bin', it's a sustainable alternative to a plastic compost bin.

The bird's nest bin is an alternative composting method to a Johnson–Su bioreactor for creating fungi–dominant compost from wood waste (such as aged woodchips, brown leaves, shredded bark, branches, woody vegetable stems and pine cones), which you use to fill your 'nest'. Fungi develop in cool temperatures and will grow in a compost heap that is carbon–rich, damp and left alone (turning your bird's nest bin disrupts the development of their root-like mycelia). You do need to be patient with this slow composting method, as it can take around two years for the organic matter to decompose. If you have the space available, then it's worth the wait – and it's fun for children to be involved in, too.

Follow these instructions to make a bird's nest bin:

1. Pick a spot in your garden for your bird's nest bin, being mindful that this slow composting pile will take a long time to fully decompose. If you want to build it in a weedy or grassy corner, make sure you cover the ground with a thick layer of moist cardboard or newspaper to smother the weeds or grass first.
2. Build the framework. The bird's nest bin can be round – drive eight to twelve branches or garden stakes into the ground to make a circle. Or it can be square – drive four branches or garden stakes into the ground roughly 1 metre apart.
3. Weave your waste materials in and out of the vertical branches or garden stakes, from the ground up. This is not an exact science, but you should weave in enough material so the bin holds its form.
4. Fill the centre of your bird's nest bin with layers of green and brown garden material (don't add food waste, as there is no way to keep vermin out of these piles). As you're building up the layers, push sticks, robust stems, hedge prunings and small branches through the framework and into the centre of the pile to help oxygen to filter through. This allows for passive composting without the need to turn your pile.
5. Over time, the centre of this composting system will slowly sink down. Add more organic matter when this happens. The sides will take longer to decompose, as they're more fibrous and hold less moisture.
6. Keep your bird's nest bin moist; hose it down during dry periods. Depending on your weather, you may want to cover the top with hessian or an old piece of wool carpet to help insulate it and reduce evaporation.
7. After about two years (three years in drier climates), you can dismantle what's left of the structure. Fish out any remaining sticks and chunkier bits, and use these as part of your next bird's nest bin. Most of what you've added to the bin will have turned into fungi–rich, black earth that is high in potassium.
8. Due to the long, slow maturation period, there is no additional curing time needed. You can use bird's nest bin compost in your garden straight away.

I personally think that bird's nest bins look romantic, especially if there are old sunflowers sticking out of the sides. But if you feel that this pile will take up too much valuable real estate while it's slowly decomposing, then you can use the vertical framework to grow climbing vegies or flowers. Add some compost to spaces on the outside of your bird's nest bin, and plant climbing peas, beans, sweet peas or even scrambling cucamelons. Once these plants die back, there's no need to discard the dead vines. Leave them in place – they're simply more organic matter that will decompose in time.

WOODCHIPS

If you have a tiny patch, then you can still harness the fertility of dead wood and bring life and bucketloads of fungi into your garden with the three simple, small-scale ideas outlined below. Use common sense about what will work for your situation and location, and be aware of termite activity in your home and garden, as well as bushfire risks.

Woodchip paths

Grass is a hungry crop that draws nutrients and water from the soil (and away from your edibles), so replace the grass around your vegie beds with woodchip paths. Grass paths are unproductive, but woodchip paths build fertility by:

- helping to prevent compaction and increase soil airflow
- attracting fungi to your soil
- harbouring hordes of hungry worms
- slowing composting down and making humus
- capturing and storing water
- helping to control weeds.

Follow these instructions to make a woodchip path:

1. If you have invasive grass (such as kikuyu) and/or lots of weeds, then do a 'hard' mow and scalp them down to the ground (or as close as possible). Depending on the weed species, you may need to hand-pull these before mowing.
2. Use a garden fork to lightly aerate your soil to improve drainage.
3. Sprinkle organic fertiliser, compost or worm castings to feed any remaining weeds, and water well. This helps them to regrow and then rot more quickly.
4. Lay down a thick layer of cardboard or a chunky wad of newspaper over your grass and weeds. Make sure these layers overlap well, otherwise opportunistic grass and weeds will easily sneak through the gaps. Water well.
5. Cover the cardboard/newspaper with a layer of woodchips that is around 5 centimetres thick.

You'll need to top up the woodchips yearly. If you see weeds and grass growing back, then get weeding. You may need to repeat the steps above a few times until you win the battle against the weeds and grass – but you'll win eventually.

Sheet mulch with woodchips

If you want to transform an area of your garden into a more productive patch, then use the powerhouse combo of sheet mulching and woodchips to smother grass and weeds. It's especially beneficial to use sheet mulching around fruit trees – if grass is growing right up to their trunks, then it will be stealing water and nutrients from the trees.

To apply sheet mulching to your garden, repeat the steps from the woodchip–path instructions above, but over the whole garden bed. Over time, this will prevent photosynthesis from occurring, and weaken and eventually kill the plants underneath the cardboard/newspaper. Invasive weeds will still sneak back in, so you'll need to proactively hand–pull them. Once the cardboard/newspaper has broken down in your sheet–mulched bed, grow vigorous plants that will outcompete weeds and feed your soil (pick a plant from the dynamic accumulators on page 221).

CHIP TIP

In an ideal world (if you have the space), it's best to age woodchips made from fresh, green wood in a separate pile for up to one year before using them in your garden or compost.

OPPOSITE:
Sheet mulching with a foundation layer of newspaper or cardboard topped with woodchips is a superb way to manage weeds without using herbicides.

LOGS AS GARDEN EDGES

One of the simplest approaches to using dead wood in your garden to build life is to make a border around your garden beds from horizontal branches or split logs. It's not a bad idea to dig these into the soil a little, to stop them from moving out of place due to foot traffic or mowing.

For a longer–lasting solution, you can edge your garden bed with a low wall made out of smaller logs or branches that have been cut to size. Position these side by side so they stand upright, and bury about half of the length of each log or branch into your soil. Over time, these edges will decompose, but that is the point! Nothing is ever fixed or finished in nature. This decomposing wood is building soil and storing carbon while also serving a purpose.

GREENS

Your neighbours will be green with envy when they see your flourishing plants after you've applied nitrogen–rich materials to your garden. From green–manure crops and grass clippings to garden weeds and seaweed, greens are the gift that keeps on giving.

GREEN–MANURE CROPS

Just like we wear a hat and sunscreen in summer, our soil needs protection, too. A fundamental principle of regenerative gardening is to never allow soil to lie fallow (or bare); instead, we should protect it with cover crops that act as a living mulch. When plants cover the soil, this stops it from degrading, drying out and disappearing – and soil microorganisms can thrive.

My favourite type of cover crop is green manure, which I grow after my main crop has been harvested. Green–manure crops are specifically grown to feed the soil, not you. If you never produce enough compost, leaf mould or worm castings for your patch, and you don't want to use commercial animal manure of questionable quality (it can be full of weed seeds or contaminated with persistent herbicides), then I highly recommend that you

grow a green–manure crop to add organic matter back into your soil. There are many benefits of using green–manure crops:

- Bare soil oxidises carbon and releases it into the atmosphere, whereas green–manure crops draw carbon dioxide from the atmosphere and sequester it, feeding the soil biology at the same time. What a win!
- There is a significant increase in mycorrhizal fungi activity in soil when green–manure crops have been grown. Fungi in your soil develop a relationship with the plant roots that allows these crops to take up available nutrients in return for sugars.
- These plants draw minerals up through the soil, making them more available to your next crop of edible plants.
- Green–manure crops protect soil from erosion, allow it to absorb and retain more water, and reduce nutrient leaching.
- The plants lower the temperature of the soil in summer and protect it from cold nights in winter.
- Acting as a living mulch, green–manure crops outcompete and suppress weeds

(they're actually more effective than dead mulch material, such as sugar-cane mulch or woodchips).

- Green-manure crops play an important role in integrated pest management.
- When green-manure crops are chopped and dropped onto the soil (see pages 220–1), they act as a soil food and improve soil structure (in all soil types, including clay and sand).

Follow these instructions to grow a green-manure crop:

1. Prepare the soil by hand-pulling weeds, then gently loosen the soil with a fork to increase drainage (rather than digging it over). Carbon is released into the atmosphere and mycorrhizal fungi are disturbed each time you dig or till your soil.
2. Scatter the seeds by hand. This helps to spread the green-manure seeds generously over the surface of your soil to maximise coverage.
3. Gently incorporate the seeds into the surface of the soil by using your hand to mix them in (if it's a larger area, then use a rake). You can also sprinkle a thin layer of cured compost over the top to cover the seeds. Make sure you push any bigger seeds (such as broad beans) into the soil.
4. Water the seeds well.
5. Once the seeds have germinated and you've got a lush carpet of green coverage, you have a few options:
   - Slash or mow the green-manure crop down to its base after six to eight weeks of growth to prevent flowering (otherwise it will start using the nutrients in the soil). Leave this plant material on the surface of the soil to decompose. Allow plants to reshoot, and then repeat the process.
   - Dig the green-manure crop through the soil to incorporate the organic matter (this isn't my favourite method, as digging releases soil carbon).
   - Slash the green-manure crop, and smother it with cardboard. Leave the bed covered for four to five weeks.

The biology in the soil will gobble up the plant material, and you'll be left with healthy soil for your next crop. You can either leave the cardboard in place and add compost on top to create a no dig garden, or pull back this layer and plant directly into the well-fed soil underneath.

SEED MIXES FOR GREEN-MANURE CROPS

You can get different seed mixes, depending on the season. Some of the best mixes include:

- legumes, broad beans and peas, which draw nitrogen from the atmosphere and return it to the soil
- rye, which can be used annually to help deter some problematic nematodes
- oat, which is a useful plant to use for clayey soils as it has fibrous roots that help to break up compaction
- vetch, which does a wonderful job of outcompeting weeds
- mustard, which helps to deter fungal pathogens and root-knot nematodes.

OPPOSITE:
Green-manure crops are food for the soil, so don't let them flower – otherwise nutrients will be drawn out of the soil to produce a crop.

GRASS CLIPPINGS

We need to eliminate the 'mow and blow' approach to gardening because continually mowing and disposing of grass clippings means that the nutrients are not being recycled. Over time, this results in the quality of the soil underneath your lawn becoming very poor. The simplest way to stop this from happening is to leave the clippings on your lawn as mulch. Grass is a hungry and thirsty plant, and mulching with the clippings themselves helps to feed it. You can also apply the clippings in thin layers as mulch around trees and shrubs.

Grass clippings are the quintessential compost ingredient, but you do need to proceed with caution. Fresh grass clippings pack a nitrogen punch and help to heat up your pile when composted correctly. However, if they're added in large amounts to your compost, they'll compact into an oxygen-free layer and quickly turn into smelly and anaerobic green slime.

Before composting grass clippings, premix them with a similar-sized carbon input (such as mowed brown leaves). Simply place whole leaves on your grass, and mow over them to cut them to size and mix them with the grass. You can then add the premixed grass to your compost in thin layers, and aerate to mix the grass with other organic matter. This will allow the grass to break down quickly without turning into a putrefied, stinky mess.

Turf the turf

Lawns are controversial: they're loved by some, and loathed by others. My attitude towards neatly manicured grass is that it no longer fits into gardens that are designed for climate resilience. Grass is resource intensive: it's just as hungry as it is thirsty, and it's a big petroleum consumer, too (due to the use of petrol-powered mowers to keep grass trimmed in summer; battery-powered mowers are better). Most frustratingly of all, it's monocultural and designed to keep biodiversity out of our gardens.

Whatever your stance on it, you can make your lawn far more sustainable by interplanting it with beneficial weeds. In particular, clover and dandelion are underrated ground covers. Here are some of their many benefits:

- **Clover is part of the legume family, so it's a nitrogen-fixing plant. It pulls nitrogen out of the air, converts it into a nutrient, and returns it to the soil.**

- Dandelion is a deep-rooted dynamic accumulator that draws nutrients up through the soil. (To learn more, turn to page 221.)
- When you interplant clover and dandelion with regular grass, they'll help to fertilise the grass. This means that you don't need inorganic fertilisers, which is a win for your wallet and the environment, too.
- Clover and dandelion are drought-tolerant plants once established, so they need far less water than regular grass to look lush.
- They produce flowers that bees and other pollinators love.
- As they grow vigorously, they can be planted in high foot-traffic areas and will outcompete weeds.
- Clover and dandelion are edible! Imagine how much food we could all be pumping out if we replaced lawns with these salad-ready ground covers.

OPPOSITE AND ABOVE:
Clover and dandelions are mowable, edible ground covers that aren't thirsty like traditional lawns. They'll stay lush and green, even during hot, dry summers.

WEEDS

Weeds might be uninvited guests in your garden, but they're not always bad news. This may seem crazy, but if I had to choose between a garden with bare earth and a weedy patch, I would always pick the garden with weeds because the soil underneath will be a lot more biologically active. There are three reasons for this:

1. Weed roots feed soil fungi, and some deep-rooted varieties help to draw up nutrients, adding fertility to the soil.
2. Weeds protect soil from erosion, water loss and heat stress by providing a living ground cover.
3. Flowering weeds attract beneficial insects (such as pollinators) to your patch.

My best piece of advice is to get rid of weeds before they produce seeds. If you stay on top of this, your soil won't become a seed bank, and you'll be able to say goodbye to weeds for good after a couple of seasons. Instead of binning weeds, thank them for their service and cycle their nutrients back into your soil by using one of these techniques:

- Smother them – If you want to take the path of least resistance, smother weeds where they're growing with thick layers of wet cardboard or newspaper. This is a quick method to kill vast swathes of weeds by stopping photosynthesis and allowing the soil food web to gobble up the remains. You may need to apply cardboard or newspaper – covered with woody mulch or compost (if you want to build a no dig bed) – more than once to get rid of highly invasive or pernicious weeds.
- Drown them – Weeds that have gone to seed, grow from root divisions or have invasive runners (such as kikuyu, couch or bindweed) are best kept out of your slow compost bins or piles. Add them to your steaming batch of hot compost, and the activity of the thermophilic microbes will stop any plant material or seeds from being viable. If you can't do death by 'fire', then do death by drowning and capture these

nutrients by brewing up some weed tea. This is a super-easy process, but it does take time and is really stinky, so keep this brew away from your neighbours. (To discover the recipe and method, turn to pages 238–9.)

- Cook them – If you don't have space for a hot compost, and you don't want to make weed tea, then your best option is harnessing the rays of the sun and solarising your weeds. This process effectively 'cooks' the weeds and their seeds. You can solarise weeds in situ by placing a tarpaulin or plastic sheet over garden beds and allowing the sun's rays to beat down on them. For urban gardeners, however, the best practice is small-scale solarising in tough black-plastic bags. Fill the bag with weeds and seeds, and leave this in the sun to cook for several weeks. Be prepared for a stinky, slimy mess when you're done, but this sludge will now be safe to add to your compost.

- Chop and drop them – Hand-pulling weeds before they've gone to seed and then laying them on the surface of your soil is an easy and effective way to return the nutrients to your soil. I only recommend doing this with weeds that don't grow from runners, nodes or root divisions. You can use this simple style of mulching with many other plant materials, too. To learn more about this style of mulching, read on.

Chop and drop

Every time we bring resources into our garden that are made elsewhere, waste is produced and emissions are released. Buying bagged mulch is costly for you and the planet. That's why growing your own mulch and applying it via the chop and drop method is such a win. Even if you can't grow enough plant material to use as coverage for your whole yard, it's worth growing at least some for the sake of your soil's health.

Chop and drop is a permaculture technique that is tied to a core practice of this form of agriculture: the idea of building self-sufficiency and resilience into our gardens by utilising renewable resources. Homegrown tender plant material (such as clippings, herbaceous leaves and weeds before they've gone to seed) is chopped and dropped directly onto the soil. Mulch that is made from fresh green plants is a rich source of nitrogen and other trace minerals. Plants are also covered in indigenous microorganisms that have adapted to the plants, your climate and your rainfall patterns, so it makes sense to keep these beneficial organisms in your own garden ecosystem.

How do you chop and drop? Cut off leaves and stems at the base of herbaceous plants, rather than pulling out the whole plant. (This allows for continual harvesting throughout the season.) Then place the plant matter directly on the surface of the soil. This technique works best with tender plant offcuts that have a bit of weight and substance to them, so they're not easily blown away. Comfrey is an ideal plant to use because the large leaves decompose rapidly and help to suppress weeds. A fast-growing plant, it can be chopped multiple times in the growing season and will reshoot.

Unlike traditional carbon-heavy mulches made from woodchips, chop and drop mulch can be applied to your vegie beds because the green plant material won't rob your soil of nitrogen as it decomposes.

I should flag something for the neat freaks out there: this style of mulching doesn't give you a consistent look. It's messy and free-form, much like forest floors, but in my experience the more that you add to it, the better it looks. Generating these resources onsite ticks so

many sustainable boxes and it's fantastic for your soil, so it's worth embracing the mess!

Dynamic accumulators

Deep-rooted plants (such as comfrey) are referred to as dynamic accumulators in permaculture. The theory is that these plants act like pumps, drawing up nutrients from deep within the soil and storing the nutrients in their leaves. When the plants naturally die back and decay, or when they're used in chop and drop mulching, added to compost or extracted into teas, the minerals become available to shallow-rooted plants.

The scientific world is still unconvinced about dynamic accumulators, and much of what has been written about them comes from 'soft data' rather than scientific studies. But many well-respected organic gardeners swear by them and attest to their usefulness, so I've chosen to include a variety of these plants in my own garden. From observing the changes in my backyard, I feel that they're part of a holistic approach to soil improvement. There's still a lot we don't know about the secrets of nature above and below ground, but what we do know is that these plants contribute to an ecologically rich garden.

Amaranth, borage, chickweed, comfrey, dandelion, sorrel and nettle are some of my favourite deep-rooted plants to tuck into food forests, plant along pathways (do be careful of nettle's stinging hairs!) or grow under fruit trees. This isn't a complete list of dynamic accumulators, but these ones are quick-growing herbaceous plants that will give you the biggest bang for your buck. Many are also medicinal or edible, and others produce beautiful flowers that are attractive to beneficial insects and pollinators.

Next, I'll dive deep into four of my favourite plants, two cultivated beauties (borage and comfrey) and two wild weeds (nettle and dandelion).

LOP AND DROP

For more robust and woody branches (such as those removed from fruit trees during their annual prune), you can use the lop and drop method to turn them into mulch. These branches must be cut into small pieces around 5–15 centimetres in length (the thicker they are, the shorter they need to be). This increases the surface area, so when the lopped branches are placed on the earth, the biology in the soil can easily consume them.

TOP LEFT:
Growing your own mulch to chop and drop saves you money, time and energy.

ABOVE:
Healthy soil is alive with plant roots that pump nutrients into the earth and feed soil biology.

OPPOSITE:
Comfrey is a great dynamic accumulator to chop and drop. A prolific grower, it can be cut back numerous times throughout the growing season.

Borage and comfrey

Almost everyone would agree that comfrey is king in permaculture gardens, but I think that borage comes a very close second. Both plants are in the Boraginaceae family and are kissing cousins, as they share a lot of similarities (and a couple of distinct differences).

Comfrey is a perennial plant, while borage is an annual; however, if you leave borage to flower and go to seed, it will readily return to your patch year after year. Comfrey spreads quickly and can be grown from root divisions. It's for this reason that it's sometimes considered a weed. To avoid this problem, grow the sterile form Bocking 14.

The leaves of both plants are rich in nitrogen, potassium and phosphorus because their deep roots mine these nutrients from the soil. To get the most from the masses of leaves and stems that these plants produce, cut them back regularly and use the plant matter for chop and drop mulch, turn them into teas or add them to your compost (comfrey is a particularly good activator).

It's best to cut back borage and comfrey just before they flower, as this will ensure that the leaves contain the greatest amounts of soil-enriching nutrients and minerals. This also stops them from spreading with wilful abandon. Personally, I like to let some flower because pollinators (such as bees and butterflies) flock to the nectar-rich blooms.

Comfrey and borage are dense plants that help to shade the soil and keep it cool. This shady understorey provides a home for beneficial predators (such as lacewings and parasitoid wasps), and these guys help to rein in unwanted pests in your patch.

Comfrey will die back in winter, but will return to its former glory year after year. It has a habit of spreading rapidly, especially from root divisions. It's therefore best to plant it as a companion for perennial crops (such as artichokes, rhubarb and asparagus) or as an understorey plant beneath fruit trees. This is because you won't be digging and disturbing the soil around these plants, as they don't have to be replanted annually. Comfrey can also be used as a barrier to keep invasive species (such as kikuyu) out of gardens. Being an annual, borage is a bit more versatile and can be planted with both your annual and perennial crops.

222

Nettle and dandelion

These wild weeds are the multivitamins of the plant world. This is because they're dynamic accumulators that are high in a broad spectrum of minerals and nutrients. You can take advantage of these often-overlooked weeds by using them in a number of regenerative gardening practices.

Nettle is a weed with bite, but I've learned to love it since moving to the far south coast of New South Wales. I never came across it when I was a city slicker, but down here it grows in abundance in moist soil that has not been disturbed (such as shady spots along creek banks).

On the other hand, dandelion thrives in disturbed soil. You'll often find the cheery yellow faces of the flowers popping up in areas where there's a lot of human activity (such as lawns, rural sites, roadsides and newly created garden beds). It's worth embracing rather than eradicating them because they're one of the first plants to flower in spring, and they provide an early source of pollen and nectar for pollinators.

I won't focus on the edible and medical uses of nettle and dandelion (there are many); instead, I'll hone in on their uses as soil food. Nettle and dandelion contain high amounts of calcium, magnesium, phosphorus and potassium. They can be made into a:

- chop and drop mulch
- green-manure crop (before they've gone to seed)
- nutrient-packed tea (see pages 238–9)
- shelf-stable fermented plant juice that's a valuable mineral amendment.

ABOVE:
Softly, softly stroke a nettle, and it stings you for your pains. Grasp it like you're made of metal, and soft as silk it remains.

OPPOSITE:
Borage blooms are irresistible to bees and other pollinators. The plant readily reseeds, so you may wish to cut it back before it flowers.

FERMENTED PLANT JUICE

I've adapted this Korean Natural Farming technique from Nigel Palmer's *The Regenerative Grower's Guide to Garden Amendments*. This fermented juice is not only rich in minerals and nutrients, but also full of enzymes and proteins, in plant–available forms. You can use the diluted solution as a soil drench to feed plant roots and soil biology several times each growing season. You can also use it as a foliar spray on leaves and bark. Fermented plant juice also helps to stimulate germination. So, soak your seeds in the diluted solution for several minutes before planting them out.

This juice is powerful stuff; a little goes a long way. It must be diluted to a ratio of 1:1000 (weaker application for a foliar spray) or 1:500 (stronger application for a soil drench). This is 1 tablespoon of fermented plant juice mixed with 20 litres of water, or 2 tablespoons at a 1:500 ratio. It's important to use dechlorinated water to dilute it, so rainwater or tank water is best.

INGREDIENTS
The ingredients can be upsized or downsized, as long as the 1:1 ratio remains.
* 225 grams of mineral–rich weeds (such as nettle or dandelion); you can use just the leaves, but if you're using the whole plant, then remove the roots and soil, and make sure to chop it thoroughly
* 225 grams of organic brown sugar

EQUIPMENT
* scale
* sharp knife
* washing–up gloves
* large bowl
* sterilised metal spoon
* 2–litre crock or glass jar
* fermenting weight, rock or glass of water
* clean cloth
* kitchen string
* sieve
* funnel
* 1–litre lidded glass jar

METHOD
1. Head out in the early morning to forage for weeds. Nettle and dandelion leaves and stems still wet with dew before the sun comes up have the most energy in them. This is not a hippy dippy belief, but fact–based science related to photosynthesis and transpiration.
2. This plant matter is covered with indigenous microorganisms, lactic acid bacteria and yeasts. You want to capture these within your fermented plant juice, so don't harvest after rain or wash the plants before use.
3. Weigh the leaves and stems, chop them roughly (wearing washing–up gloves if handling stinging nettle), and place them into a large bowl. Sprinkle three–quarters of the sugar over the plant matter, and mix thoroughly with a sterilised metal spoon.
4. Place the mixture into your crock or glass jar, and cover it with the remaining quarter of the sugar. Pop your choice of weight on top. This weight helps to initiate fermentation by pressing the sugar and plant matter together and releasing the liquid.
5. Cover the opening of the crock or glass jar with the clean cloth tied with kitchen string, and store out of direct sunlight in a dry and well–ventilated position. It's important that the container stays at around 20 degrees Celsius; if it gets colder than this, then the process will slow down significantly.
6. You can remove the weight when enough liquid has formed so that all of the plant matter is fully submerged. This may take a day or so. The fermentation is now considered active. Allow it to process for several days, and regularly check that all leaves and stems remain submerged. You may need to use a sterilised metal spoon to push escaping leaves back under the liquid.

7. After a week, the fermentation is complete. It should smell funky but not off-putting. Use the sieve and funnel to strain the fermented plant juice into the second, lidded glass jar.

8. If foam appears on top of the fermented liquid after extraction, add a small amount of sugar to eliminate it.

9. Store the fermented plant juice out of direct sunlight in a well-ventilated area with a consistent temperature of 20 degrees Celsius or cooler. If stored correctly, this liquid will be shelf-stable until it's all used up.

SEAWEED

I have fond childhood memories of time spent by the ocean playing with seaweed. My older sister and I would pretend to be mermaids, and we'd 'bedazzle' ourselves with seaweed 'strings of pearls' and kelp wigs. I'm still addicted to it, but for very different reasons. Seaweed is supercharged stuff, but its magic seems to be amplified when it's applied fresh or as a nutrient–rich extract to garden soil.

Whichever way you use it – as mulch, as a compost addition or as tea – seaweed is a hardworking soil conditioner, rich in many nutrients that are vital for plant health. When it breaks down in the soil or compost, it creates a nutrient smorgasbord that attracts all sorts of microbiology, which in turn convert the nutrients into forms that plants can use. In particular, it stimulates root growth and chlorophyll production.

It's a valuable supplement in organic gardening, as the mineral content of seaweed is ten times that of land plants, and it contains a combination of substances not commonly found in plants grown in soil. It's jam–packed full of stuff your plants need – no wonder it's tempting to buy bottles of seaweed extract at a premium price. But you can avoid the plastic packaging by sustainably foraging for seaweed at a beach near you – for free!

You should only collect seaweed that has washed up on the beach, rather than cutting it off from wherever it's growing. There are beaches where seaweed can be legally collected, and others where you aren't allowed to collect any beach–cast seaweed at all, so always have a look at local regulations in your area.

Seaweed makes a great mulch for your garden, although it does break down faster than conventional mulches (such as woodchips or straw) because it's a juicy green not a fibrous brown. But long–term coverage is not the point: it's free, it's food for the soil, and it does the job of a mulch and a pest deterrent.

Unlike many straw mulches, seaweed won't be contaminated by weed seeds or aminopyralid herbicides (see page 198), and it's a natural slug and snail deterrent because they don't like the salt. You don't need to worry about washing it

in fresh water before you use it because seawater itself is a mineral source when used in moderation and contains a lot of the macro and trace minerals needed in the garden.

A WORD OF WARNING

Seaweed denatures when it's out of water, and it soon turns into funky sludge. Apply it to your garden on the day you collect it (or the day after), otherwise you'll have to deal with a stinky bag of slime. This slime isn't really a concern, but it does take some getting used to if you're more accustomed to neat and tidy mulches (such as pea straw or lucerne [alfalfa]). Worms and springtails adore this nitrogen–rich gloop and will quickly feast on it. But it's worth being mindful of the thickness of your seaweed mulch layer – if it's applied too thick (more than 3 centimetres), it may become anaerobic, super stinky and attractive to flies.

WHITES, GREY AND BLACK

Your soil needs to be fed more than just nitrogen–rich materials (the greens) and carbon–rich organic matter (the browns) to fulfil your plants' broad nutritional and mineral needs. That's where the whites (eggshells, bones and seashells), grey (rock minerals) and black (biochar) come into play.

Eggshells are high in calcium carbonate, and bones are rich in phosphorus and calcium. Biochar is a source of stable, long–lasting carbon (unlike the unstable carbon in woody materials), and rock dust is jam–packed with minerals that your soil needs. So, instead of buying plastic–packaged commercial fertilisers from non–renewable sources, use the regenerative techniques I outline below to capture fertility from these often–overlooked everyday items.

THE WHITES

Heavy–feeding crops growing in pots or your patch (such as tomatoes, eggplants and capsicums) need plenty of calcium to produce a healthy harvest without blossom–end rot, as do leafy vegies (such as spinach, chard and broccoli). You can compost your eggshells, which will provide trace amounts of this micronutrient to your plants, or crush them and use the grit in worm farms to help balance the pH (see page 137). However, to obtain the most plant–available calcium from eggshells, it's best to extract it using vinegar.

Eggshell extraction

I've adapted this Korean Natural Farming recipe and method from Nigel Palmer's book, *The Regenerative Grower's Guide to Garden Amendments*. This simple garden supplement is super potent, so it needs to be diluted in a ratio of 1:500 – which is the equivalent of 1 tablespoon to 10 litres of water – when used as a soil drench

(or 1:1000 when used as a foliar spray). Once diluted, it can be used as part of your regular fertilising routine. It actually works best when used in conjunction with other homemade fermented products (such as fermented plant juice; see pages 224–5). The supplement is shelf-stable, so it can be kept for years and used at the beginning of each growing season.

You'll need these materials and equipment:

- eggshells
- oven or wood-fired stove
- mortar and pestle, or tea towel and rolling pin
- glass jar with lid
- vinegar (either homemade apple cider or scrap vinegar, or shop-bought white vinegar)
- muslin or cotton cloth
- strainer.

Follow these instructions to perform the eggshell extraction:

1. Remove water and other contaminants from the eggshells by cooking them in an oven on low (150 degrees Celsius) for 10–20 minutes (monitor them, as they can quickly burn). You can also place them on a tray in a wood-fired stove overnight when there are only embers left.
2. Roughly crush the dried eggshells, either with a mortar and pestle or in a tea towel bashed with a rolling pin.
3. Fill 10–15 per cent of the glass jar with eggshells, and top up with vinegar. Leave space at the top (around 2.5 centimetres) because this brew will fizz and bubble.
4. Loosely place a piece of muslin or cotton cloth over the jar to allow gases to escape.
5. Leave the jar for a week or two in your pantry (away from direct sunlight), strain the extraction, and compost the remains.
6. Return the liquid to the jar, and close the lid. Store in a cool, dark pantry.

Bonemeal and shell meal

All plants need phosphorus for photosynthesis. So, let's stop disposing of our leftover mineral-rich bones and shells from oysters, mussels, clams or eggs, and instead mine their goodness by drying them out and grinding them down. This allows the phosphorus (and calcium) to be more available for plants.

This is how I make ground bonemeal and shell meal at my place:

1. I add my bones with remaining meat or sinew to my Bokashi bin to ferment them, then I compost the bones.
2. Once the compost is cured, I fish out the well-picked-over bones and dry them out in an oven set to low (150 degrees Celsius) for an hour. A word of warning – this process is quite smelly, so keep your windows open while the bones are cooking. If using shells, I skip the composting part and simply cook them fresh in an oven set to low (150 degrees Celsius) for 20 minutes.
3. Using a mortar and pestle, I grind the bones and shells into a fine powder. I sprinkle it around my hungry plants, pop it into my compost, use it as grit for my worm farms and feed it to my chickens.

THE GREY

I think that a lot of kids go through a rock- or crystal-collecting phase. I certainly did. In the 1990s, I would save up my hard-earned pocket money to spend on a hypercolour T-shirt or multicoloured gemstones. My T-shirt may have lost its glow, but my rainbow gemstones are now being enjoyed by my kids. Today, as an organic gardener, I'm still fascinated with rocks, but now I'm interested in how they can improve soil health and stimulate microbial activity in compost.

There is certainly a buzz around rock dusts and rock minerals (made from a mix of rock dusts – including basalt, gypsum, lignite and rock phosphate – that are 'prilled' to form pellets and inoculated with microbes). Lots of companies are selling them, and their pitch is that rock dusts (combined with microbes) will add plant-accessible minerals to the soil. This is not a new idea. Over 100 years ago, German agricultural chemist Julius Hensel wrote a book called *Bread from Stones*, in which he theorised that a lot of the nutrients required by food plants can be found in volcanic rock dust.

This idea is now being championed by large mining companies, including Boral in Australia. It's no wonder, really, because rock dusts are by-products of their mining activity, so they're creating a market for something that would otherwise be wasted. I do want to note that the sustainability of rock dusts is questionable, as they're mined from the earth. That said, if we can return these minerals to the earth in order to help remineralise our soils, then I think that this is a good thing.

The following points are certainly true:

1. Our soil – especially intensively farmed land – is often depleted of minerals, so much of the food we eat is lower in nutritional value today than it was a century ago.
2. Rock dusts are full of minerals (such as magnesium, sulphur, calcium, manganese and zinc).

There are claims that trials have shown that rock minerals improve 'soil pH, water retention capacity, microbial activity, root-to-shoot ratio, plant health generally, seed germination rates, and the humus complex, while [increasing] plant height and weight and [reducing] plant mortality'. But there are also papers that have concluded, from trials, that rock minerals are probably inert and have no demonstrable effect on the soil.

The knockers say that while rock dusts contain loads of minerals, they're not in a form that can be easily and quickly accessed by plants. Others are more positive about the potential for nutrients to be made available to plants when rock dusts are combined with the biology present in compost.

Like many things, the science is not entirely clear, but I certainly understand where both sides are coming from. My personal attitude is that at a macro level, it would probably help the soil to have minerals returned to it, and so I'll add rock minerals to my compost if I have them on hand. I think that the little girl in me who loved rocks and crystals wants to believe that they help.

Using rock dusts and minerals

Here are three considerations before you start using rock dusts and minerals on your patch:

1. It's important to test the pH of your soil (see pages 194–5) before using rock minerals in your garden. Don't use them on alkaline soils, as they will raise the pH.
2. Make sure you wear a mask when spreading dry rock dusts and minerals. The particles can become airborne, and this can be a dangerous lung irritant. Rock dusts and minerals are safe to handle once they're moist and settled in your compost or on your soil.
3. Not all rock dusts have the same mineral content and properties as the excellent volcanic rock basalt. When buying it from landscaping suppliers, make sure you check the type of rock from which the dust has been made.

Rock dusts and minerals can be used:

*   in compost to add minerals and increase biological activity
*   as slow–release trace–mineral amendments to build soil fertility
*   as long–lasting inorganic surface mulches on garden paths
*   in clayey soil to help open it up and aerate it
*   to improve soil drainage and help to prevent waterlogging
*   as natural soil amendments to increase the pH of acidic soils (they're quite alkaline, with a pH of 9).

To apply rock dusts and minerals to your compost, add up to 6 per cent rock dusts/minerals relative to the volume of green and brown inputs (this is around three handfuls per 400 litres of other organic materials). Keep the rock minerals moist, so the microbes will thrive. When the compost is fully decomposed and cured, add it to your garden.

THE BLACK

Supercharge leftover organic matter that's not going to rapidly decompose in your soil (such as bones from meat and fish; mussel, abalone, clam and oyster shells; woody prunings; or even the hard outer shells of nuts) by transforming it into biochar. An extremely stable form of carbon, biochar is magical stuff. It offers wide–ranging benefits to soil and plant health.

Biochar is formed when organic matter is burned at a high temperature in a low–oxygen environment, in a process called pyrolysis. This transforms the organic matter into a carbon–rich 'skeleton' with an open pore structure. If you looked at a cross–section of biochar under a microscope, you'd see something that looks like honeycomb – lots of tiny holes (micropores) packed tightly together, with bigger holes (macropores) interspersed throughout. This structure is highly porous and acts like a sponge, sucking up nutrients, water and microbes.

Think of the many holes in biochar as empty high–rise apartments, and microbes as the soon–to–be residents. Biochar only becomes a potent garden amendment when the pores are filled or 'charged' with nitrogen, which is a food source for our microbial mates. This can be done by creating a 50:50 mix of well–cured compost (or worm castings) and biochar, and leaving it for around two weeks to allow the new microbial tenants to move in. Alternatively, you can soak the biochar in tea made from compost or worm castings – or even in fresh urine – for a minimum of three days to fill the pores with nitrogen and microbes. Once activated and added to soil, biochar holds a stockpile of nutrients that can be provided to plants when needed.

Benefits of biochar

There is a long and rich history of biochar being used as a soil amendment. One of the most fertile soils in the world – called *terra preta* – comes from the Amazon basin and was enriched with biochar over 2000 years ago. To this day, it's more fertile than the surrounding soil that was not amended by humans.

Biochar complements compost in your garden, as the carbon from these two sources performs differently. Carbon from plant materials in your compost is unstable, as it continues to decompose in the soil. The carbon in biochar stubbornly resists degradation and can remain intact in soil for hundreds of years. Once activated and added to your soil, the stable carbon in biochar helps by improving:

* fertility
* nutrient retention
* aeration and soil structure
* moisture retention
* soil carbon (for healthier plants) and carbon sequestration (helps fight climate change by capturing carbon in soil and preventing it from being released into the atmosphere).

How do you make biochar?

Making biochar is simple once you've sorted out the required equipment – you'll need access to fire and a kiln or hole in the ground to hold the organic matter. If you're worried about burning carbon to make biochar, then you can take heart from the fact that biochar is considered a negative emissions technology because it can store carbon away from the atmosphere for centuries.

The easiest way to make biochar – if you have the space – is in a pit dug into the ground. Position your biochar pit away from overhanging branches or shrubs, and only do this on a day without wind. You may need a permit to light a fire in your area, and check for any existing fire bans. Make sure you have a water source nearby in case things go awry, and to extinguish the fire at the end of the process. Here's the equipment you'll need:

* shovel
* matches or lighter
* organic matter of your choice (this must include a mix of dried wood waste, which will be used as fuel for the fire, and can also include shells and bones)
* water
* hessian sack or chicken–feed bag
* hammer or mallet.

~~~~~~~~~~~~~~~~~~~~~~~~~~~~~~~~~~~

RIGHT:
I remove chunky bits and bobs (such as bones, corncobs, avocado stones, mango seeds and oyster shells) from my cured compost and turn them into biochar to feed my soil.

Follow these instructions to make the biochar:

1. Dig a hole with a diameter of around 1 metre. It needs to taper to a point once it reaches a depth of around 1 metre, so the hole is cone-shaped. This helps to create a low-oxygen environment, so you end up with layers of biochar rather than ash.
2. Build a fire in the bottom of the pit, and slowly add dried branches to the fire. Place the woody materials evenly over the surface of the fire, so that branches cover larger gaps. This helps to keep oxygen at a low level and prevents full combustion of the materials.
3. You can add bones, shells and other organic matter at this point, too, along with the wood to fuel the fire.
4. This is a slow process, so be patient – it can take several hours, depending on how much organic matter you're turning into biochar. You can gauge the speed required when adding more organic matter to the fire by the amount of smoke or ash being produced – if smoke is billowing, then you're adding organic matter too quickly; if you see ash forming at the bottom of the pit, then you're not adding new material quickly enough.
5. When you no longer have material to add, and everything has caught alight, extinguish the flames with plenty of water.
6. Leave overnight. Once the biochar has fully cooled, but is still moist, crush and grind it into a powder. Do this by placing the biochar into a sack or bag, and smashing it with a hammer or mallet.

You need to 'charge' the biochar by mixing it in a container with an equal volume of worm castings or cured compost, or soaking it in compost/casting tea, fresh urine or seaweed or fish solution. Leave it for a minimum of three days to activate, then apply the activated biochar to your soil as a surface mulch or add it to planting holes.

Alternatively, you can add biochar as a compost ingredient when building a pile or filling a bin. It facilitates faster decomposition and enhances bacterial life in your pile. The ideal application rate of biochar is 5–20 per cent of the volume of the other carbon and nitrogen inputs in your compost.

IS CHARCOAL THE SAME AS BIOCHAR?

Biochar and charcoal look similar and have some shared properties: both are alkaline and hydrophobic when taken straight from the fire. But charcoal can't be used in the same way as biochar in your garden because its structure is quite different. The process of pyrolysis results in biochar having significantly more surface area than charcoal, allowing it to be a lot more absorptive. Also, regular charcoal decomposes at a much faster rate than biochar when added to soil. Another important difference is that biochar generally has a lower pH. Depending on the feedstock used and the temperature range of the production, biochar can have a pH between 4.6 and 9.3; charcoal's pH is higher, sitting at 9 to 11.

PINT-SIZED POWER

Biochar doesn't need to be made on a large scale. I make small batches in a mini biochar kiln that fits into our wood-fired stove. This kiln works a treat to transform bones, large fruit stones and corn husks into biochar. Pyrolysis (see page 230) only takes two hours. When the biochar has cooled down, I crush it up using a mortar and pestle, then charge it by mixing it with cured compost or worm castings, or soaking it in urine.

TEAS

It's likely that at some point your demand for compost will exceed your supply. Healthy garden ecosystems quickly gobble up the organic matter in compost, worm castings, processed Bokashi material, leaf mould, and more. So, a convenient way to spread the love further is by brewing up teas.

All organic matter, both living and dead, is heaving with local microscopic life forms. As gardeners, we can capture and extend the application of this biology by making potent living soil conditioners and foliar sprays from water extractions. Using teas on your edible and ornamental garden beds helps to distribute beneficial biology over the entire surface of your plants. This is an important string to your bow as an organic gardener because these microscopic minibeasts will help to protect your plants from attacks by pests and diseases.

When it comes to teas, there are two different types: actively aerated teas, and slow brews with no introduced oxygen. In the past, many gardeners have used compost, worm castings and manure to make oxygen–free slow brews, but after seeing the evidence from the most up–to–date research, I personally recommend that you don't do this. Anaerobic bacteria can take over these solutions, and the resulting tea can be damaging to plants and your soil.

If you're still interested in slow brews, I've included recipes on pages 238–43 that employ a lengthy maturation period – this helps to overcome the stinky anaerobic period and transforms plant material into a valuable soil amendment. Read on to find a detailed explanation of both tea types, their benefits and recipes, so you can decide what will work best for your garden.

ACTIVELY AERATED TEAS

Make your compost and worm castings work harder – and spread a lot further – by brewing them into microbially rich aerated teas. Rather than fertilisers, think of these as biological

supplements for your soil that are quickly absorbed by plant roots.

Dr Elaine Ingham, a world-renowned microbiologist and soil-biology researcher, recommends brewing compost extract (see below) in a short and sharp fashion. To do this, you'll need to use an air pump that pushes enough oxygen into the dechlorinated water to create a soft, rolling 'boil'. The forceful turbulence created by the water pressure (around 80 psi) will dislodge the microorganisms from the parent material (compost or castings) into the water in around 30 minutes.

You can use this compost extract immediately on your garden by diluting it at a minimum of 50:50 (or more) with dechlorinated water. Or you can transform this extract into an actively aerated compost tea by feeding the microbes that are now floating around in the water to encourage particular strains to reproduce. Using targeted food sources (such as liquid kelp and fish hydrolysate/emulsion) allows the microbiology in your tea to be customised to match the needs of your garden.

Once you've added these delectable delicacies to the water, ideally it should be kept at around 20 degrees Celsius for 24 hours (18 hours if the overnight temperature exceeds 20 degrees Celsius, and 48 hours in winter), with the air pump still going to allow microbes time to feast and multiply before you apply the tea to your garden. Your actively aerated compost tea should be diluted one part tea to four parts dechlorinated water (at a minimum), and can be used as a foliar spray or soil drench to provide biology from the roots to the tips of your plant babies.

The biggest benefit of actively aerated compost tea is that the highly oxygenated process captures the aerobic life forms (depending on the quality of your compost) and stops anaerobic bacteria proliferating. To put this more simply, your aerated tea shouldn't stink, and you'll be able to make the finished brew quickly.

The aerated tea recipes on pages 235-6 have been adapted from those by the Soil Foodweb Institute, and they use a tea brewer. There are lots of different permutations of this set-up, but in basic terms it involves placing an air pump (also known as an aquarium blower) into a food-grade barrel, bin or bucket that has a compost tea bag (a 450-micron tea bag or elastic-top paint strainer) suspended inside so that it doesn't touch the bottom (to help prevent anaerobic areas from forming).

Dr Ingham recommends using a 90-watt air pump. Don't use an aquarium air stone, as these can be hard to clean and can build up a colony of anaerobes that can contaminate your next batch of tea. Speaking of cleaning, once you've made your tea or extract, you'll need to thoroughly clean the brewing container with detergent. Soak your tea bag in water with a dash of bleach for an hour, then rinse and sun-dry before using it again.

Due to the equipment involved, I suggest that you only try to make actively aerated compost teas if you want to take your organic gardening practices to the next level.

Compost extract

This is the easiest way to stretch your compost. Simply place 200 grams of well-cured compost or worm castings (or a 50:50 mix of both) into a clean compost tea bag, and suspend it in 20 litres of dechlorinated water. Have an air pump blowing enough oxygen into your container so that the surface of the water looks like it's boiling.

After 30 minutes, your extract is ready to be diluted with dechlorinated water (at a minimum ratio of 50:50, but you can go a lot weaker to spread it further) and applied to your garden. This extract is lower in microbiology than actively aerated compost teas, but is still very effective.

A CONVENIENT WAY TO SPREAD THE LOVE FURTHER IS BY BREWING UP TEAS.

A trio of targeted teas

These three recipes will increase beneficial bacteria and fungi in your patch. All include an ingredient called fish hydrolysate, which is full of fish oils that fungi adore. Make sure you check that your fish hydrolysate has been produced using enzymes rather than heat, otherwise it won't work. If you struggle to track it down, you can replace it with a good–quality organic fish emulsion.

Each of these recipes makes about 20 litres of potent tea. This can be diluted and used to cover up to 4000 square metres of soil, but can also be used on much smaller gardens, as you can't really apply too much. All three teas need to be brewed for 24–30 hours and used on your garden within four hours of the pump being switched off, otherwise anaerobes will start to multiply as the oxygen level drops. Reduce the brew time to 18 hours if the overnight temperature is above 20 degrees Celsius.

- The 'all–rounder' tea – This recipe will make a balanced fungal and bacterial brew that can be used throughout your yard on ornamental shrubs, edible plants and even your lawn. Here's what you'll need:
    - 20 litres of dechlorinated water
    - 80 millilitres of fish hydrolysate
    - 40 millilitres of liquid kelp
    - 200 grams of compost or worm castings (in a compost tea bag)
    - 1 cup of homemade humic acid (see page 239).

- The 'pumping produce' tea – This bacterially rich tea is the ideal regenerative amendment for your vegie patch, as most vegetables (especially brassicas) love bacterially dominant soil. Check the tea's aroma while it's brewing because the blackstrap molasses can also feed anaerobic bacteria. If you're brewing up some baddies, then the tea will start to stink. Here's what you'll need:
    - 20 litres of dechlorinated water
    - 30 millilitres of fish hydrolysate
    - 60 millilitres of liquid kelp
    - 10 millilitres of blackstrap molasses
    - 200 grams of compost or worm castings (in a compost tea bag).

- The 'orchard' tea – Three days before you plan to brew up this fungal tea, place the compost or worm castings in a cardboard box (this will soak up excess moisture and help to keep the compost/castings aerobic). Mix the 10 millilitres of fish hydrolysate with the 20 millilitres of dechlorinated water, and sprinkle this over the compost/castings. Fungal spores should develop within three days (there'll be a distinctive fuzz over the surface; if no fuzz grows, then this is a sign that your compost is low in fungi and needs to cure for a longer time). Once the fuzz has developed, the fungi–activated compost/castings can be placed into a compost tea bag and brewed with the remaining ingredients and water. Here's what you'll need:
    - 200 grams of compost or worm castings (in a compost tea bag)
    - 10 millilitres of fish hydrolysate
    - 20 millilitres of dechlorinated water
    - 80 millilitres of fish hydrolysate
    - 40 millilitres of liquid kelp
    - 1 cup of homemade humic acid (see page 239)
    - 20 litres of dechlorinated water.

BE WISE WITH YOUR WATER

All recipes for aerated teas and slow brews must be made with dechlorinated water. Town water has chlorine added to kill parasites, bacteria and viruses, but unfortunately it also kills the beneficial biology that you want to breed in your teas. Thankfully, you can dechlorinate your water in several ways:

- Fill up your brewing container with town water, and leave it uncovered for 24 hours. The chlorine will off-gas into the atmosphere.

- Fill up your brewing container with town water, add your air pump, and set it to high. Within six to eight hours, most of the chlorine will have disappeared.

- Add a water-filtering unit to your hose, and this will extract most of the chlorine.

Remember, with all of these recipes, the quality of your compost and worm castings will determine the quality of your finished tea. To use the tea, dilute it with rainwater or dechlorinated water at a minimum ratio of 1:4. If applying the tea to very young and tender seedlings, then make it more diluted. You can use the diluted tea on your ornamental and edible plants as well as your potted plants.

SLOW BREWS

If you want to make teas without investing in specialised equipment and are happy to patiently wait for the finished product, then a slow brew might be the right choice for you. Simply place the parent material (seaweed, weeds, leaf mould) into a bucket or barrel filled with dechlorinated water, and wait. Microbes clinging to the parent material become suspended in the water and digest the organic matter, moving the mineral content into the water. Over time, these soupy solutions transform into broad–spectrum mineral and biological amendments for your soil.

Please be aware that slow–brewed seaweed and weed tea will stink, so be mindful of where you're storing these witchy garden potions. The stench is produced when anaerobic bacteria take over the water extraction. If you use these teas when they're super stinky, then the phototoxic chemicals produced by the anaerobes can stunt or kill plants.

What you must do when making a slow brew is to leave the tea for a couple of months to ensure that all food sources have run out and the anaerobic bacteria have stopped reproducing. At this point, oxygen will naturally move back into the tea and help to wake up the dormant aerobic microbes. These beneficial bacteria will start to multiply by growing on the waste that the anaerobes produced. You'll know that this has happened when your tea is no longer 'peg on the nose' stinky, but rather just a little 'funky'. At this point, you can use the tea on your garden.

Seaweed and weed tea

Seaweed and weeds can be made into mineral–rich teas that can be stored for use throughout the year. Homemade seaweed tea helps plants to become more resilient to temperature extremes (heatwaves and frosts); it helps to prevent transplant shock; it works as an antifungal against powdery mildew; and it's a great first liquid feed for seedlings. Broad–spectrum weed tea made from a mix of different plants and weeds is useful for most hardworking soils in your vegie patch.

Brewing these teas is simple – it's just a matter of steeping the ingredients in water – however, it does take several months for the process to be complete. I've adapted the recipe from Kirsten Bradley and Nick Ritar's *Milkwood* and Nigel Palmer's *The Regenerative Grower's Guide to Garden Amendments*.

INGREDIENTS
* fresh or dried seaweed, or freshly foraged weeds (roots and all) plus a mix of borage, comfrey, dandelion and nettle leaves
* dechlorinated water
* a couple of handfuls of leaf mould (optional extra)

EQUIPMENT
* lidded bucket or barrel (it doesn't matter what size, but the bigger the better)
* clean piece of cloth
* string

METHOD
1. Fill three–quarters of your bucket/barrel with seaweed or weeds/plants.
2. Top up the bucket/barrel with dechlorinated water (rainwater is best), making sure the plant material is completely covered. As a general rule, you need about 15 litres of water for every 1 kilogram of greenery.
3. Cover the bucket/barrel with the clean cloth, and tie it on with string to keep vinegar flies out. Pop the lid on top of this lightly (not tightly) because you want your brew to breathe. Leave it alone for two to three months.
4. Initially the tea is populated with aerobic bacteria, but as the decomposition of the plant matter continues, it will become anaerobic – and stinky! To combat this, add a generous handful or two of well–made leaf mould to the mix. (To find out how to make leaf mould, turn to pages 202–3.) Leaf mould is jam–packed with beneficial bacteria, fungi and other life forms, and their presence in your brew helps to reduce odours (it will still smell, but not quite as pungently).
5. After a few months, another aerobic stage will start as more beneficial bacteria move in. You'll know that this has happened when the stench changes and your brew starts to smell tolerable again. This process will occur more rapidly in summer than in winter. You may notice bacterial and fungal white blooms on the surface of the tea. This is normal and shows that an active extraction is occurring. The process is still working even if this doesn't occur.
6. Once the tea has brewed for a few months, most of the plant material will have broken down entirely, but there'll be some sludge left. This sludge is full of nutrients and beneficial bacteria but is quite strong, so instead of applying it directly to your soil, add it to your compost to give your pile a boost.

Brew this tea in a shady spot in your yard, shed or garage. It's important that the container is positioned out of direct sun (and not near your neighbours, as it will smell bad for a while). If you plan on storing this tea long–term, choose a spot that will remain above freezing during winter and in the shade in summer.

Once the tea is ready, use it as a soil drench, add it to your compost pile as a bacterial activator, or use it as a foliar spray on leaf surfaces. The longer you leave the tea to brew, the more mineral content will be transferred into the water from the plant matter, so follow these rules of thumb:

* When the tea has reached maturity, you can dilute it to a ratio of 1:10 and use it once or twice a month, or go weaker (1:30)

if you want to apply it to your plants every week (a good way to remember this is 'weakly, weekly').

- I use this liquid on any plant that needs a feed during its active growing season; once a week for hungry plants (such as chillies, tomatoes, eggplants or cucumbers) and fruit–bearing trees once the flowers appear; and every two weeks for crops in pots.

HOW TO MAKE HUMIC ACID

Take 1 cup of well–cured compost, place it in a piece of cheesecloth, and tie it off so it becomes a tea bag. Then run dechlorinated water over the tea bag without agitating or squeezing it (this passive water movement will release water–soluble humic acid), and collect the liquid in a bowl (this liquid should be a very pale golden–brown colour). Simply scoop out 1 cup of this liquid, and add to your tea brewer.

Leaf mould tea

Leaf mould is rich in fungi, mycelia and microbes. You can harness this biology by brewing it into a tea that offers many benefits:

- When applied as a foliar spray, it helps plants to resist pests and diseases.
- Used as a soil drench, it helps to build soil ecology.
- The fungi and bacteria present will improve soil structure and make nutrients and minerals more available to plants.
- When applied to compost, it will increase microbial activity.
- Spray it on leaf mould piles to speed up decomposition.
- Apply it to hydrophobic mulch, as the tea biology will digest the carbon and allow the mulch to absorb water.

This Korean Natural Farming recipe has been adapted from Nigel Palmer's *The Regenerative Grower's Guide to Garden Amendments* and Youngsang Cho's *JADAM Organic Farming*. Before making the tea, position the brewing bucket near where the tea will be applied.

INGREDIENTS
- 1 medium potato (the starch provides a food source for the microbes)
- 2 handfuls of leaf mould (to make leaf mould, turn to pages 202–3)
- 20 litres of dechlorinated water
- 1 tablespoon of sea salt (this small amount of salt adds trace minerals to the tea and will not cause issues associated with excessive salinity)

EQUIPMENT
- small rocks (heavy enough to keep the tea bag submerged in the water)
- large cotton sock, piece of muslin or paint strainer to make a tea bag
- two pieces of twine
- lidded bucket (that holds at least 20 litres of water)
- peg

METHOD
1. Boil the whole potato until it's soft. Allow it to cool.
2. Place the cooled potato, two handfuls of leaf mould and the rocks into the tea bag, and secure the top with twine.
3. Fill the bucket with 20 litres of dechlorinated water (rainwater is best).
4. Add the sea salt to the water, and mix to dissolve the salt.
5. Add your leaf mould tea bag to the water, and spend a few minutes squeezing it to release the starch and biology. When this is done, the water should be the colour of weak tea.
6. Tie a piece of twine around the top of the bucket and then from one side to the other (like a clothesline), and peg your tea bag in place so it hangs in the water. (You don't want it to sit on the bottom because this will create anaerobic areas.)
7. Place the lid loosely on the bucket – don't seal it firmly shut, as you need air to flow.
8. Leave for two to five days or until foam appears on the surface of the water. When the weather is hot, this will happen quickly; it will take longer in cold weather.
9. Remove the tea bag (rinse and sun-dry it before storing it, ready for your next brew).
10. Dilute the leaf mould tea with dechlorinated water in a ratio of 1:50. This amendment doesn't get better with age, so use it all within a few days.

Lactic acid bacteria brew

Rice and milk are staple foods in many homes around the world, and they can be used to make a bacteria–rich brew for your garden. 'Lactic acid bacteria' refers to a large assortment of bacteria that produce lactic acid when they ferment carbohydrates. As well as being used to make cheese and sourdough, they have been used for decades in agricultural systems to improve soils, control diseases and promote plant growth.

You can make a brew with these lactic acid bacteria, but you need to dilute your brew with dechlorinated water before use. Korean Natural Farming practices suggest a ratio of 1:1000 (1 millilitre per litre of dechlorinated water). The diluted mixture can then be applied via a watering–can or spray bottle. It has many garden uses:

* Water your soil with the diluted mixture a couple of weeks before planting to improve soil aeration and general health.
* Sprinkle it over your compost pile, where it will work as an activator.
* If you're going to plant seedlings, then soak their roots in the diluted mixture before transplanting them to encourage growth.
* Spray it on leaves to control fungal and bacterial pathogens.

The recipe involves just a few ingredients and pieces of equipment. However, there are two parts to the method: producing the 'stock', and making the lactic acid bacteria brew. Fortunately, both tasks are simple!

INGREDIENTS
* 500 grams of white rice
* 1 litre of dechlorinated water
* 1 litre of organic milk (raw milk is ideal, if you can get it)

EQUIPMENT
* bowl and sieve
* two wide–mouthed jars (one with a lid)
* muslin or cheesecloth
* rubber band or string

METHOD
Stage 1: produce your 'stock':
1. Soak the rice in 1 litre of dechlorinated water, and give it a thorough stir. The water will become creamy and white. Strain the rice, and reserve this liquid.
2. Put 1 litre of the rice water into one of the wide–mouthed jars. Cover the jar with muslin or cheesecloth, and secure with a rubber band or string.
3. Place the jar in a cool, dark area, and leave it for three to five days. It should start to have a sour smell. You'll end up with a thin layer of white scum on top and sediment at the bottom.
4. Spoon off the scum, pour out the liquid (but not the sediment) into the second wide–mouthed jar, and place the lid on. You now have a colony of lactic acid bacteria that you can store in the fridge and use to mix up a brew. Label the airtight jar so you don't confuse it for any other potions.

Stage 2: make your lactic acid bacteria brew:
5. Mix 100 millilitres of the 'stock' with 1 litre of milk. (I've seen suggested ratios of 1:10 – which I'm using here – and 1:3, but you don't have to be exact. You're just giving the lactic acid bacteria in the stock some food so they can multiply.)
6. Place the mix of 'stock' and milk into a wide–mouthed jar. Cover the jar with muslin or cheesecloth, and secure with a rubber band or string.
7. Place the jar in a cool, dark area, and leave it. How long depends on the temperature: in summer, it could be three days; in winter, it could be seven days. You'll end up with three layers: a thick layer that looks like ricotta cheese on top, a clear(ish) liquid in the middle, and sediment on the bottom.
8. Spoon off the top layer, and pour out the liquid (but not the sediment) into another wide–mouthed jar. Again, you can store this in the fridge in an airtight jar (for years), or dilute and use it straight away. Add the top layer to the compost, or feed it to your chooks.

REGENERATIVE CONTAINER GARDENING

If you live in an apartment and don't have a garden, you may be wondering how regenerative gardening practices can work for you. These next few pages will show you that you can, in fact, employ many of these techniques when container gardening in pots or planters.

Growing plants in pots is an entirely human idea, and in many ways it's harder than planting directly into the earth. To experience container–garden success, it's best to replicate the way plants grow in the wild. Think of your potted plants – both indoor and outdoor – as little islands that aren't connected to the mainland (the soil food web). Left to their own devices, these plants will be hungry and lonely without your help. Poor things! This is where the six Cs of container care come in: compost, castings, conditioners, cosy covers, capacity and conscious care. This might sound a bit New Age, but I promise that it's sensible advice!

COMPOST AND CASTINGS

Successful container gardens are teeming with life – good bacteria, fungi, worms, and bugs – and have happy, nutrient–dense soil. This can't come out of a bag. I suggest that you slowly wean yourself off commercial potting mix by collecting brown leaves in autumn, making leaf mould, and using this as one of the main ingredients in homemade potting mix. (To discover two recipes for potting mix, turn to page 203.) Leaf storage needn't take up much space: you can store moist brown leaves in old potting–mix bags until you've broken the habit of buying potting mix.

Another sustainable method for filling containers is to use no dig layers that break down over time and form beautifully crumbling potting soil. Simply fill your pot with layers of greens and browns – this could be a combination of compost, worm castings and shredded brown leaves or paper. You could also incorporate tender green prunings from comfrey (that hasn't gone to seed), or even a thin layer of grass clippings or seaweed. Just make sure that the brown layers are thicker than the green layers – aim for 10 centimetres for each brown layer and 5 centimetres for each green layer. Wet each layer thoroughly as you're filling the pot, and repeat the layers until your container is full. The level of pots filled in this way will drop over time; simply add more alternating layers until the pot is topped up.

If you want to plant out the pot immediately, then dig out a small pocket and fill it with well–cured compost mixed with a sprinkle of worm castings. This will nurture your rapidly growing seedlings and allow them to blossom into robust plant teenagers. Castings and compost are the perfect first foods for your pot plants. Otherwise, wait six to twelve months or until the layers have broken down, and then plant out the pot.

If you're currently using commercial potting mix, then adding compost and worm castings to your containers will start to create a planting environment that is more closely aligned to what happens in nature. You can feed your potted plants with both compost and worm castings in solid form, just below the mulch layer, and in liquid form to get down to the root zone. Put your castings or compost in a bucket or watering-can (without the rose on the spout), add dechlorinated water, and then pour this yummy soil drench into your pots. Or if you want to take this regenerative practice up a notch, then brew up some aerated compost teas (see pages 234–6).

MIX AND MATCH

You can whip up your own low-waste potting mix for indoor plants using materials you've composted at home. My favourite recipe combines the following ingredients:

- 2 parts leaf mould
- 2 parts composted woodchips (if you don't have the space to make this, then use orchid potting mix made from decomposing bark)
- 2 parts coarse river sand (from a garden centre or hardware store)
- 1 part cured compost
- 1 part worm castings.

When making potting mix from scratch for your house plants, you can experiment with the ingredient ratios to match each plant's needs – but ensure that the potting mix always has these four important properties:

1. organic matter that has a water-holding capacity (such as leaf mould or aged sawdust)
2. inorganic matter that provides drainage and air pockets (such as coarse river sand, biochar, perlite or pumice)
3. organic material that provides structure (such as composted woodchips or orchid potting mix)
4. organic matter that provides nutrients (such as worm castings, compost, organic slow-release fertiliser or composted cow manure).

CONDITIONERS

Conditioners are needed for all potted plants, especially hungry fruit–bearing trees (such as citrus) and heavy croppers (such as tomatoes and cucumbers). I'm using 'conditioners' here as an umbrella term for any additions to your containers that boost the biology or nutrients in the potting mix. Here are some of the best:

- Bokashi 'juice' – This is a fabulous DIY conditioner that you can make even in small apartments. The diluted 'juice' (2 teaspoons or 10 millilitres per litre of water) is brimming with nitrogen and microbes that feed the soil and help to keep potted plants strong and disease-resistant. Try to avoid watering the leaves of tender plant babies; if you haven't diluted the 'juice' enough, then it might burn them.
- Manure – If you want to garden regeneratively, then it's important to avoid synthetic fertilisers and instead use well–aged animal manures to feed your potted plants. Plants and worms alike love aged cow poo and pelletised chicken manure.
- Worm wee – A misnomer (worms can't wee), it's the run–off from food waste breaking down in your worm farm, which drains through worm castings before it hits the collection bucket. Even though worms don't produce it, it's a useful conditioner for your pot plants when diluted so it's the colour of weak black tea. However, it can be a bit variable in quality, as it hasn't been processed in the gut of worms – so if it smells bad, don't use it.
- Seaweed tea – This is a nutrient booster shot for plants (see the recipe on pages 238–9.) If you don't have the time to brew seaweed tea, you can just chop up fresh seaweed and use it as mulch for your pots.
- Rock minerals – A sprinkle below mulch once a season helps to grow healthy plants and produce in containers. (To learn more, turn to pages 229–30.)

COSY COVERS

Have you ever had a nightmare about turning up somewhere naked? Well, a denuded potted plant – stripped bare of mulch – is living out this bad dream! The roots of plants growing in the wild are protected by leaf litter, or living mulch from another plant. We need to re–create this in our container gardens by tucking in our plants with a cosy cover made from mulch.

Mulch helps to keep potted plants' roots cool and moist, and prevents potting mix from baking in the sun, which sends soil biology downhill fast. Mulch feeds the plant with extra nutrients and captures carbon, suppresses weeds, provides food and habitat for worms, and stops potting mix from washing away.

As the weather heats up in summer, your pots will need frequent watering. Mulch dramatically decreases the evaporation rate, which saves water. Before watering, remember to stick a finger into the potting mix, below the layer of mulch, to check if it's dry and ready to be watered. Constantly wet roots are almost as bad as constantly dry roots.

You can make your own mulch by using the chop and drop method. Instead of pruning plants that are growing in pots and then ditching that plant matter, place it on top of the potting mix as a DIY mulch. (To learn more about this permaculture practice, turn to pages 220–1.)

Another sustainable mulch is shredded brown leaves that you've collected from local hard surfaces. (For leaf–collecting tips, turn to page 200.) This avoids the use of plastic packaging, the consumption of fuel while getting the mulch home, and other environmental impacts of crop farming for mulches (such as sugar cane and hay).

CONSCIOUS CARE

As a potted plant parent, you'll have to act like Mother Nature and provide your container plant babies with all the food, water and care they need. This takes regular observation and a proactive response. Conscious care involves watching your plants and promptly responding to what they're telling you. Keep an eagle eye out for the following, and respond accordingly:

- Yellow leaves during the growing season – Feed your plant more compost or worm castings, as this may be a sign that it's exhausting its chlorophyll and nitrogen reserves.
- Wilted leaves – Water your plant the whole way around the plant's root zone, not just in one spot.
- Little piles of black or brown poo on leaves – Go caterpillar hunting, and feed them to your local birds.
- New holes in the middle of leaves, and silvery trails, in the morning – Go slug and snail hunting at night.
- Stunted growth – Check if your pot is big enough to sustain the plant's full potential.
- Scale, whiteflies, aphids, spider mites, thrips and powdery mildew – Make a natural pesticide by mixing 10 millilitres of unscented Castile soap with 500 millilitres of water, and spray the whole plant (top and underside of leaves, stems and buds) as well as the soil surface. Repeat the application every two or three days for as long as needed to stop the life cycle

of these pests and to prevent them from laying more eggs.
- Mealy bugs – Make a natural pesticide by mixing one part isopropyl alcohol (64 per cent rubbing alcohol) with two parts water, and follow the application advice in the point above.

CAPACITY MATTERS

When choosing a pot for a particular plant, always look at the suggested width of the full–grown plant. This is usually listed on the plant tag or seed packet. Divide the width by two to work out how big your pot should be. For example, a tomato plant with a suggested width of 60 centimetres will need to be planted in a 30–centimetre pot as a minimum.

FINAL THOUGHTS

I love making compost – can you tell? I love the way that I can take the waste from my kitchen, my garden and my life, and make something beneficial with it that cycles nutrients back into my soil.

It's been a journey. It started with my mum: I got my love of gardening, plants and compost from her. I kept making compost (and gardening) because it felt like a magical, purposeful and rewarding activity. As I got older, and my gardens got larger, I made more and more compost, and I became more conscious of how I managed all of my household waste. Making compost started to tie in with other ways that I could minimise my family's impact on the environment and take responsibility for how we lived and affected others.

Compost is a gateway activity to caring for the planet in other ways. Once you act and start to manage your food waste responsibly, it has an effect on other aspects of your life. You start to think about where your food comes from, how it's grown and what sort of packaging it comes in. You might then rip up a bit of lawn and grow some food and flowers for the bees, or decide to reduce plastic packaging by shopping at bulk–food stores and buying 'nude food' from local markets. Then maybe you'll start to think about other ways to tread more gently on our beautiful, old planet.

Our balconies, backyards and bigger blocks are like patches on a handmade quilt. These gardens – big or small, manicured or wild – are all different, but ultimately they're connected. What I do in my backyard affects yours, and vice versa. Soil is the foundation fabric on which each of our patches is sewn together.

I hope this book gives you confidence and inspiration to get out and get dirty. Composting (and regenerative gardening) will connect your household with the natural world around you, and your community. It lets you see your household as part of the cycle of nutrients from the earth to your family, and back again. Most of all, it's great fun.

With love and compost,

Kate

NOTES

Chapter 1: The What

14   If you have soil that lacks nutrients ...: Nigel Palmer, *The Regenerative Grower's Guide to Garden Amendments*, Chelsea Green Publishing, White River Junction, 2020, p. 47.

14   Various compost microorganisms protect ...: Nigel Palmer, *The Regenerative Grower's Guide to Garden Amendments*, p. 17.

14   Compost doesn't dramatically change ...: Nicky Scott, *How to Make and Use Compost*, Green Books, Cambridge, 2021, p. 15.

15   In one of my favourite books ...: Matthew Evans, *Soil*, Murdoch Books, Sydney, 2021, p. 36.

15   As Evans says ...: Matthew Evans, *Soil*, pp. 47, 48.

16   It acts like glue ...: Nicky Scott, *How to Make and Use Compost*, p. 14.

16   Compost binds with soil particles ...: Stu Campbell, *Let It Rot!*, 3rd edn, Storey Publishing, North Adams, 1998, p. 10.

Chapter 2: The Why

20   Bagged scraps piled on top ...: Lauren Rothman, 'In Today's Landfills, Food Is Embalmed for Decades at a Time', *Vice*, ‹www.vice.com/en/article/aeyxxz/in-todays-landfills-food-is-embalmed-for-decades-at-a-time›, 28 January 2014, accessed 19 July 2022.

21   But did you know ...: IPCC, 'Climate Change and Land', *Intergovernmental Panel on Climate Change*, ‹www.ipcc.ch/srccl/›, 2019, accessed 19 July 2022.

21   Food that is produced ...: WWF, 'Food Waste', *World Wildlife Fund*, ‹www.worldwildlife.org/initiatives/food-waste›, 2022, accessed 19 July 2022.

21   The global emissions ...: OzHarvest, 'Fight Food Waste', *OzHarvest*, ‹www.ozharvest.org/fight-food-waste/›, 2022, accessed 19 July 2022.

21   The food wasted just ...: Waste Management Review, 'National Food Waste Strategy in discussion', *Waste Management Review*, ‹https://wastemanagementreview.com.au/national-food-waste-strategy/›, 6 February 2018, accessed 19 July 2022.

21   If global food waste ...: FAO, 'Food wastage footprint: Impacts on natural resources, Summary Report', *Food and Agriculture Organization of the United Nations*, ‹www.fao.org/3/i3347e/i3347e.pdf›, 2013, accessed 19 July 2022.

21   Today, one in nine people ...: FAO, 'The State of Food Security and Nutrition in the World', *Food and Agriculture Organization of the United Nations*, ‹www.fao.org/publications/sofi/2021/en/›, 2021, accessed 19 July 2022.

21   If as little as one-quarter ...: FAO, 'The State of Food Security and Nutrition in the World'.

22   Households in Australia lose ...: Department of Climate Change, Energy, the Environment and Water, 'Tackling Australia's food waste', *Australian Government*, ‹www.awe.gov.au/environment/protection/waste/food-waste›, 26 April 2022, accessed 19 July 2022.

22   This wastage equals ...: Department of Climate Change, Energy, the Environment and Water, 'Tackling Australia's food waste'.

22   Almost half of all fruits ...: OzHarvest, 'Food Waste Facts', *OzHarvest*, <www.ozharvest.org/food–waste–facts/>, 2022, accessed 19 July 2022.

22   The fresh, edible food wasted ...: WWF, 'Fight climate change by preventing food waste', *World Wildlife Fund*, <https://www.worldwildlife.org/stories/fight–climate–change–by–preventing–food–waste>, 2022, accessed 19 July 2022.

23   The good news is ...: Project Drawdown, 'Reduced Food Waste', *Project Drawdown*, <www.drawdown.org/solutions/reduced–food–waste>, 2022, accessed 19 July 2022.

Chapter 3: The How

28   Adding carbon is important ...: Cornell Composting, 'Compost Chemistry', *Cornell Waste Management Institute*, <http://compost.css.cornell.edu/chemistry.html>, 1996, accessed 19 July 2022.

31   A happy heap will feel ...: Nicky Scott, *How To Make and Use Compost*, Green Books, Cambridge, 2021, p. 22.

31   This is because microbial decomposition ...: Nancy M. Trautmann and Marianne E. Krasny, 'Composting in the Classroom', *Cornell University*, <http://cwmi.css.cornell.edu/compostingintheclassroom.pdf>, 1997, accessed 19 July 2022.

32   This gives microbes 16 parts ...: USDA Natural Resources Conservation Service, 'Carbon to Nitrogen Ratios in Cropping Systems', *USDA NRCS East National Technology Support Center*, <https://www.hamiltonswcd.org/uploads/3/7/2/3/37236909/nrcs_carbon_nitrogen.pdf>, 2011, accessed 19 July 2022.

33   Woodchips and sawdust made ...: Nancy M. Trautmann and Marianne E. Krasny, 'Composting in the Classroom'.

38   You can create an open structure ...: Marina Bistrin, 'Cold composting', *Local Food Connect*, <https://localfoodconnect.org.au/community–gardening/cold–composting/>, 2019, accessed 19 July 2022.

40   The active decomposition of materials ...: HOTBIN Composting, 'Core principles of hot composting', *HOTBIN Composting*, <www.hotbincomposting.com/blog/core–principles–of–hot–composting.html>, 2012, accessed 21 July 2022.

40   The temperature range and length ...: Cornell Composting, 'Compost Physics', *Cornell Waste Management Institute*, <http://compost.css.cornell.edu/physics.html>, 1996, accessed 21 July 2022.

41   Microbially induced decomposition ...: Cornell Composting, 'Compost Physics'.

44   If you dig into the core ...: Not to be confused with actinomycetes that grow like white spider webs on the surface of your compost – read more about these beneficial fungus–like bacteria on page 148.

44   This process of aeration ...: Cornell Composting, 'Compost Physics'.

50   Many of these composting buddies ...: Palisa Anderson, '"You don't need a fancy bin": hard–won lessons from farming worms', *The Guardian*, <www.theguardian.com/lifeandstyle/2020/apr/11/you–dont–need–a–fancy–bin–hard–won–lessons–from–farming–worms>, 11 April 2020, accessed 21 July 2022.

52   Studies have shown that ...: Barbara Pleasant and Deborah L. Martin, *The Complete Compost Gardening Guide*, Storey Publishing, North Adams, 2008, p. 150.

52   If you can smell an ammonia ...: NYC Compost Project, 'How to Use Compost', *NYC Department of Sanitation*, <https://earthmatter.org/wp–content/uploads/2016/08/tip–sheet–how–to–use–compost–cpts–htuc–f.pdf>, 1993, accessed 19 July 2022.

53   An aerobic (oxygen–rich) compost ...: Cornell Composting, 'Monitoring Compost pH', *Cornell Waste Management Institute*, <http://compost.css.cornell.edu/monitor/monitorph.html>, 1996, accessed 21 July 2022.

53   Organic acids increase ...: Cornell Composting, 'Monitoring Compost pH'.

53   Old–school composting guides ...: Cornell Composting, 'Monitoring Compost pH'.

56 Soil that is pale brown ...: Department of Primary Industries, 'Healthy soil: healthy garden', *NSW Government*, <www.dpi.nsw.gov.au/agriculture/soils/guides/soil–types–and–condition/garden>, 2022, accessed 19 July 2022.

67 Some compost microorganisms produce ...: Planet Natural Research Center, 'Compost Science', *Planet Natural Research Center*, <www.planetnatural.com/composting–101/science/>, 2022, accessed 19 July 2022.

Chapter 4: The Kit

76 If you do end up with ...: Sustainable Gardening Australia, 'Composting How–To', *SGA*, <www.sgaonline.org.au/composting–how–to/>, 2022, accessed 19 July 2022.

102 I've adapted this recipe ...: Rebecca Louie, 'How To Make DIY Bokashi Flakes', *The Compostess*, <https://thecompostess.com/2015/04/22/how–to–make–bokashi/>, 22 April 2015, accessed 19 July 2022.

Chapter 5: The Worms

125 Worm castings are jam–packed ...: Rajiv Sinha, Sunil Herat, Dalsukhbhai Valani and Krunalkumar Chauhan, 'Earthworms Vermicompost', *Griffith University*, <https://research-repository.griffith.edu.au/bitstream/handle/10072/30336/62923_1.pdf>, 2009, accessed 19 July 2022.

125 In exchange for their services ...: Tim Miner, 'In a Worm's Gut', *Edible Learning Lab*, <http://ediblelearninglab.com/in–a–worms–gut/>, 2022, accessed 19 July 2022.

125 As bacteria enter the worm's ...: Steve Churchill, 'Vermicomposting 101: What Happens In A Worm Bin?', *Urban Worm Company*, <https://urbanwormcompany.com/what–happens–in–a–worm–bin/>, 14 May 2019, accessed 19 July 2022.

126 This is then deposited ...: Steve Churchill, 'Vermicomposting 101: What Happens In A Worm Bin?'.

132 They're classified as epigeic ...: Mary Appelhof and Joanne Olszewski, *Worms Eat My Garbage*, Storey Publishing, North Adams, 2017, p. 44.

Chapter 6: The Who

146 They're both an important part ...: Mary Appelhof and Joanne Olszewski, *Worms Eat My Garbage*, Storey Publishing, North Adams, 2017, p. 129.

146 It's true that a treasure trove ...: Dr Elaine Ingham, 'Compost Food Web Information', *Soil Foodweb Institute*, <www.soilfoodweb.com.au/about–our–organisation/compost–food–web–information>, 2022, accessed 21 July 2022.

147 Energy flows from one organism ...: Mary Appelhof and Joanne Olszewski, *Worms Eat My Garbage*, p. 116.

148 They help to consume organic matter ...: Nancy Trautmann and Elaina Olynciw, 'Compost Microorganisms', *Cornell Composting*, <http://compost.css.cornell.edu/microorg.html>, 1996, accessed 21 July 2022.

149 True maggots ...: Angela Libal, 'The Difference Between Soldier Fly Larvae and Maggots', *Pets on Mom*, <https://animals.mom.com/difference–between–soldier–fly–larvae–maggots–8917.html>, 2022, accessed 21 July 2022.

150 They perform important functions ...: Mary Appelhof and Joanne Olszewski, *Worms Eat My Garbage*, 2017, p. 120.

152 Nematodes are free–ranging ...: Pauline Pears, *Organic Book of Compost*, IMM Lifestyle Books, London, 2020, p. 161.

152 Protozoa and nematodes help ...: Dr Elaine Ingham, 'Compost Food Web Information', *Soil Foodweb Institute*, <www.soilfoodweb.com.au/about–our–organisation/compost–food–web–information>, 2022, accessed 21 July 2022.

154 Ants are beneficial ...: The Daily Gardener, '6 Tips To Control Ants In Compost Bin', *The Daily Gardener*, <www.thedailygardener.com/control–ants–in–compost–bin>, 2022, accessed 19 July 2022.

156 Alys Fowler shares some useful ...: Alys
Fowler, *The Thrifty Gardener*, Kyle Cathie,
London, 2008.

156 Instead of poison ...: Deborah Metters,
'Pest Rodent Control without Harming
Owls', *Land for Wildlife*,, 2022, accessed 19 July 2022.

156 If you do need to use poison ...: Owl
Friendly Margaret River Region, 'Rodent
Control', *Owl Friendly Margaret River
Region*, <https://owlfriendly.org.au/rodent–
control/>, 2022, accessed 19 July 2022.

156 ... not leaving pet food ...: Deborah
Metters, 'Pest Rodent Control without
Harming Owls'.

Chapter 7: The Scraps

165 Such products are typically made ...:
Adam Sarfati, 'What is the Difference
Between Biodegradable and Compostable
Packaging?', HeapsGood, <https://
heapsgoodpackaging.com.au/blogs/
news/biogradeable–vs–compostable>,
2 February 2021, accessed 19 July 2022.

165 Testing has shown that ...: NSW EPA,
'FOGO information for households',
NSW EPA, <www.epa.nsw.gov.au/your–
environment/recycling–and–reuse/
household–recycling–overview/fogo–
information–for–households>, 2022,
accessed 19 July 2022.

165 The cobs, stalks and husks ...: Nancy
M. Trautmann and Marianne E. Krasny,
'Composting in the Classroom', *Cornell
University*, <http://cwmi.css.cornell.edu/
compostingintheclassroom.pdf>, 1997,
accessed 19 July 2022.

166 To ensure that you've eradicated ...: Nicky
Scott, *How To Make and Use Compost*,
Green Books, Cambridge, 2021, p. 113.

168 If you're interested in learning ...: Joseph
Jenkins, 'The Humanure Handbook',
Weblife.org, <https://weblife.org/humanure/
index.html>, 1999, accessed 19 July 2022.

168 The World Health Organization classifies ...:
WHO, 'Dioxins and their effects on human
health', *World Health Organization*, <www.
who.int/news–room/fact–sheets/detail/

dioxins–and–their–effects–on–human–
health>, 4 October 2016, accessed
19 July 2022.

169 People became concerned about ...:
Philip Shabecoff, 'Traces of Dioxin Found
in Range Of Paper Goods', *The New York
Times*, <www.nytimes.com/1987/09/24/us/
traces–of–dioxin–found–in–range–of–
paper–goods.html>, 24 September 1987,
accessed 19 July 2022.

169 ... one particular manufacturer claims ...:
LD Davis Glues & Gelatins, 'Glue Used to
Make Corrugated Fiberboard', *LD Davis
Glues & Gelatins*, <https://blog.lddavis.
com/glue–corrugated–fiberboard>,
10 May 2016, accessed 19 July 2022.

169 ... many contain mineral oil ...: Food
Standards Australia New Zealand,
'Mineral oil hydrocarbons in food and
food packaging', *Food Standards Australia
New Zealand*, <www.foodstandards.gov.
au/publications/Documents/Mineral%20
oil%20hydrocarbons.pdf>, August 2018,
accessed 19 July 2022.

170 These bad hydrocarbons ...: Food
Standards Australia New Zealand,
'Mineral oil hydrocarbons in food
and food packaging'.

170 The authors suggest that ...: Sang–
Hwan Lee, Bang–Il Oh and Jeong–gyu
Kim, 'Effect of various amendments
on heavy mineral oil bioremediation
and soil microbial activity', *Bioresource
Technology*, vol. 99, no. 7, May 2008,
pp. 2578–87.

170 As with any manufactured paper ...: Nancy
Trautmann and Tom Richard, 'Frequently
Asked Questions', *Cornell Composting*,
<http://compost.css.cornell.edu/faq.html>,
1996, accessed 19 July 2022.

170 So, make sure you rip ...: Nancy Trautmann
and Tom Richard, 'Frequently Asked
Questions'.

170 A very concerning problem ...: OECD,
'PFASs and Alternatives in Food
Packaging', *OECD*, <www.oecd.org/
chemicalsafety/portal–perfluorinated–
chemicals/PFASs–and–alternatives–
in–food–packaging–paper–and–
paperboard.pdf>, 2020, accessed
19 July 2022.

170 The Australian government has set up ...:
     Australian Government, 'Per- and
     Polyfluoroalkyl Substances (PFAS)',
     Australian Government, <https://www.
     pfas.gov.au/>, 2022, accessed
     19 July 2022.

170 Thankfully, you can conduct ...: Dr Kerry J.
     Dinsmore, 'Forever chemicals in the food
     aisle: PFAS content of UK supermarket
     and takeaway food packaging', *Fidra*,
     <www.pfasfree.org.uk/wp-content/uploads/
     Forever-Chemicals-in-the-Food-Aisle-
     Fidra-2020-.pdf>, February 2020,
     accessed 19 July 2022.

170 The results of a study of 92 ...: Dr Kerry
     J. Dinsmore, 'Forever chemicals in the
     food aisle'.

170 The highest concentrations of PFAS ...:
     Dr Kerry J. Dinsmore, 'Forever chemicals
     in the food aisle'.

170 According to the Australian Packaging ...:
     APCO, 'PFAS in Fibre-Based Packaging',
     *Australian Packaging Covenant
     Organisation*, <https://documents.
     packagingcovenant.org.au/public-
     documents/PFAS+in+Fibre-Based+
     Packaging>, December 2021, accessed
     19 July 2022

171 According to Food Standards ...: Food
     Standards Australia New Zealand,
     'Bisphenol A (BPA)', *Food Standards
     Australia New Zealand*,, November 2018,
     accessed 19 July 2022.

171 The US Food & Drug ...: US Food & Drug
     Administration, 'Bisphenol A (BPA): Use
     in Food Contact Application', *FDA*, <www.
     fda.gov/food/food-additives-petitions/
     bisphenol-bpa-use-food-contact-
     application>, November 2014, accessed
     19 July 2022.

172 Animal worm medications ...: Mary
     Schwarz and Jean Bonhotal, 'The Fate
     of Ivermectin in Manure Composting',
     Cornell Waste Management Institute,
     <https://cwmi.css.cornell.edu/ivermectin.
     pdf>, 2016, accessed 21 January 2023.

177 The microorganisms in the bran ...:
     EnviroShop, 'EnsoPet In-ground Pet
     Waste Kit', *EnviroShop*, <https://enviroshop.
     com.au/products/ensopet-kit>, 2022,
     accessed 19 July 2022.

179 According to the NSW Environment ...:
     NSW Environment Protection Authority,
     'FOGO information for households',
     NSW EPA, <www.epa.nsw.gov.au/your-
     environment/recycling-and-reuse/
     household-recycling-overview/fogo-
     information-for-households>, 2022,
     accessed 19 July 2022.

Chapter 8: The Soil

193 Overworked or compacted soil ...: Flowful,
     'Session 6: Basics of Soil', *Flowful*, <www.
     flowful.org/permaculture-community-
     resilience-course/s6-soil-basics>,
     16 April 2020, accessed 19 July 2022.

194 These soil tests are adapted ...: Costa
     Georgiadis, *Costa's World*, HarperCollins,
     Sydney, 2021.

195 Biodynamic gardeners warn ...: Alanna
     Moore, 'Rock Dust Can Improve Our
     Soils', *Eco Farming Daily*, <www.
     ecofarmingdaily.com/build-soil/soil-
     inputs/minerals-nutrients/rock-dust-
     can-improve-soils/>, June 2005,
     accessed 19 July 2022.

196 Professor Mark Taylor ...: Costa Georgiadis,
     Costa's World, p. 71.

196 Organic matter can't remove lead ...: Kat
     Lavers, 'Soil', *Kat Lavers*,,
     24 April 2020, accessed 19 July 2022.

198 Hay and straw harvested ...: Penny
     Woodward, 'Herbicide Alert', *ABC Organic
     Gardener*, <www.organicgardener.com.au/
     blogs/herbicide-alert>, December 2013,
     accessed 19 July 2022.

198 Cows, horses and sheep ...: Penny
     Woodward, 'Herbicide Alert'.

198 Red flags are poor seed germination ...:
     Penny Woodward, 'Herbicide Alert'.

201 The combination of bacteria and
     nitrogen ...: permies.com, 'Camphor
     laurel leaf mulch – denaturing the
     aromatics', *permies.com*, <https://permies.
     com/t/94333/Camphor-laurel-leaf-
     mulch-denaturing>, 2019, accessed
     19 July 2022.

202 Leaf mould has little available nitrogen ...: Alys Fowler, 'How to make leaf mould', *The Guardian*, <www.theguardian.com/lifeandstyle/2020/nov/14/how-to-make-leaf-mould>, 14 November 2020, accessed 19 July 2022.

202 Depending on the variety of leaves ...: Millie Ross, 'Leaf Mould = Garden Gold!', *Gardening Australia*, <www.abc.net.au/gardening/how-to/leaf-mould=garden-gold!/11281974>, 5 July 2019, accessed 19 July 2022.

210 It's also a great idea to seed ...: Sulyn Lam, 'Forest Floor Compost Inspired by Birds', *Salad Days*, <https://mesclun.wordpress.com/2009/10/30/forest-floor-compost-inspired-by-birds/>, October 2009, accessed 19 July 2022

215 Green-manure crops protect soil ...: James J. Hoorman and Alan Sundermeier, 'Using Cover Crops to Improve Soil and Water Quality', *Ohioline: Ohio State University Extension*, <https://ohioline.osu.edu/factsheet/anr-57>, 12 May 2017, accessed 19 July 2022.

218 We need to eliminate the 'mow and blow' ...: Nicky Scott, *How To Make and Use Compost*, Green Books, Cambridge, 2021, p. 117.

221 The scientific world is still unconvinced ...: John Kitsteiner, 'The Facts about Dynamic Accumulators', *Permaculture Research Institute*, <www.permaculturenews.org/2015/04/10/the-facts-about-dynamic-accumulators/>, 10 April 2015, accessed 19 July 2022.

221 There's still a lot we don't know ...: Amy Stross, '6 Reasons to Grow Borage in the Permaculture Garden', *Tenth Acre Farm*, <www.tenthacrefarm.com/grow-borage/>, 13 June 2022, accessed 19 July 2022.

222 Both plants are in the Boraginaceae family ...: Amy Stross, '6 Reasons to Grow Borage in the Permaculture Garden'.

222 It's therefore best to plant it ...: Hannah Moloney, 'Everything I Know About Comfrey (So Far)', *Good Life Permaculture*, <https://goodlifepermaculture.com.au/everything-i-know-about-comfrey-so-far/>, 8 April 2016, accessed 19 July 2022.

223 These wild weeds are the multivitamins ...: Nigel Palmer, *The Regenerative Grower's Guide to Garden Amendments*, Chelsea Green Publishing, White River Junction, 2020, p. 91.

224 This fermented juice is not only rich ...: Nigel Palmer, *The Regenerative Grower's Guide to Garden Amendments*, p. 134.

226 It's a valuable supplement ...: Ole G. Mouritsen, 'The science of seaweeds: Marine macroalgae benefit people culturally, industrially, nutritionally, and ecologically', *American Scientist*, vol. 101, no. 6, Nov–Dec 2013, pp. 458–65.

226 Unlike many straw mulches, seaweed ...: Kirsten Bradley and Nick Ritar, *Milkwood*, Murdoch Books, Sydney, 2018, p. 219.

226 You don't need to worry about ...: Nigel Palmer, *The Regenerative Grower's Guide to Garden Amendments*, p. 122.

227 I've adapted this Korean ...: Nigel Palmer, *The Regenerative Grower's Guide to Garden Amendments*, p. 129.

229 There is certainly a buzz ...: Josh Byrne, 'Rock Minerals', *Gardening Australia*, <www.abc.net.au/gardening/how-to/rock-minerals/9436038>, 1 November 2014, accessed 19 July 2022.

229 There are claims that trials ...: Alanna Moore, 'Rock Dust Can Improve Our Soils'.

229 But there are also papers ...: Atefeh Ramezanian, A. Sigrun Dahlin, Colin D. Campbell, et al., 'Addition of a volcanic rockdust to soils has no observable effects on plant yield and nutrient status or on soil microbial activity', *Plant and Soil*, vol. 367, 2013, pp. 419–36.

229 Others are more positive about ...: Nigel Palmer, *The Regenerative Grower's Guide to Garden Amendments*, p. 117.

230 This transforms the organic matter ...: Albert Bates, 'How to Make Your Own Biochar', *Pip Magazine*, <https://pipmagazine.com.au/grow/make-biochar/>, 31 March 2020, accessed 19 July 2022.

230 This structure is highly porous ...: Albert Bates, 'How to Make Your Own Biochar'.

231 If you're worried about burning carbon ...: Pete Smith, 'Soil carbon sequestration and biochar as negative emission technologies',

Global Change Biology, vol. 22, no. 3, March 2016, pp. 1315–24; IPCC, 'Global warming of 1.5°C' (Ch. 4, FAQ 4.2, 'What are Carbon Dioxide Removal and Negative Emissions?'), <https://www.ipcc.ch/sr15/>, 2018, accessed 19 July 2022.

232 You can gauge the speed ...: Lindsay Campbell, 'Make Your Own Biochar Using the Cone Pit Method', *Modern Farmer*, <https://modernfarmer.com/2021/11/how-to-make-biochar/>, 7 November 2021, accessed 19 July 2022.

232 Depending on the feedstock used ...: Nastaran Basiri Jahromi, Amy Fulcher and Forbes Walker, 'What Is Biochar and How Different Biochars Can Improve Your Crops', *University of Tennessee Institute of Agriculture*, <https://extension.tennessee.edu/publications/Documents/W829.pdf>, 2022, accessed 19 July 2022.

235 To do this, you'll need ...: Joe Gardener, '117 – Compost, Compost Tea and the Soil Food Web, with Dr. Elaine Ingham', *Joe Gardener*, <https://joegardener.com/podcast/compost-tea-dr-elaine-ingham/>, 15 August 2019, accessed 19 July 2022.

235 All four recipes outlined ...: Simon Webster, 'How to Make Compost Tea', *ABC Organic Gardener*, <www.organicgardener.com.au/articles/how-make-compost-tea>, March–April 2012, accessed 19 July 2022.

237 Microbes clinging to the parent ...: Nigel Palmer, *The Regenerative Grower's Guide to Garden Amendments*, p. 44.

237 These beneficial bacteria will start ...: Simon Webster, 'How to Make Compost Tea'.

238 I've adapted the recipe from Kirsten ...: Kirsten Bradley and Nick Ritar, *Milkwood*, p. 221; Nigel Palmer, *The Regenerative Grower's Guide to Garden Amendments*, p. 122.

240 Apply it to hydrophobic mulch ...: Nigel Palmer, *The Regenerative Grower's Guide to Garden Amendments*, p. 153.

240 This recipe has been adapted from Nigel ...: Nigel Palmer, *The Regenerative Grower's Guide to Garden Amendments*, p. 150; Youngsang Cho, *JADAM Organic Farming*, JADAM, Daejeon, 2016, n.p.

242 As well as being used to make cheese ...: John R. Lamont, Olivia Wilkins, Margaret Bywater-Ekegärd and Donald L. Smith, 'From yogurt to yield: Potential applications of lactic acid bacteria in plant production', *Soil Biology and Biochemistry*, vol. 111, August 2017, pp. 1–9.

THANK YOU

Writing this book while in peak–hour parenting mode – caring for my three gorgeous but very busy small humans, Tully, Woody and Sunday (who were six, four and two at the time) – was a marathon. My partner, Lee, needs to be thanked (and given a couple of nights off), as he has provided me with unwavering love and support from start to finish throughout this process.

I also want to thank Honey Atkinson, my photographer and fabulous friend. Honey is a firecracker of a human and a visionary to work with. Her photos truly bring the book to life.

It was a privilege to work with Melinda Berti as my illustrator. I'm so proud of being able to show off her joyous drawings in my book.

A virtual hug and celebratory toast to Jane Willson from Murdoch Books. Whenever I turned to Jane for help, she would always provide me with uplifting encouragement and guidance without an ounce of bullshit. Thank you for believing in my message and getting down 'n' dirty with me!

To Sarah, Dannielle, Justin and Andy from Murdoch Books – thank you for shaping and elevating my manuscript into this wonderful book. As a first–time author, I was extremely grateful to have you all on my team, as you were very patient with my questions and queries.

Finally, a wholehearted thanks to my online compost community. Without you following and supporting me, I wouldn't have had this opportunity to bring my words and message from the online world into the real world.

INDEX

Published in 2023 by Murdoch Books, an imprint of Allen & Unwin

Murdoch Books Australia
Cammeraygal Country
83 Alexander Street
Crows Nest NSW 2065
Phone: +61 (0)2 8425 0100
murdochbooks.com.au
info@murdochbooks.com.au

Murdoch Books UK
Ormond House
26–27 Boswell Street
London WC1N 3JZ
Phone: +44 (0) 20 8785 5995
murdochbooks.co.uk
info@murdochbooks.co.uk

For corporate orders and custom publishing,
contact our business development team at
salesenquiries@murdochbooks.com.au

Publisher: Jane Willson
Editorial Manager: Justin Wolfers
Design Manager: Sarah Odgers
Designer: Andy Warren
Editor: Dannielle Viera
Photographer: Honey Atkinson
Illustrator: Melinda Berti
Production Director: Lou Playfair

*Murdoch Books acknowledges the Traditional Owners
of the Country on which we live and work. We pay our
respects to all Aboriginal and Torres Strait Islander Elders,
past and present.*

ISBN 978 1 92261 645 6

 A catalogue record for this
book is available from the
National Library of Australia

A catalogue record for this book is available from the
British Library

Colour reproduction by Splitting Image Colour Studio Pty
    Ltd, Wantirna, Victoria
Printed by 1010 Printing International Limited, China

The information provided within this book is for general
inspiration and informational purposes only. While we try
to keep the information up–to–date and correct, the author
and publisher do not assume and hereby disclaim any
liability to any party for any loss, damage, or disruption
caused by errors or omissions, whether such errors or
omissions result from negligence, accident, or any other
cause. Be sure to check with your local council and use
common sense when handling any potentially harmful
equipment or materials.

10 9 8 7 6 5 4 3 2